Women and health services

Women and health services
An agenda for change

Edited by **Lesley Doyal**

Open University Press
Buckingham · Philadelphia

Open University Press
Celtic Court
22 Ballmoor
Buckingham
MK18 1XW

email: enquiries@openup.co.uk
world wide web: http://www.openup.co.uk

and
325 Chestnut Street
Philadelphia, PA 19106, USA

First Published 1998

A catalogue record of this book is available from the British Library

ISBN   0 335 20137 7 (hb)   0 335 20136 9 (pb)

Library of Congress Cataloging-in-Publication Data
Women and health services: an agenda for change/edited by Lesley
   Doyal.
      p.   cm.
   Includes bibliographical references and index.
   ISBN 0–335–20137–7. – ISBN 0–335–20136–9 (pbk.)
   1. Women's health services – Great Britain.   2. Health care reform –
Great Britain.   I. Doyal, Lesley.
RA564.85.W6548   1998
362.1'082'0941 – dc21   98–4891
                                                                      CIP

Typeset by Graphicraft Limited, Hong Kong
Printed in Great Britain by Biddles Ltd, Guildford and King's Lynn

For Tamsin Wilton with many thanks for sharing both her weaknesses and her many strengths at a crucial moment in my life.

Contents

Acknowledgements

This book began as a joint effort with Pamela Charlwood and Lyn Harrison and I am grateful for their enthusiasm and ideas that helped get it off the ground. Thanks are due also to Jean Trainor and Caroline Langridge who contributed material which eventually had to be excluded due to lack of space.

My own illness intervened twice during the book's gestation making the delivery especially difficult. Without the support of friends and family it would not have been possible and I thank them all very much. Linda Price kept the paper work and computer disks in order, was calm and collected under pressure and generally provided more help and support than I could reasonably have expected. Friends in both London and Bristol were there when needed especially Tamsin Wilton and Norma Daykin who saw me through some long, dark nights.

And most important of all, thanks to my family without whom everything might have been aborted. Dan Wilsher played *Scrabble*, held my hand, and made food while Hannah Doyal travelled thousands of miles from tropical sunshine to a cold English winter when I needed her. Len Doyal – what can I say? My comrade in arms and partner for life, he hung on in there when the going got tough and I will never forget it. Thanks a million.

Notes on contributors

Amanda Amos is Senior Lecturer in Health Promotion at the Department of Public Health Sciences, Edinburgh University. She has a long-standing interest in women's health particularly in relation to smoking. Other research interests include investigating social and cultural influences on smoking uptake and cessation such as the media and tobacco industry tactics. She is a member of the Board of ASH Scotland and has been an adviser to WHO on women and tobacco.

Sara Arber is Professor and Head of the Department of Sociology at the University of Surrey. She is well known nationally and internationally for her work on ageing and on class and gender inequalities in health. She is co-author with Jay Ginn of *Gender and Later Life* (Sage 1991) and *Connecting Gender and Ageing* (Open University Press 1995), which won the 1996 Age Concern Prize for the best book on ageing. Her research is mainly based on the secondary analysis of national surveys, such as the General Household Survey. She is currently working on a Health Education Authority-funded study of health promotion among older people.

Katharine Bell qualified as a midwife in 1983. In 1990 she became Associate Director of Family Services at Mount Vernon and Watford Hospital NHS Trust. Katharine has always been very interested in improving the services available to women, hence the Gynaecology Assessment Clinic Project. In 1996 Katharine became the Local Supervising Authority Midwife for the West London Consortium of Health Authorities.

Rosa Benato has been Practice Manager at Hoxton Health Collective for seven years. She is also a King's Fund Organisational Audit Surveyor and local Organisational Audit Facilitator, and is doing a degree in communication and cultural studies.

Jean Bradlow is a specialist in public health, leading on developing women's health strategy in Oxfordshire. Her background is in primary care and health services research.

Alison Clarke trained as a general nurse in Dublin, Ireland, before her midwifery training at St Bartholomew's College of Nursing and Midwifery. She then worked as a midwife at Homerton Hospital before joining Hoxton Health Collective as Women's Health Worker in 1995. She actively campaigns for reproductive rights and against violence directed towards women and is involved in providing information and access to abortion for Irish women. She is currently reading for a BSc in Combined Women's Health Studies.

Elizabeth Crossan is a Research Fellow at the Centre for Social Research on Dementia at the University of Stirling. Her research focuses on health issues, with a particular interest in mental health. Previously she was the project coordinator for the 'Under a Cloud' pilot project at Edinburgh University.

Norma Daykin is a Senior Lecturer in Health Sciences in the Faculty of Health and Social Care at the University of the West of England. She has been involved in research on women's health for a number of years and is a member of the Bristol Women and Health Research Group.

She is also interested in occupational health issues and is currently researching the occupational health implications of changes in work organization and employment conditions.

Jenny Douglas is a Lecturer in Health Education and Health Promotion in the School of Education, University of Birmingham. She has undertaken research and written about the health experiences and health needs of black and minority ethnic communities in the United Kingdom. Her current research interests are in 'race', ethnicity, gender and health, health promotion and black and minority ethnic communities, and cigarette smoking in adolescence. She is presently undertaking research on smoking and identity in African–Caribbean adolescent women.

Lesley Doyal is Professor of Health and Social Care in the School for Policy Studies, University of Bristol and a member of the Bristol Women and Health Research Group. She has published extensively on gender and health issues both in the UK and also in an international context. Her most recent book, *What Makes Women Sick: Gender and the Political Economy of Health* was published by Macmillan in 1995.

Paula Gaunt-Richardson has worked with young people and their families in both the statutory and voluntary sectors in community and residential settings. She has a first degree in Applied Social Science, a postgraduate certificate in Community Education and an MSc in Social and Public Policy. She currently manages the three-year Women, Low Income and Smoking Project which is based in ASH Scotland.

Hilary Graham is Professor of Social Policy at Lancaster University and is Director of the ESRC Health Variations Programme. Her research has focused on the experience of promoting family health in circumstances of disadvantage, looking in particular at the patterns of women's smoking and the place of cigarettes in the lives of mothers caring for children on a low income. She has conducted research for the Department of Health, the Economic and Social Research Council and the Health Education Authority. Her published work includes *Hardship and Health in Women's Lives* (1993) and *When Life is a Drag: Women, Smoking and Disadvantage* (1993).

Sian Griffiths was appointed as Director of Public Health and Health Policy for Oxfordshire in 1993. Her previous public health experience was at both district and regional levels. She trained and worked in East London before joining Oxford region as a consultant in 1989. From 1990 to 1993 she was Regional Director of Public Health for South West Thames, where she was lead RDPH for primary care. Her main interests are in health strategy and policy. She is currently Treasurer of the Faculty of Public Health Medicine and Co-Chair of the Association of Public Health.

Diana Harcourt is a Research Psychologist at the Breast Care Centre, Frenchay Healthcare Trust, Bristol, and is conducting a PhD at the University of the West of England. She is an Associate Member of the Centre for Appearance and Disfigurement Research.

Victoria Holt trained as a doctor at Cambridge University and the London Hospital, and as a GP on the St Bartholomew's and Hackney GP vocational training scheme before joining Hoxton Health Collective in 1989. She was active in Women in Medicine in the 1980s, and co-commissioned and co-researched the educational video and teaching pack, *Lesbian Health Matters*, produced in 1995.

Victoria Lack trained at Manchester University, taking a degree in General and Community Nursing. She worked as a Practice Nurse at Hoxton Health Collective for three years and is currently College Nurse at King's College University, London.

Sue Laughlin is currently Women's Health Coordinator for Greater Glasgow Health Board. In this post, she is responsible for coordinating the implementation of the Glasgow Women's Health Policy within the health service. She is also chairperson of the Glasgow Healthy City Partnership Women's Health Working Group. Glasgow has recently been appointed as a WHO Collaborating Centre for Women's Health.

Sarah Payne lectures in Health Policy at the School for Policy Studies, University of Bristol. Her research interests include gender and mental health and the delivery of mental health services, inequalities in health and deprivation, particularly in relation to women's experience of poverty and the experience of deprivation in rural areas.

Nichola Rumsey is a Principal Lecturer in Psychology at the University of the West of England, Bristol, and Research Director of the Centre for Appearance and Disfigurement Research.

Imogen Sharp is Director of the National Heart Forum, the leading alliance of over 35 national medical, health and consumer groups working to reduce the high rates of coronary heart disease in the UK through prevention strategies. She is editor of several Forum reports, including *Coronary Heart Disease: Are Women Special?*, and has led a campaign through the National Heart Forum to increase awareness of women's risk of heart disease. She has been a participant in several *Health of the Nation* Task Forces (including physical activity, nutrition, and workplace), in the development and implementation of the national health strategy. She is also an Honorary Member of the Faculty of Public Health Medicine, and has honorary lectureships in Public Health Policy at the London School of Hygiene and Tropical Medicine, and at University College London.

Fenella Starkey undertook her undergraduate degree in Social and Political Sciences at the University of Cambridge, and then moved on to work in the voluntary sector as a Research and Development Worker. She has worked at the University of the West of England (UWE) since 1995 on various research projects, including a project commissioned by Maternity and Health Links to assess the need for health service interpreting and advocacy provision for women whose first language is not English. Fenella is currently Research Fellow in Health Promotion at UWE, and is studying part-time for a PhD with the University of Bristol's School for Policy Studies.

Hilary Thomas is a Lecturer in the Department of Sociology, University of Surrey. Her research interests include the sociology of reproduction and gynaecology. She is a joint editor of *Locating Health: Sociological and Historical Explorations* (Avebury 1993) and *Private Risks and Public Dangers* (Avebury 1993). She was formerly convenor of the British Sociological Association Medical Sociology Group and is currently a member of the executive committee of the European Society for Health and Medical Sociology.

Tamsin Wilton is Senior Lecturer/Senior Research Fellow in Health Sciences at the Faculty of Health and Social Care, University of the West of England, Bristol, and a member of the Bristol Women and Health Research Group. She has written widely on sexuality and health and her most recent publications include *En/Gendering AIDS: Deconstructing Sex, Texts and Epidemic* (Sage 1997), and *Good for You: A Handbook on Lesbian Health and Wellbeing*

(Cassell 1997). She is currently writing a textbook on sexuality for health and social care professionals, to be published by the Open University Press.

Kate Woodhouse has been involved in smoking prevention since 1980, when she became incensed by tobacco advertising. She was Research Officer at the HEA smoking prevention unit, HELIOS, where she produced a number of publications on women and smoking. She has also done consultancy for the HEA's Adult Smoking and Smoking in Pregnancy programmes, and for No Smoking Day.

Part 1

●

Women and health services: the case for change

Introduction: women and health services

•

Lesley Doyal

Introduction

When the National Health Service (NHS) was set up in 1948 it received widespread acclaim with visitors coming from many parts of the world to see this new model for meeting the healthcare needs of an urban industrial population. Despite major financial constraints it continues to deliver good quality care at relatively low cost and compares well on most criteria with provision in other countries at similar levels of economic development. Yet there continues to be considerable disquiet about the way the service treats women.

The NHS has changed dramatically over the past two decades and the effects of these changes have been complex. There is some evidence of a stronger voice for consumers and of greater accountability of both doctors and senior managers to the populations they serve (Robinson and Le Grand 1993). However, this has made relatively little impact on the responsiveness of the service to the particular needs of women. This is especially surprising against the background of the women's health advocacy movement that has developed in so many countries over the past 25 years (Garcia-Moreno and Claro 1994; Doyal 1995: ch. 8). Though British women have been active in some of these wider campaigns their impact on the NHS itself has been relatively limited (Doyal 1983, 1993).

The factors underlying this are complex. On the one hand it highlights women's lack of power in the wider society and the failure of successive governments to take them seriously as a political constituency. On the other it reflects the structure of the service itself. Though the NHS represented a major step forward in the organization and financing of healthcare it was never a model for democratic planning. Few mechanisms of accountability or participation were built into the system with the result that the majority of users (and most workers) have had little opportunity to influence its operation.

However this situation has been changing. Since the 1980s increasing pressures to deliver more effective and efficient services within the purchaser/provider framework have generated innovative ways of thinking about the organization of care. At the same time, traditional patterns of power and control have been at least partially disrupted and new mechanisms set up to express the views of the wider community. Of course the resulting developments have not always been to the benefit of patients. Indeed they have often been against their better interests. But new opportunities have also been created to exert pressure for a more equitable and responsive service. This potential for change was further enhanced by the election of a new government in 1997, creating an environment in which the interests of women (and other groups with particular needs) could be moved higher up the agenda of both purchasers and providers (Stationery Office 1997).

Women's health advocates and their supporters have long claimed that the NHS treats women unfairly (Doyal 1985, 1993; Roberts 1985; Stacey 1985). They have amassed considerable evidence to show that women are treated differently from men in ways that objectively disadvantage them and they have campaigned for the removal of these discriminatory practices. However this does not mean that a genuinely equitable healthcare system would treat men and women in identical ways. If equality of outcome is to be achieved, services need to be based on a clear understanding of both the biological and the social differences between women and men and the impact that these have on their healthcare needs.

These are complex issues that will be spelled out in more detail in the remainder of this chapter. We look first at feminist critiques of medical practice to identify the gender discrimination that too often characterizes female patients' encounters with the healthcare system. Having seen how women can be damaged by perceptions of their 'difference' we will then explore what could be called the 'positively' gendered approach. This will involve an examination of how 'maleness' and 'femaleness' affect health needs in ways that need to be acknowledged if services are to be both equitable and effective. The final section of the chapter will look in more detail at the spaces for change that have opened up in the NHS and explore the ways in which these could be occupied by those seeking to promote women's health.

Women and the NHS: difference and discrimination

Many critics of the NHS have drawn attention to women's lack of influence in a system in which they make up about 75 per cent of workers as well as the majority of users (Miles 1991; Doyal 1993). Most of the power remains with the medical profession and with senior managers, the majority of whom are male. Though the last few years have seen a marked curtailment of their 'clinical freedom', doctors still exercise a significant degree of control both over medical research and over the allocation of scarce medical resources. They also have a major influence on the quality of the treatment given to individuals. This disadvantages many women employed in the health sector and also has profound effects on women using its services.

In medicine itself women now make up over 50 per cent of the student body but only about a quarter of hospital doctors and 30 per cent of GPs. As these new entrants move through the system the population of women at different levels will increase but it is apparent that they are unlikely to pursue their careers on equal terms with men (Witz 1992). Only about 17 per cent of consultants are female and they are concentrated in a few specialties, most of which have relatively low status (IHSM Consultants 1994). As a result women continue to be under-represented on the ruling bodies of the profession such as the General Medical Council and the British Medical Association.

In management too women are conspicuously absent from senior positions. Though their situation has improved in recent years they still hold only about 16 per cent of top NHS management posts (IHSM Consultants 1994). Female influence is also limited on those bodies designed to facilitate public participation. Again the percentage of women is increasing, but nationally, men still make up about 60 per cent of the membership of health authorities and NHS Trusts (Department of Health 1997a).

Thus women's predominance in the healthcare labour force and as unpaid carers is not reflected in their access to power and decision making. In particular the vast numbers of female nurses who play such a central role in running the service continue to have a subordinate role in relation to their medical colleagues. Individual nurses may be able to negotiate greater autonomy in their own work setting. However, the profession as a whole remains in a position of structured dependence and there is clearly a gender dimension to these divisions in the healthcare labour force (Davies 1995).

These continuing gender inequalities are sustained by a range of discriminatory practices, which act as an arbitrary constraint on the benefits women can obtain from the health service both as workers and as users. Of course the origins of these practices and the motivations of those who carry them out are often complex and sometimes contradictory. Indeed they will sometimes be designed to meet what are genuinely perceived to be women's 'real' needs. But whatever the subjective intentions of those involved, their objective effects can be damaging. In their attempts to map the impact of this discrimination on service users, women's health advocates have focused on two key issues: access and quality of care.

Around the world, many millions of women continue to be denied access to basic healthcare as a result of social, economic and cultural inequalities (Jacobson 1992; Koblinsky *et al.* 1993). One of the main achievements of the NHS was to remove obstacles of this kind for British women through the introduction of care free at source and the setting up of a national network of general practitioners. Indeed, in the first years after its inception, working-class women were among the main beneficiaries of the service as their pent-up need for items such as gynaecological surgery, dental care and spectacles was at last met. However this does not mean that access is no longer a problem.

Some women still have difficulty in obtaining appropriate care and these problems have intensified as the pressures on NHS spending have increased. Though waiting lists and other symptoms of financial strain have an impact on both sexes there is evidence that women are disproportionately affected in particular areas. Family planning services for instance have been significantly reduced in many parts of the country (Kennir 1990), while their longer life expectancy means that older women are more likely than their male counterparts to be affected by the withdrawal of the NHS from the provision of continuing care beds (Whitehead 1993; see also Arber, this volume). Women are also more likely than men to find their access limited by increasingly demanding domestic responsibilities (Young 1996), by lack of transport and in some instances by cultural or linguistic barriers (Smaje 1995: ch. 6; see also Starkey; Douglas, this volume).

When they do receive services there is evidence that women may experience particular problems in their relations with those who are paid to care for them. Though men too may find it difficult to communicate with their carers, women seem to face additional difficulties, relating both to their own socialization and to the stereotypical views that others may hold of them (Roberts 1985; Fisher 1986; Miles 1991). Many doctors are still reluctant to let women speak for themselves and women may feel unable to assert their own wishes. Poor women in particular, as well as those from ethnic minorities, are sometimes treated by health workers as though they were less rational, less capable of complex decision making and sometimes as simply less valuable than men (Douglas 1992; see also Douglas, this volume).

Women's own experience is often devalued by comparison with 'expert' medical knowledge and many doctors are unwilling to admit ignorance and uncertainty (Graham and Oakley 1981). As a result female patients may become the passive recipients of doctors' ministrations. For some this will be a distressing and demeaning experience as a number of personal accounts have described (O'Sullivan 1987). More seriously perhaps, failure to respect women's autonomy represents a significant breach of the generally accepted codes of medical ethics (Beauchamp and Faden 1986). Informed consent for instance can have little reality in a situation where women's own beliefs and desires are accorded little value or respect (Faulder 1985; Sherwin 1992: ch. 6).

These issues have generated particular concern in the context of reproductive healthcare where the price of access to technology can be loss of autonomy (Holmes and Purdy 1992; Sherwin 1992; Tong 1997). Women seeking to use modern methods of fertility control, for instance, may need to negotiate with a doctor whose personal judgements about the appropriateness of particular methods may constrain the woman's own choice (Bruce 1987;

see also Thomas, this volume). In surgery too, women are sometimes denied the opportunity to participate fully in treatment decisions. Of course individuals will vary greatly in how active a part they wish to play, but in the case of breast cancer surgery and hysterectomy in particular, many still report lack of support in their attempts to make an informed choice (see Rumsey and Harcourt; Thomas, this volume).

Concerns about the quality of caring relationships continue to be high on the agenda of women's health advocates both in the UK and around the world. But alongside them has been a growing concern about the technical quality of the care offered to many women, with reproductive health services again receiving particular attention. It is clear that the development of contraceptive devices is often influenced more by effectiveness and cost criteria than by concern for women's health (World Health Organisation and International Women's Health Coalition 1991). As a result women may be prescribed devices that prevent them from conceiving but only at significant cost to their well-being (Mintzes 1992). Though these criticisms are most frequently levelled at services in the developing countries, it is clear that in the UK too there are women who have difficulty finding a contraceptive that meets all their needs (Pollack 1985).

Even more seriously, breast cancer treatment in the NHS has come under critical scrutiny as a growing body of evidence shows that many women are continuing to die unnecessarily. Though the incidence of the disease in Britain is not especially high the mortality rate is the highest in the world. In 1992 there were nearly 40 deaths per 100,000 of the population, compared with a rate of 34 per 100,000 in the US. Yet the US has an incidence of 89 cases per 100,000 compared with the UK rate of only 56 (House of Commons Health Committee 1995). While some of these differences may be due to variations in reporting practices, the conclusion of a recent report was that most were due to the way care is currently organized, particularly the huge variations in women's access to specialist treatment (House of Commons Health Committee 1995). This makes the deaths potentially preventable if services were properly organized to take advantage of existing knowledge and skills (see also Rumsey and Harcourt, this volume).

In recent years it has become evident that problems with the quality of clinical care are not confined to specialist 'women's' areas. In the US in particular a number of studies have shown that even where women and men have the same health problems, women may be denied a fair allocation of clinical resources (Kirchstein 1991; United States National Institutes of Health 1992; Giacomini 1996). Men on dialysis for example are significantly more likely than women with the same symptoms to obtain a kidney transplant (Held *et al.* 1988). A number of US studies have shown that men with cardiac symptoms are more likely than women to be given diagnostic catheterization (Fiebach *et al.* 1990; Wenger 1990) and UK studies are beginning to show similar patterns (see Sharp, this volume). Men in the South West Thames Region for instance are 60 per cent more likely than women with the same condition to be offered coronary artery bypass operations or angioplasty (Kee *et al.* 1993; Petticrew *et al.* 1993).

Evidence of this kind highlights the ways in which differential treatment of men and women can sometimes lead to unacceptable outcomes. It therefore offers clues about how healthcare should not be delivered. However, we need to take the analysis a stage further if we are to identify those genuine differences that require positive action in the planning of equitable and effective services.

Sex, gender and healthcare: different but equal?

Differences between men and women are now receiving greater attention in healthcare planning. However, discussion is frequently hampered by confusion about the ways in which 'maleness' and 'femaleness' affect health. If we are to make a credible case for change in the NHS we need to have a much clearer model of the ways in which being a man or being a woman can affect both the need for healthcare and the form that healthcare should take. This will provide a basis for gender-sensitive planning that is better informed about the needs of all service users.

The term 'gender' is increasingly used in debates about healthcare but its meaning is often imprecise. Indeed, it is often used interchangeably with the term 'sex' when the two actually refer to very different things (Oakley 1972; Birke 1986). If we are to make sense of the varying health needs of men and women we need to start by making a clear distinction between the biological (or sex) differences between them and the social (or gender) differences. Both are important in understanding human health and illness but their policy implications may well be very different. And both need to be taken seriously if services are to meet the needs of women as well as those of men.

The most obvious differences between the sexes are, of course, the biological ones since their distinctive reproductive systems generate health problems specific to each sex. Only a woman will need screening for cancer of the cervix for instance, while only men have to fear diseases of the prostate. However women's capacity for pregnancy and childbirth gives them additional needs for healthcare. Unless they are able to control their fertility and give birth safely women can determine little else about their lives. This is reflected in the fact that contraceptive use is by far the commonest reason for women visiting their GPs while childbirth is the major reason for hospital stays (see Thomas, this volume).

The importance of meeting women's reproductive health needs has been widely recognized and pregnant women in particular have received a great deal of attention in the NHS. Indeed the specialty of obstetrics and gynaecology has become a powerful force in the medical arena, and has played its part in ensuring that Britain now has amongst the lowest maternal and infant mortality rates in the world. However this should not be taken as an indication that all the health needs specific to women have been met. The territory staked out by obstetricians and gynaecologists does not exhaust the biological differences between the sexes but other dimensions of difference have been largely ignored in the planning and delivery of services.

In the case of coronary heart disease for example, we know that there are marked sex differences in the age of onset of the disease and possibly in its progression (see Sharp, this volume). However, the continuing failure to include women in sufficient numbers either in epidemiological research or in clinical trials has made it difficult to investigate these or to assess their overall significance in the delivery of effective care (Mastroianni *et al.* 1994; Rosser 1994; Hamilton 1996). Similar concerns have been expressed in relation to HIV and AIDS where there is still considerable ignorance about sex differences in the transmission of the virus and in the progression of the disease (Healy 1991; Korvick 1993).

It is clear then, that biological differences between the sexes play a significant part in determining patterns of health and illness and that this influence is not confined to the reproductive process itself. Further research on these issues is urgently needed so that they can be more accurately reflected in the planning and implementation of clinical care. But however seriously we take the biological differences between the sexes, this can provide only a partial picture of the impact of femaleness and maleness on health and illness. Gender or social differences also have an important role and need equally careful exploration (Doyal 1995; Sargent and Brettell 1996).

All cultures assign particular characteristics to those they define as female and those they define as male (Moore 1988). Men and women are defined as different types of beings with different duties, different responsibilities and different rights and rewards (Moore 1988; Papanek 1990). The most obvious illustration of this is the split between the public world of work and politics which is seen as 'naturally' male and the private arena of the family and domesticity which is seen as 'naturally' female. In most societies these are not merely differences but inequalities, with women having less access than men to a whole variety of economic and social resources (UNDP 1995).

The reality of these gender divisions is apparent in the different lives led by women and men and these can influence health in a number of ways. Men and women will be exposed to different health risks, both physical and psychological. They have access to different amounts and types of resources for maintaining or promoting their own health and may also have different levels of responsibility for the care of others. If they become ill they may have very different strategies for coping. They may define their symptoms in very different ways, will probably seek help from different sources and may respond very differently to treatment. These gender differences clearly have profound implications for the planning of healthcare but thus far they have received little attention from those trained in the biomedical tradition.

Women's 'caring' responsibilities, for instance, can be physically hard and emotionally demanding especially for those with few financial or social resources (Doyal 1995: ch. 2). This work is undervalued and usually unpaid and often has to be combined with employment outside the home which can itself involve unrecognized hazards. Both the labours themselves and the broader cultural devaluation of the 'female' go some way towards explaining why women continue to report twice as much anxiety and depression as men (Busfield 1996: ch. 10; see also Payne, this volume). Men, on the other hand, are more likely to die prematurely from work-related accidents or illness or from risky activities traditionally defined as 'masculine' (Gibbs 1988; Sabo and Gordon 1993).

Thus, both their biological characteristics and the similarities in their social circumstances mean that women have certain health needs in common and that these are sometimes different from those of men. However, this should not lead us to assume that they can be treated as a homogeneous group for planning (or any other) purposes. Sex and gender are not the only determinants of health and illness and we also need to explore the biological, social and cultural factors that separate different groups of women from each other. These differences too will have to be taken seriously if the healthcare needs of all women are to receive equal attention.

Women and health: dimensions of diversity

The ageing process is a fundamental determinant of health so that women's healthcare needs will vary markedly across the lifespan. The physiological processes of ageing are undeniable and women in particular experience major bodily changes as they move through different stages of their reproductive cycle. However, the ageing process is also shaped by life experiences and by social attitudes towards people of different ages (see Arber, this volume). Thus the low income and lack of support experienced by so many older women can contribute directly to physical and psychological ill health (World Health Organisation 1996). The stereotype of older people in general is a predominantly negative one but older women are often treated especially badly and this is reflected in their continuing invisibility in many areas of healthcare planning.

Women's health needs will also vary with their economic and social status, with poverty remaining a major cause of ill health in both men and women. Despite the existence of the NHS, a British woman in social classes I or II still has almost four years' greater life expectancy than a compatriot in social classes IV or V as well as having significantly less chance of dying during pregnancy or childbirth (Drever and Whitehead 1997). Of the 70 major causes of death in women, 64 are more common in those married to men in unskilled or semi-skilled occupations, with breast cancer being the only major exception (NHS Executive 1995). These differences are also reflected in patterns of morbidity, with 15 per cent of professional women reporting limiting and long-standing illness compared with 31 per cent of women in unskilled occupations (Office for National Statistics 1997).

Race and ethnicity too affect health status in a variety of ways that are still being disentangled (Smaje 1995; see also Douglas, this volume). Racist practices are one element in the structural disadvantage that members of many ethnic minority communities still experience. Different cultural beliefs, demographic structures and levels of access to a range of economic and social resources also contribute to the variations in patterns of health and illness found between ethnic groups. As yet there have been few attempts to explore the influence of gender on these complex processes (Smaje 1995) but some interesting findings are beginning to emerge. There is growing evidence for instance of the mental health problems facing young South Asian women (Fenton and Sadiq 1995; Smaje 1995). However, other aspects of life in the same communities seem to be protective of women's health. Smoking for example (as well as tranquillizer use) is much less common in Asian and African–Caribbean women in Britain than it is among white women (Gabe and Thorogood 1986; see also Woodhouse, this volume).

It is clear from this very brief account that women are not a single homogeneous group. They have extremely varied experiences, interests, needs and desires. Any policy designed to meet the needs of all women will therefore need to take the differences between them as seriously as the similarities. This is a complex task that poses considerable challenges but it is one that can no longer be ignored. The current state of the NHS offers considerable opportunities for change and these need to be exploited if more women are to realize their potential for health.

Time for change?

The Thatcher review of 1988 set in train a series of changes in both the culture and the organization of the NHS. Central to these developments was the creation of an internal or managed market with a separation of roles between purchasers and providers of healthcare. This was achieved through the setting up of NHS Trusts to take responsibility for the management of both hospital and community services. Health authorities were then given the responsibility for purchasing these services for the people living in their area. Primary care too was changed, with some general practitioners becoming fundholders and purchasing a range of both community and hospital services.

These developments have had far-reaching effects, often disrupting traditional ways of doing things. Established relationships were unlocked and new alliances began to form. The power of those controlling acute medicine was threatened both by health authorities and by fundholding GPs and the clinical practice of senior members of the medical profession has come under increasing scrutiny. The effects of these developments on patient care have been complicated, often contradictory and sometimes damaging and they have certainly not led to the dramatic increase in patient power trumpeted at their inception (Robinson and Le Grand 1993). However, the process of change itself opened up possibilities for developing models that are more sensitive to the varied needs of NHS users in general and women in particular.

This has been especially evident in the last few years as severe constraints on resources, combined with an increase in patient throughput, has led to ever-increasing pressure on providers. At the same time the reduction in junior doctors' hours and associated reforms in the medical career structure have led to severe shortages of junior staff in some specialties. Under these conditions old models may become unsustainable and the pressures for change irresistible. New ways have been sought of deploying staff and of organizing services and ideally these opportunities can also be used to improve patient care.

One example of this has been the development of new nursing roles, in which the postholders themselves take on greater professional autonomy and greater responsibility. In some cases these new roles have also delivered greater continuity of care and improvements in interpersonal communication which women in particular have found extremely valuable (Read and Graves 1994; Doyal *et al.* 1997). Thus the need for Trusts to rationalize their activities can simultaneously facilitate the development of services that meet the needs of users in more sensitive and appropriate ways (see Bell, this volume).

As part of the move towards greater effectiveness and efficiency, there is also an increased concern with 'evidence-based medicine' and a rapid growth in the monitoring and evaluation of clinical practice. These developments have particular significance for women since historically some of the most serious examples of ineffective treatment have been inflicted on female patients. Radical mastectomies for example are now out of fashion while the value of continuing to perform such large numbers of hysterectomies has been widely questioned (Coulter *et al.* 1988). Many aspects of the new obstetrics have also been criticized both for their ineffectiveness and also for their potential to damage both mothers and babies (Chalmers *et al.* 1980).

Despite this record there is little evidence that either sex or gender differences are routinely incorporated into the criteria being used for the development of new processes of evaluation and review. However, it is likely that women would be major beneficiaries if clinical audit in particular were opened up and the findings subject to wider public scrutiny. Recent work in the area of coronary artery disease for instance has highlighted the importance of identifying male and female differences in diagnostic procedures and therapeutic outcomes (see Sharp, this volume). It is important, therefore, that these issues should be taken seriously by the new National Institute for Clinical Excellence (Department of Health 1997b).

Purchasers as well as providers have been given new opportunities to promote better quality care for women since the 1988 reforms. Under the internal market, they were given responsibility for meeting the needs of the population they serve in ways that are open to public scrutiny for the first time in the history of the service. This has led to more open debate about the determination of priorities in settings where the particular concerns of women can legitimately be raised (see Laughlin; Griffiths and Bradlow, this volume). The question of whether or not to fund infertility treatment, for example, is now being openly discussed in a number of authorities in ways that would previously have been done behind closed doors. As the internal market disappears with the 'New NHS' these processes can hopefully be opened up still further (Department of Health 1997b).

The commissioning process requires health authorities to carry out needs assessments of the population for whom they are responsible. If these are carried out with a gender perspective they can be used to identify gaps in services which might previously have gone unnoticed as well as revealing the systematic biases that continue to limit the effectiveness of many data collection methods in common use. Assessing the need for community mental healthcare for women is one example which has posed considerable challenges for a number of authorities (Abel *et al.* 1996).

As part of the process of needs assessment, health authorities are required to initiate consultation with the various groups they serve and a growing number have recognized women as a key constituency requiring special attention (see Griffiths and Bradlow; Laughlin, this volume). Though such exercises are often limited in their scope, they do offer to individuals and to groups representing women's interests an opportunity to have their voices heard by those who can take action on their behalf. In the case of abortion services for example, many health authorities have listened to GPs, women's groups and community health councils who condemned the inadequacy of previous levels of provision. These campaigns were a major factor behind the increase in NHS funding for abortions taking place in some areas over the past five years (Abortion Law Reform Association 1997).

The management of the system requires the placing of formal contracts or service agreements between health authorities and trusts and here too there are opportunities for raising women's concerns. Recognizing the importance of this stage of the planning process, some advocacy organizations have already developed guidelines for the purchasing of good quality care in particular areas such as abortion and mental health (Birth Control Trust, n.d.). After the original contracting process has been completed many authorities are monitoring the performance of providers to ensure adherence to specified quality standards. Again this offers the opportunity to raises issues of gender sensitivity and awareness (see Laughlin, this volume). Trusts may be required to offer mentally ill women a choice of male or female doctor for instance (Abel *et al.* 1996).

Some fundholding general practices have also been functioning as direct purchasers of care, giving them important opportunities to influence the delivery of care in line with the expressed needs and desires of their female (and male) patients. At the same time the emergence of 'the locality' as a focal point in the purchasing process has increased the role of all primary healthcare teams in determining the policies and priorities of commissioning authorities and in the 'New NHS' this will be formalized in Primary Care Groups (Department of Health 1997b).

As well as playing a greater part in the planning of care, some general practices have also responded to these developments by changing the way in which their own work is organized (Harrison and Neve 1996). Some health visitors, for example, have been active in developing community-based provision for 'at risk' women with the fewest economic and social resources (Blackburn 1996). Most practices also offer a wider range of services in their own surgeries, some using the skills of a variety of different practitioners. These include 'outreach' clinics moving traditionally hospital-based provision nearer to the patients, as well as a range of counselling services and complementary therapies. Women make greater use than men of most of these new provisions and they have been especially valuable for the large numbers of women who report depression and other forms of mental distress (Abel *et al.* 1996; see also Payne, this volume).

Alongside the changes within primary care there has been a shift towards community-based provision as well as a growth in joint initiatives across different areas of health and social services. Again, this process will be intensified in the 'New NHS' (Department of Health 1997b). Like so many other developments these moves have had complex and contradictory effects for women. On the one hand they have intensified their role as carers as they take up some of the responsibilities that institutions have shed. However, they have also created space for small-scale projects which can serve as models for larger developments (see Wilton; Amos *et al.*; Laughlin; Payne, this volume). Among the most creative have been those developing new approaches to the care of HIV-positive women, women with AIDS and those with mental health problems. Many have involved collaboration between the NHS and the voluntary sector. The Shanti project in Brixton for example is an intercultural psychotherapy centre which began as a pioneering project for an Inner City Partnership but is now a free service within a community trust (Mills 1996).

As the physical and economic shape of the NHS has changed there has also been a gradual transformation in the basic philosophy underlying it. Around the world, medicine has been widely criticized for its emphasis on the biological at the expense of the social, on the physical at the expense of the psychological. In response to these concerns there is evidence of a shift towards what has been called a social model of health. Internationally this has been led by the World Health Organisation (WHO) initiative *Health For All by the Year 2000*.

The response to these developments has been more muted in the UK than in many other parts of the world, and not surprisingly perhaps the 'holistic' approach it embodies is more evident in some parts of the NHS than in others. The *Health of the Nation* document and its associated policies have been widely criticized for their 'victim blaming' approach and also for their failure to take gender issues seriously (Daykin and Naidoo 1995; see also Graham; Daykin, this volume). However the basic philosophy of *Health of the Nation* does reflect a growing commitment to prevention and attempts to put it into practice have generated a more sophisticated understanding of the impact on health of class, race and gender inequalities in daily life.

Gender issues in the social causation of health and illness are clearly a matter of concern for men as well as women. However, it is women who have developed the most rigorous and clearly documented account of the social, economic and cultural influences on their well-being (Doyal 1995; Sargent and Brettell 1995). If the goals of *Health of the Nation* (Secretary of State for Health 1992) and its successor *Our Healthier Nation* (1998) are to be realized these links need to be acted upon. In the case of smoking for instance, or exercise, nutrition or mental health, effective strategies cannot be developed without taking the differences between women and men seriously. This offers an important opportunity to demonstrate the potential damage imposed by gender inequalities on all aspects of women's well-being (Doyal 1995).

Developing a strategy

As we have seen, the history of the NHS has been one of continuing transformation under both Conservative and Labour governments. Within this environment, strategies to promote women's health could flourish but this will require considerable commitment from those working both inside and outside the service. It will also require a willingness to learn from others. There is now a considerable volume of writing from academics, health advocates and planners around the world which could be used as a resource in making the NHS more gender-sensitive while important models of good practice outside the UK could provide exemplars for change (Sen *et al.* 1994; World Health Organisation 1994; Commonwealth Secretariat 1996).

Closer to home, many organizations in the voluntary sector in the UK have developed examples of high-quality care for specific groups of women. Some provide valuable examples of gender-sensitive services but few of these lessons have yet been transferred into mainstream NHS practice. Within the NHS itself there have also been notable pioneers in the process of enhancing gender awareness but the lessons learned have rarely been diffused through the service as a whole. The main aim of this book is to bring some of these examples of good practice to a wider audience and to explore in more detail the philosophies that underlie them.

The introductory chapter has provided a preliminary overview of the case for change and the articles that follow elaborate on the various issues raised. They cover a range of both practical and conceptual concerns and spell out their implications for a future National Health Service. The authors come from a variety of backgrounds and approach their subject in very different ways. Some are engaged primarily in a critique of existing policies while others describe new initiatives and assess their potential for wider dissemination. Some write as academics, some as policy makers, some as health practitioners and some as activists, and many occupy several of these roles simultaneously. What they share is a commitment to maintaining what is good about the NHS while at the same time enhancing its capacity to meet women's need for effective and appropriate healthcare.

Part 1 begins with four articles exploring the needs and interests of different groups of women. Hilary Graham examines the relationship between poverty, gender and health. Focusing on the daily lives of poor women, she explores the limitations of the *Health of the Nation* strategy as a way of conceptualizing risk. She argues for a social rather than a medical approach to public health and stresses the need for multi-sectoral models of intervention that recognize the reality of the choices poor women in particular face. Hilary Thomas then looks at the healthcare needs common to all women during their reproductive years. She identifies the unique challenges created when most service users are well rather than sick and stresses the continuing tensions between the perspectives of women themselves and the professionals who are paid to care for them.

This is followed by Sara Arber's exploration of the health concerns of older women. She identifies both the biological and the gender issues in ageing as well as the divisions of race and class that make the lives of older women so diverse. Gender blindness in both health and social care policies are discussed in some detail and implications for future planning highlighted. Jenny Douglas then discusses the needs of women from minority ethnic groups. Looking at their healthcare needs across the lifecycle, she examines the common experiences of racism and disadvantage that many of these women share. At the same time she emphasizes their diversity and the difficulties this poses for the planning of culturally sensitive and genuinely empowering services.

The next two articles take a slightly different approach, looking not at particular groups of women but at the ways in which specific health problems impact differentially on women as a (diverse) group. Sarah Payne begins with a discussion of mental health policy. She provides a brief overview of gender differences in the epidemiology of mental illness and the explanations offered for these variations. This is followed by a discussion of the form and content of mental health policy itself and the assumptions about women and men that lie behind it. She explores the impact of these ideas on those who use the services and begins to identify alternative ways of organizing care that might benefit both male and female users. This is followed by Imogen Sharp's account of women and coronary heart disease where gender bias is identified both in the knowledge base of medicine and in a range of medical practices. The article calls for much greater awareness of the differences between men and women in epidemiological research, clinical trials, surgical and medical treatment and also in the design of preventive strategies.

In the final article in Part 1, Kate Woodhouse analyses the growing hazard of female tobacco consumption. She begins with an account of current trends in smoking patterns, highlighting in particular the effects of disadvantage, and then examines the impact of these developments on women's health. The chapter includes an outline of gender differences in both the initiation and the continuation of the smoking habit and concludes with a discussion of the implications of these differences for cessation and prevention policies.

Part 2 focuses more directly on existing initiatives in the National Health Service. The articles describe a wide variety of projects in different parts of the service, linking them to broader women's health concerns. None presents a simple blueprint for change and few have been formally evaluated. This reflects a continuing failure within the NHS to audit organizational change with as much rigour as clinical innovation. However the range of initiatives described here can serve as illustrative examples of changes that can realistically be achieved within the current confines of the NHS.

The section begins with three case studies in the general area of sexuality and reproduction. Fenella Starkey gives a historical account of interpreting and advocacy services set up for Asian mothers in various parts of the country. She links them with broader developments in consumerism in the NHS and explores some of the issues of empowerment that lie behind the shift towards advocacy. The example of Maternity and Health Links in Bristol is then used to explore the position of voluntary organizations funded by providers to offer specialized services within the contract culture. This is followed by Katharine Bell's account of the development of a nurse-led gynaecology assessment unit in Watford which offers an illustration of women-centred innovation in the context of Trust rationalization. Tamsin Wilton then explores issues of sexuality in healthcare, describing the limitations of current provision for all users. She gives an account of the new services being set up for lesbian women in various parts of the country and calls for the ideas behind them to be given much wider circulation.

Nichola Rumsey and Diana Harcourt also concentrate on what is a predominantly 'female' problem in their account of current developments in the organization of care for women with breast cancer. Through an examination of 'one-stop' clinics and the introducton of counselling services they highlight the gap that continues to exist between research and policy. They stress the requirement to take the psychosocial needs of women with breast disease more seriously but emphasize that this will only be possible if innovations are properly evaluated and the results acted upon.

This is followed by two articles in the general area of health promotion. Amanda Amos and colleagues in Edinburgh describe a project funded by the Health Education Board in Scotland to develop new approaches to smoking cessation with poor women. Health promotion practitioners from different backgrounds worked together to develop principles of good practice in this area of work. From this a number of community-based projects were set up and these are briefly outlined so that lessons can be drawn for those undertaking similar work elsewhere. Norma Daykin then reviews broader developments in health promotion for women. Based on two recently completed case studies she compares the workplace and primary care as settings for the promotion of women's health and points out the implications for revisions to the *Health of the Nation* strategy.

Primary care is also the theme of the contribution by Rosa Benato and colleagues who describe the setting up of a collective general practice in East London. This offers illuminating examples of the ways in which both women and men can benefit from improvements in the relationships between healthcare workers and their patients. It provides an honest account of the difficulties faced by both groups in moving towards a more egalitarian approach and stresses the need for personal as well as organizational change if innovations of this kind are to succeed.

The last two articles in this section focus on the role of purchasers in developing a more gender-sensitive approach to the organization of healthcare. Sian Griffiths and Jean Bradlow describe their experiences of consulting the women of Oxfordshire about the county's health plan. They stress the benefits of consultation and outline some of the policy initiatives that resulted, while at the same time acknowledging the significant limitations of the process. In the final article in this section, Sue Laughlin describes the women's health policy implemented in Glasgow. This initiative is based on a social model of health. It is multi-sectoral in its approach and represents the most advanced strategy for women's health yet developed in the UK. The article gives an account of its historical development while also looking forward to the next stages. It outlines the basic principles underlying the strategy and places them in the broader context of current debates about women and health. In a concluding chapter, Lesley Doyal draws together the main themes from the book and sets an agenda for change.

References

Abel, K., Buszewicz, M., Davison, S., Johnson, S. and Staples, E. (1996) *Planning Community Mental Health Services for Women: A Multiprofessional Handbook*. London: Routledge.

Abortion Law Reform Association (1997) *A Report on NHS Abortion Services*. London: ALRA.

Beauchamp, J. and Faden, R. (1986) *A History and Theory of Informed Consent*. Oxford: Oxford University Press.

Birke, L. (1986) *Feminism and Biology*. Brighton: Wheatsheaf.

Birth Control Trust (n.d.) *Purchasing Abortion Services*. London: Birth Control Trust.

Blackburn, C. (1996) Building a poverty perspective into health visiting practice. In P. Bywaters and E. McLeod (eds) *Working for Equality in Health*. London: Routledge.

Bruce, J. (1987) Users' perspectives on contraceptive technology and delivery systems: Highlighting some feminist issues. *Technology in Society*, 9: 359–83.

Busfield, J. (1996) *Men, Women and Madness: Understanding Gender and Mental Disorder*. London: Macmillan.

Chalmers, I., Enkin, M. and Keirse, M. (eds) (1980) *Effective Care in Pregnancy and Childbirth*. Oxford: Clarendon Press.

Commonwealth Secretariat (1996) *Models of Good Practice Relevant to Women's Health*. London: Commonwealth Secretariat.

Coulter, A., McPherson, K. and Vessey, M. (1988) Do British women undergo too many or too few hysterectomies? *Social Science and Medicine*, 27 (9): 987–94.

Davies, C. (1995) *Gender and the Professional Predicament in Nursing*. Buckingham: Open University Press.

Davis, J., Andrews, S., Broom, D., Gray, G. and Renwick, M. (eds) (1995) *Changing Society for Women's Health. Proceedings of the 3rd National Women's Health Conference.* Canberra: Australian Government Publishing Service.

Daykin, N. and Naidoo, J. (1995) Feminist critique of health promotion. In R. Bunton, S. Nettleton and R. Burrows (eds) *The Sociology of Health Promotion: Critical Analyses of Consumption, Lifestyle and Risk.* London: Routledge.

Department of Health (1997a) *NEFU Appointments Database.* Personal communication.

Department of Health (1997b) *The New NHS: Modern and Dependable.* London: Stationery Office.

Department of Health (1998) *Our Healthier Nation: A Contract for Health,* Cm 3852. London: Stationery Office.

Douglas, J. (1992) Black women's health matters: putting black women on the research agenda. In H. Roberts (ed.) *Women's Health Matters.* London: Routledge.

Doyal, L. (1983) Women, health and the sexual division of labour: a case study of the women's health involvement in Britain. *Critical Social Policy,* 7: 21–33.

Doyal, L. (1985) Women and the National Health Service: the carers and the careless. In E. Lewin and V. Oleson (eds) *Women, Health and Healing: Towards a New Perspective.* London: Tavistock.

Doyal, L. (1993) Changing medicine? Gender and the politics of health care. In J. Gabe, D. Kellahar and G. Williams (eds) *Challenging Medicine.* London: Tavistock.

Doyal, L. (1995) *What Makes Women Sick: Gender and the Political Economy of Health.* London: Macmillan.

Doyal, L., Dowling, S. and Cameron, A. (1997) *Challenging Roles: An Evaluation of New Nursing Posts in the South West.* Bristol: Policy Press.

Drever, F. and Whitehead, M. (eds) (1997) *Health Inequalities: Decennial Supplement.* Series DS: 15. London: Stationery Office.

Faulder, C. (1985) *Whose Body Is It? The Troubling Issue of Informed Consent.* London: Virago.

Fenton, S. and Sadiq, A. (1995) *The Sorrow in My Heart: Sixteen Asian Women Speak about Depression.* London: Commission for Racial Equality.

Fiebach, M., Viscoli, C. and Horwitz, K. (1990) Differences between men and women in survival after myocardial infarction. *Journal of the American Medical Association,* 63: 1092–6.

Fisher, S. (1986) *In the Patient's Best Interest: Women and the Politics of Medical Decisions.* New Brunswick, NJ: Rutgers University Press.

Gabe, J. and Thorogood, N. (1986) Tranquillisers as a resource. In J. Gabe and P. Williams (eds) *Tranquillisers: Social, Psychological and Clinical Perspectives.* London: Tavistock.

Garcia-Moreno, C. and Claro, A. (1994) Challenges from the women's health movement: women's rights versus population control. In G. Sen, A. Germain and L. Chen (eds) *Population Policies Reconsidered: Health, Empowerment and Rights.* Boston: Harvard University Press.

Giacomini, M. (1996) Gender and ethnic differences in hospital-based procedure utilisation in California. *Archives of Internal Medicine,* 156: 1217–24.

Gibbs, J. (1988) *Young, Black and Male in America: An Endangered Species.* Dover, MA: Auburn House.

Graham, H. and Oakley, A. (1981) Competing ideologies of reproduction: medical and maternal perspectives on pregnancy. In H. Roberts (ed.) *Women, Health and Reproduction.* London: Routledge and Kegan Paul.

Hamilton, J. (1996) Women and health policy: on the inclusion of females in clinical trials. In C. Sargent and C. Brettell (eds) *Gender and Health: An International Perspective*. Upper Saddle River, NJ: Prentice-Hall.

Harrison, L. and Neve, H. (1996) *A Review of Innovations in Primary Health Care*. Bristol: Policy Press.

Healy, B. (1991) The Yentl syndrome. *New England Journal of Medicine*, 325: 274–6.

Held, P., Pauly, M. and Bovberg, R. *et al.* (1988) Access to kidney transplantation: has the US eliminated income and racial difference? *Archives of Internal Medicine*, 148: 2594–600.

Holmes, H. and Purdy, C. (1992) *Feminist Perspectives in Medical Ethics*. Bloomington and Indianapolis: Indiana University Press.

House of Common Health Committee (1995) *Breast Cancer Services*, vol. 1. London: HMSO.

IHSM Consultants (1994) *Creative Career Paths in the NHS. Report No.1: Top Managers*. London: Department of Health.

Jacobson, J. (1992) *Gender Bias: Roadblock to Sustainable Development*. Worldwide Paper 110. Washington, DC: Worldwatch Institute.

Kee, F., Gaffney, B., Currie, S. and O'Reilly, D. (1993) Access to coronary catheterisation: fair shares for all? *British Medical Journal*, 308: 883–6.

Kennir, B. (1990) *Family Planning Clinic Cuts: A Survey of NHS Family Planning Clinics in Greater London*. London: Family Planning Association.

Kirchstein, R. (1991) Research on women's health. *American Journal of Public Health* 81 (3): 291–3.

Koblinsky, M., Timyan, J. and Gay, J. (1993) *The Health of Women: A Global Perspective*. Boulder, CO: Westview Press.

Korvick, J. (1993) Trends in federally sponsored clinical trials. In A. Kurth (ed.) *Until the Cure: Caring for Women with HIV*. London and New Haven: Yale University Press.

Mastroianni, A., Faden, R. and Federman, D. (eds) (1994) *Women and Health Research: Ethical and Legal Issues of Including Women in Clinical Studies*, vols 1 and 2. Washington, DC: National Academy Press.

Miles, A. (1991) *Women, Health and Medicine*. Milton Keynes: Open University Press.

Mills, M. (1996) Shanti: An intercultural psychotherapy centre for women in the community. In K. Abel, M. Buszewicz, S. Davison, S. Johnson and E. Staples (eds) *Planning Community Mental Health Services for Women: A Multiprofessional Handbook*. London: Routledge.

Mintzes B. (ed.) (1992) *A Question of Control: Women's Perspectives on the Development and Use of Contraceptive Technology*. Amsterdam: Women and Pharmaceuticals Project, Health Action International and WEMOS.

Moore, H. (1988) *Feminism and Anthropology*. Oxford: Polity Press.

NHS Executive (1995) *Variations in Health: Report of the Variations Sub-group of the Chief Medical Officer's Health of the Nation Working Group*. London: HMSO.

Oakley, A. (1972) *Sex, Gender and Society*. London: Temple Smith.

Office for National Statistics (1997) *Living in Britain: Results from the 1995 General Household Survey*. London: Stationery Office.

O'Sullivan, S. (1987) *Women's Health: A Spare Rib Reader*. London: Pandora Press.

Papanek, H. (1990) To each, less than she needs, from each, more than she can do: allocating entitlements and value. In I. Tinker (ed.) *Persistent Inequalities: Women and World Development*. Oxford: Oxford University Press.

Petticrew, M., McKee, M. and Jones, J. (1993) Coronary artery surgery: are women discriminated against? *British Medical Journal*, 306: 1164–6.

Pollack, S. (1985) Sex and the contraceptive act. In H. Homans (ed.) *The Sexual Politics of Reproduction*. Aldershot: Gower.

Read, S. and Graves, K. (1994) *Reduction of Junior Doctors' Hours in the Trent Region: The Nursing Contribution,* Report to the Trent Task Force. Sheffield: Sheffield Centre for Health and Related Research (SCHARR).

Roberts, H. (1985) *The Patient Patients: Women and their Doctors.* London: Pandora.

Robinson, R. and Le Grand, J. (1993) *Evaluating the NHS Reforms.* London: King's Fund Institute.

Rosser, S. (1994) Gender bias in clinical research: the difference it makes. In A. Dan (ed.) *Reframing Women's Health: Multidisciplinary Research and Practice.* London: Sage.

Sabo, D. and Gordon, G. (1993) *Men's Health and Illness: Gender, Power and the Body.* London: Sage.

Sargent, C. and Brettell, C. (eds) (1996) *Gender and Health: An International Perspective.* Upper Saddle River, NJ: Prentice-Hall.

Secretary of State for Health (1992) *The Health of the Nation: A Strategy for England.* London: HMSO.

Sen, G., Germain, A. and Chen, L. (1994) *Population Policies Reconsidered: Health Empowerment and Rights.* Boston: Harvard University Press.

Sherwin, S. (1992) *No Longer Patient: Feminist Ethics and Health Care.* Philadelphia: Temple University Press.

Smaje, C. (1995) *Health, 'Race' and Ethnicity: Making Sense of the Evidence.* London: King's Fund Institute.

Stacey, M. (1985) Women and health: the United States and the United Kingdom compared. In E. Lewin and V. Oleson (eds) *Women, Health and Healing: Towards a New Perspective.* London: Tavistock.

Tong, R. (1997) *Feminist Approaches to Bioethics: Theoretical Reflections and Practical Applications.* Boulder, CO: Westview Press.

United National Development Programme (1995) *Human Development Report 1995.* Geneva: UNDP.

United States National Institutes of Health (1992) *Opportunities for Research on Women's Health.* NIH publication 92–3457. Washington, DC: US Department of Health and Human Services.

Wenger, M. (1990) Gender, coronary artery disease and coronary bypass surgery. *Annals of Internal Medicine,* 112: 557–8.

Whitehead, M. (1993) Is it fair? Evaluating the equity implications of the NHS reforms. In R. Robinson and J. Le Grand (eds) *Evaluating the NHS Reforms.* London: King's College Institute.

Witz, A. (1992) *Professions and Patriarchy.* London: Routledge.

World Health Organisation (1994) *Quality of Health Care for Women. Report of a Workshop held in Budapest, Hungary, October 1994.* Geneva: UNDP/World Bank/WHO.

World Health Organisation (1996) *Women, Ageing and Health: Controlling Health across the Lifespan.* Geneva: WHO.

World Health Organisation and International Women's Health Coalition (1991) *Creating Common Ground: Report of a Meeting between Women's Health Advocates and Scientists.* (WHO/HRP/ITT/91). Geneva: WHO.

Young, R. (1996) The household context for women's health care decisions: impact of UK policy changes. *Social Science and Medicine* 42 (6): 949–63.

1

•

Health at risk: poverty and national health strategies

•

Hilary Graham

Introduction

The chapter is set against the backdrop of the widening gap between rich and poor in the UK. It examines the implications of this widening gap both for national strategies to improve the nation's health and for the individual health strategies of women living and caring in the shadow of poverty. The central theme of the chapter is that national strategies are grounded in concepts of health and in measures of risk which obscure the health experiences and risk exposures shaping the domestic strategies of women caring for children in poverty.

The chapter explores the complex relationships between poverty, risk and health strategies in three sections. The first section discusses the income trends which frame the *Health of the Nation* (*HOTN*) strategies that have been pursued in the UK, as elsewhere in Europe and the US. The section notes how income inequality has widened across the last two decades and an increasing proportion of the population are living on incomes insufficient for their needs.

The second section examines the national health strategies which were established in the UK in the early 1990s – and subsequently revised as part of the Labour government's commitment to tackling health inequalities. These strategies seek to improve the health of the population by reducing the prevalence of health-damaging behaviours, like cigarette smoking and fat-rich diets. While such behaviours display a strong socio-economic gradient, the strategies rest on concepts of health and risk derived, not from qualitative data on how individuals protect health in the face of social disadvantage, but from quantitative data on the predictors of mortality.

The third section explores what *HOTN* concepts of health and risk obscure – and what in contrast women's accounts illuminate – about the health experiences and risk exposures of low-income families.

Income trends among households with children

There is no official poverty line in Britain. However, the European Commission has adopted a poverty standard, defining as poor those whose resources are so limited as to exclude them from the minimum acceptable way of life of the member states in which they live (CEC 1989: 9). This concept is measured by a poverty threshold of 50 per cent of average disposable income per equivalent adult. Roughly translated, this means you are poor if you live in a household with an income below half the average of all households, adjusted for size and composition.

Between 1939 and 1976, the risk of living below the EC poverty threshold fell in the UK, as differences in the income and living standards of rich and poor households narrowed and the poorest households were able to afford more of the resources that better-off families took for granted. Since the mid-1970s, the trend towards greater income equality has been reversed. Figure 1.1 tracks this reversal, plotting the proportion of the population living in households below the EC poverty threshold between 1961 and 1991. In 1976, 8 per cent of the population lived in households with incomes below the EC poverty line. By 1991, the proportion was not 8 per cent, but 24 per cent; not 1 in 13 but 1 in 4 were living in households with incomes below half the national average. Today, 14 million people in Britain are living on incomes below the EC decency threshold (Goodman and Webb

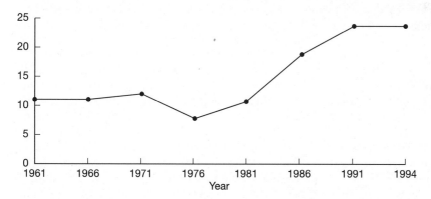

Figure 1.1 Proportion of the population below 50 per cent of average income (after housing costs) 1961–94, UK
Source: Goodman and Webb (1994: Figure 2.8 (a) + (b)); DSS (1997: Table F2 (AHC))

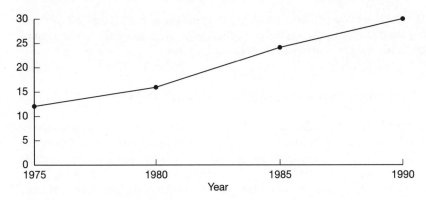

Figure 1.2   Proportion of children in poverty UK 1975–90
Source: Goodman and Webb (1994: Figure 2.8 (a) + (b)); DSS (1997: Table F2 (AHC))

1994). Those in receipt of income support (nearly 10 million people) make up the largest group among Britain's poor (DSS 1996).

Among those on the very lowest incomes, real incomes have not even stood still; they have declined. In the decade from 1979, households in the top decile of the income distribution saw their real incomes rise by over 60 per cent (calculated after housing costs). Between 1979 and 1990/91, the real incomes of households in the lowest income decile fell by 14 per cent (after housing costs) (House of Commons 1993).

National trends can mask changes in the distribution of income within the population. The rise in poverty has impacted disproportionately on households with children, on households in which adult patterns of health and health-related behaviours are being laid down among today's generation of children. Figure 1.2 presents the same data on trends in poverty, not for the population as a whole but for children. As the figure makes clear, the proportion of children in poverty is greater than the proportion of the population as a whole. Two decades ago, one child in eight in the UK was growing up in poverty; by the mid-1990s, it was one in three. In 1976, there were 1.8 million households with children under the age of 16 in households below the poverty line. By 1991, the number of poor families had trebled, to 5.5 million.

Figure 1.2 presents a chilling picture of the scale of childhood disadvantage in the UK, both in absolute terms and relative to its industrial neighbours. But because it maps the national incidence of poverty year by year, it underestimates the number of children exposed to poverty in the process of growing up. For example, in the US, while 18 per cent of children were in poverty in 1990, more than twice that proportion (38 per cent) will experience poverty at some time in their childhood (Ashworth *et al.* 1992). Figure 1.2 also masks the inequalities of 'race' and ethnicity which are deeply etched into the upward trend in childhood poverty. While national data are limited, they indicate that African–Caribbean and Asian households are much more likely to be reliant on income support, the major means-tested benefit for households without an adult in paid employment. While 17 per cent of white households receive income support, the proportion is 25 per cent among Indian households, 39 per cent among Black Caribbean households, and 54 per cent among Pakistani/Bangladeshi households (Oppenheim and Harker 1996).

Trends in family poverty are also deeply gendered. It is the women who are living and caring for children in poor households. Women are represented in almost all poor households with children in the UK, as partners in couples and as lone mothers. In the majority of families on income support, mothers and children are the primary domestic unit: they live and cope as lone parent families (Department of Social Security 1996).

The UK evidence suggests that households with children are not only more likely to be poor than other types of households; they also face more difficulties in meeting basic needs than other low-income households (Heady and Smyth 1989; Berthoud and Kempson 1992). Studies of income support, for example, suggest that the safety net benefit does not cover the basic needs of households with children. The cost of a healthy diet, low-cost clothes, warm shelter with enough space for each family member and the opportunity to participate in community activities absorbs more than the income support received by claimant families (Oldfield and Yu 1993). In other words, women find themselves caring for children on incomes where basic health needs are sacrificed in the struggle for financial survival.

The health effects of poverty have been measured not directly and qualitatively, through surveys of the health experience of low-income families, but indirectly and quantitatively, through the analysis of mortality data. These analyses rely on a proxy measure of living standards, based on occupation. They suggest that health inequalities have increased across the last two decades. Thus, between 1971 and 1981, death rates (all-cause Standardized Mortality Ratios) fell for women in England and Wales, but the differentials between women in manual and non-manual households increased (Macintyre 1994). The evidence for 1971–91 confirms this trend (Denver *et al.* 1996). In the early 1970s, the all-cause mortality rate for men aged 20–64 was twice as high in social class V as in social class I; by the early 1990s, men at the bottom of the class ladder were three times more likely to die before the age of 65 as men in the highest social class.

Analyses based on occupation are known to underestimate the scale of inequalities in health among women and children. Sharper and more finely graduated differences in mortality emerge using measures like tenure and car access, either as alternative measures or in combination with own occupation (Moser *et al.* 1990). Childhood mortality provides a powerful and chilling example of what is lost and what is obscured in the standard measures of social class.

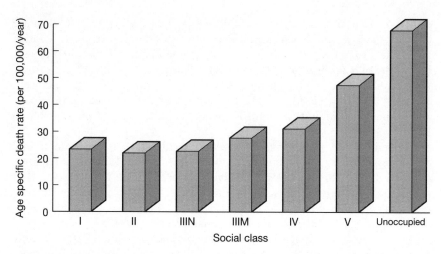

Figure 1.3   Childhood mortality (ages 1–15) in England and Wales, 1979–83
Source: Judge and Benzeval (1993: Table 1)

Figure 1.3 maps out the class gradient in mortality among children aged 1 to 15 who lived with a parent whose occupation was recorded at the registration of death (Judge and Benzeval 1993). As the figure indicates, the gradient in mortality captured through the conventional measure of living standards rises sharply when the class distribution is extended to include children who fall outside the Registrar General's classification: from 48 to 69 deaths per 100,000. An analysis of the 'unoccupied' category has revealed that it consists of parents whose occupation was not recorded at the registration of death, a group made up largely of economically inactive lone mothers, where living standards are constrained by the levels of income support (Judge and Benzeval 1993). It appears that class inequalities in health are at their sharpest among those excluded from a schema designed to capture these inequalities: among women whose socio-economic circumstances are mediated, not through a man, but through the social security system.

While the health effects of economic disadvantage have been tracked primarily through indirect quantitative measures of socio-economic status, there is an important seam of qualitative research which taps more directly into the lives of those with first-hand experience of disadvantage. In these studies, mothers – and more rarely children and fathers – have spoken about their lives. The accounts they give are of chronic hardship and deepening crises, where motherhood is structured around an unending conflict between caring enough and economizing enough, a conflict which seeps into the fabric of family relationships and eats away at women's emotional health (Cohen *et al.* 1992; Graham 1993a; Kempson 1996). The accounts that mothers have given to researchers reveal how patterns of care are structured, too, by risks built into their physical and social environment: by open stairwells, rubbish chutes and unprotected balconies and by harassment from older children and the constant danger of traffic. Women describe how strategies designed to protect their children from these dangers, like restricting their movement to and within the home, can have negative effects on the well-being of mother and child, and on the quality of the relationship between them (Mayall 1986; Roberts *et al.* 1995).

Before exploring mothers' accounts of health promotion and child protection in poverty, the chapter looks briefly at current national health strategies.

National health strategies

In the early 1990s the UK, like many other countries, launched national health strategies, setting targets and identifying mechanisms to improve the health of the population. While there are important differences between them, these *Health of the Nation* (*HOTN*) strategies rest on the targeting of major health problems and risk factors (Figures 1.4 and 1.5).

As is widely recognized, strategic targeting marks a major political and organizational advance in health planning. Framed by the WHO *Health for All* charter, it represents a political commitment to improving the overall health of the population, with progress to be measured against precise, scheduled national targets. In organizational terms, the strategies require

Key areas/main targets	Risk factor targets
• CHD and stroke • Cancer • Mental illness • HIV/AIDS • Accidents	• Cigarette smoking • Nutrition • Alcohol consumption • Blood pressure • STDs and injection drug use

Figure 1.4 Health of the Nation: a strategy for England
Source: Secretary of State for Health (1992: 16–20)

Priority areas	Risk reduction targets
• Coronary heart disease • Cancers • HIV/AIDS • Accidents • Dental and oral health	• Smoking • Diet • Alcohol misuse • Exercise

Figure 1.5 Scotland's health: a challenge to us all
Source: Scottish Office, Edinburgh (1992: 9–16)

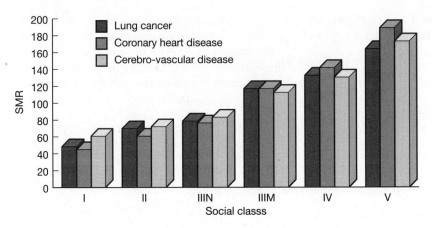

Figure 1.6 Mortality among married women, aged 20 to 59, by social class (partner's occupation) 1979–80, 1982–3, selected causes
Source: Wells (1987: 61)

cross-sectoral investment in health promotion and disease prevention, with an ongoing review of priorities and achievements built into the target-setting process (Secretary of State for Health 1992; Department of Health 1993; NAO 1996).

HOTN strategies have been introduced against the backdrop of increasing poverty and widening inequalities in health. However, the *HOTN* checklist of health priorities and risk factors is not grounded in the everyday experiences of those at the sharp end of class disadvantage. The model of health and risks is informed, instead, by the analysis of population mortality statistics. It is, as commentators have observed, an approach based on quantitative data on mortality and not on qualitative accounts of health (Davison *et al.* 1991; Lupton 1993; Popay and Williams 1994).

The *HOTN* model of health addresses the major causes of death in the population, and cardiovascular disease and cancer in particular, rather than the quality of people's health across the life course. The strategies identify disease-specific factors, like dietary fat, cigarette smoking and alcohol consumption, which are represented as unequivocally and uniformly health-damaging, because they raise the odds of death from these diseases. In contrast, the strategies place in shadow common social factors linking these causes of death to the disease-specific factors associated with them. And, as Figures 1.6 and 1.7 indicate, the most important common social factor is the experience of socio-economic disadvantage, an experience which is increasing for families with children at a pace and to a depth unprecedented in the post-war period. However, as is now widely recognized, socio-economic disadvantage figures as neither a key health area nor as a risk factor in the national health strategies for England, Scotland, Wales and Northern Ireland (see Figures 1.4 and 1.5 as examples). As a result, those living and caring in

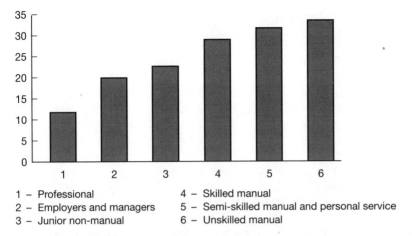

1 – Professional
2 – Employers and managers
3 – Junior non-manual

4 – Skilled manual
5 – Semi-skilled manual and personal service
6 – Unskilled manual

Figure 1.7 Prevalence of smoking among women aged 16 and over by socio-economic group in Britain, 1994
Source: DSS (1996: Table 4.9)

circumstances of disadvantage are likely to confront risks to individual health and to the welfare of their families which are obscured in the national health strategies.

While obscured in national strategies, the health risks of poverty and inequality figure prominently in the domestic strategies women have described to qualitative researchers. As the next section notes, the strategies of mothers living and caring in poverty are structured around environmental, financial and social risks to health. The behavioural risks targeted by *HOTN* strategies constitute only one part of the 'landscapes of risk' which frame and infuse their everyday lives (Davison *et al.* 1991). Moreover, set within these broader risk landscapes, health-related behaviours like diet and smoking can have divergent and variable relationships to health, simultaneously increasing the risk of future disease and death, and containing immediate risks to health and survival.

Risking and protecting health in poverty

In most households, it is mothers rather than fathers who take responsibility for health. It is mothers who take on the tasks of keeping the home warm and clean and keeping children protected from physical and moral danger; who ensure that their children's diets are sufficient in quantity and quality to meet their nutritional needs; who try to socialize partners and children into healthy habits with respect to personal hygiene, sleep and addictive behaviours. Given these complex health responsibilities, it is not surprising that *HOTN* strategies, with their emphasis on personal behaviour, have a moral edge for women, as expectant mothers and as the caretakers of children's health. The moral edge can be particularly sharp for mothers who are working to meet their health responsibilities on incomes insufficient for health needs. The conflicts that are faced and the compromises that are forged can be glimpsed by focusing on two risk factors targeted in *HOTN* strategies: diet and cigarette smoking.

Diet is often the area in which the impact of poverty on health is most acutely felt. It represents both a basic necessity, to be protected in the struggle to survive, and an enforced economy, where cutbacks are made. The rich seam of poverty research, both qualitative and quantitative, has recorded how poor families cut back on items that are or can be treated as individual 'luxuries', like family outings and clothes and shoes for parents, in order to give priority to necessities, like rent, fuel, food and clothes and shoes for children (Graham 1993a). However, weekly incomes are often insufficient to cover basic necessities. In such circumstances, mothers 'are forced to assign priorities within their necessities' (Kempson *et al.* 1994: 106). The enforced priorities tend to reflect external constraints rather than individual preferences. Where deductions from benefit are made automatically (rent, and often fuel and social fund deductions) and where penalties for non-payment are high (like repossession for mortgage arrears), fuel, housing and debt repayments take precedence over necessities which more directly protect and promote the welfare of children.

Within the limited space marked out by automatic deductions on the one hand and unavoidable bills and debt repayments on the other, is spending on food. A collective and priority necessity, it is also the area in which cutbacks are most likely to be made. This is because it is both the largest single item of household spending in low-income families, and the one over which women exercise most direct control. Other major items of expense, like rent, fuel and debt repayments, are increasingly paid at source – deducted from social security benefits before they are paid, or controlled and monitored by external agencies. In contrast, families, and typically women in families, retain financial independence with respect to food and manage the food budget without the involvement of outside agencies. Patterns of food purchase and consumption are governed by the need to maximize both the quantity and quality of the children's diet while minimizing cost and wastage. Financial management strategies which promote a family's survival, like buying fuel stamps and using key meters, can further constrain food choices and worsen the family's diet (Dowler and Calvert 1995).

Within these constraints, mothers tend to buy the same limited range of food each week, avoiding new foods that may not be eaten in favour of filling cheap meals of chips, potatoes, burgers, processed meals and pies, frozen vegetables, beans and bread (Dobson *et al.* 1994). The cultural patterns that mark out the process of growing up – having friends round to tea, eating meals separately from one's parents, buying take-outs and snacking on chocolates and biscuits – all have to be carefully regulated. Women find themselves forced to cut back on the purchase of food they know is healthy, and to ration the consumption of the limited supply of healthy food they can afford to buy. Fresh fruit is an example of such a restricted purchase and rationed item:

> I find increasingly that I can't afford to buy fresh fruit and vegetables. It really has gone down to the minimal things to keep yourself going. When you have to pay for your phone bill, the first thing you economise on is food. We live on rice and beans and porridge. Everything is so expensive. Weeks go by and I can't experiment with fruit. I can't offer (my son) a lot of choice, because if he wastes it, it hurts to throw it away. It could be two weeks or so that I won't buy any fruit and the same with vegetables, the sort of things I do buy are carrots, or potatoes, the safe vegetables.
>
> (Kempson *et al.* 1994: 114)

> I buy apples and bananas every fortnight. It's horrible when she has a banana and then says, 'Can I have an apple?' and you've got to stop her because it's got to last.
>
> (Dowler and Calvert 1995: 36, 38)

> My son likes expensive things like oranges and grapefruit, and I just can't afford them very often.
>
> (Dobson *et al.* 1994: 107)

Restrictions and rationing extend beyond expensive items like fresh fruit, to what most mothers regard as the basic staples of a family diet, like milk and bread (Dowler and Calvert 1995: 36, 38):

> The kids can't just come and help themselves to food. They don't have access to milk just to drink, milk goes on their cereal. Their hot chocolate at night is mostly water.
>
> I normally buy four packets of bread but if I'm running out of money for food, we just buy two. So those who take six slices I tell them to take four, those taking four I tell them to take three and I don't eat. When we don't have enough, say one boy comes and says, 'Mummy, I'm hungry', I say, 'Wait until the others come and we can divide it' or if he's badly hungry I give him a portion and say, 'Don't take any more – the rest has to go to the other children'.

As the comment 'I don't eat' in the last account indicates, protecting the nutritional standards of children is central to the process of meeting health needs on an insufficient income. Research across the century has recorded how parents cut back to protect the diets of children. Recent studies confirm this historical pattern: for households in poverty, the intake adequacy of such nutrients as iron, NSP (fibre), folate and vitamin C is low for mothers but not for their children (Lee and Gibney 1985; Dowler and Calvert 1995). Parents, it seems, are protecting their children from the worst nutritional consequences of poverty. Despite parents' strategies, poverty leaves its imprint on the diet of their children. Diets deteriorate across the week as benefit money runs low and then runs out (Kempson 1996). Young children in low-income households have higher intakes of saturated fatty acids and sugar than toddlers in higher income households. Conversely, they have lower intakes of dietary fibre and most minerals and vitamins (Low Income Project Team 1996).

Can smoking be seen in a similar light, as a way of protecting – however paradoxically – children from the adverse consequences of poverty? The prevalence of smoking is high among mothers in low socio-economic groups (Figure 1.7). Among mothers in claimant households in Britain, around six in ten are smokers (Marsh and McKay 1994; Graham 1996). The patterns of prevalence reflect smoking habits laid down in adolescence, when the majority of smokers take up smoking. These habits are sustained despite and against their health beliefs: most women, and most mothers in low-income households, recognize the health risks of smoking for their own health and the health of their children (Blaxter 1990; Ben-Shlomo *et al.* 1991; Graham 1993b). What mothers' accounts highlight is how smoking habits are woven into the domestic strategies through which they cope with the gendered burdens of health-keeping and housekeeping in poverty (see also Woodhouse; Amos, Crossan and Gaunt-Richardson, this volume).

Caring for children on a low income means living in cramped overcrowded accommodation in the residualized rented sector of the housing market (Marsh and McKay 1994; Graham 1996). In contrast to the majority of families, families in poverty typically live their lives without a car and without the money to access the shopping, leisure and play facilities that other mothers take for granted. In circumstances where physical space is limited, mothers describe how they find ways of making a symbolic space from their children, ways of temporarily escaping without leaving the room. Cigarettes can help to structure these time-outs, providing moments, however temporary, when the pressures of everyday life can be suspended, as the lottery advertising tells us, 'for an instant'.

> The kids know that when I sit down and have a fag then they've not to bother me. When I do this it means I'm not in and I've gone out and they have to sort themselves out until I've finished. That probably sounds awful but I don't go out and I'm always with the kids, you can see for yourself that there's not much room here and I can't really leave them on their own, so this is what I do. I would rather be hungry than not have any fags.
>
> (Dobson *et al.* 1994: 21)

> I tend to say to the kids, 'Just let Mummy have this smoke in peace.' It's something like it's my time that I've put down to thinking about what I have to do.
>
> (Greaves 1996: 47)

Cigarettes can figure in mothers' lives not only as a routine and anticipated bonus, but in times of crisis. Thus, when talking about how they handle the stress and exhaustion of caring for children, women in low-income households suggest that cigarettes provide an important self-help child protection strategy (Graham 1993b: 58):

(I am very likely to smoke) when the baby is screaming and won't shut up.

(I am very likely to smoke) when my eldest son won't do as he's told and he answers me back.

(I am very likely to smoke) when I'm making the tea. The two older ones come home from school, the baby's hungry and all four of them are hungry. They are all fighting and screaming and the dinner's cooking in the kitchen. I'm ready to blow up so I light a cigarette. It calms me down when I'm under so much stress. Since the baby was born, you feel at the end of your tether – a cigarette makes me feel better, helps me cope. I feel it's better than throwing him about and tearing my hair out.

The research of Lorraine Greaves, a Canadian feminist researcher, points to the ways in which gender inequality, and the threat and fact of domestic violence in particular, can shape women's use of cigarettes (Greaves 1996). Women in violent relationships describe how lighting up a cigarette can subtly shift the tempo and power imbalance of violent relationships. As for women seeking to deflect and defuse the impact of poverty, smoking cigarettes in the context of a violent relationship can be both a risk-taking activity and a risk-avoidance strategy (Greaves 1996: 49):

I figured it worked a couple of times, if I have a cigarette in my hand or stuck in my mouth, then he's not going to hit me at least until I put that cigarette down . . . when I had the cigarettes right there I (could light up and) break his concentration without him knowing it. I'm saying 'yes, yes, I'm listening', then I light one up. I'm looking at him, listening to him and yet he's getting side tracked by it. He doesn't know what's happening.

I don't think I could be as brave if I don't smoke. I'm pretty brave when I have a cigarette in my mouth. I light up a cigarette and get all the courage in the world.

What women appear to be emphasizing in their accounts of class and gender inequality is that cigarette smoking is a situated routine, fashioned in and against the material and relational pressures of everyday life. For smokers for whom life is a continuing struggle, cigarettes emerge as one of the few constants, one of the few resources that they control and can rely on:

I just gotta have cigarettes by my side 'cos they're the only stable thing in my life. Just not having them is the hardest thing. I won't smoke them, but I've gotta have them 'cos they're my best friend.

(Lawson 1993: 12)

I couldn't face a day without cigarettes. That's all we've got now.

(Simms and Smith 1986: 78)

I try to cut down on cigarettes to save money but cigarettes are my one luxury and at the moment they feel a bit like a necessity.

(Graham 1988: 379)

I think smoking stops me getting irritable, I can cope with things better. If I was economising, I'd cut down on cigarettes but I wouldn't give them up. I'd stop eating. That sounds terrible, doesn't it? Food just isn't that important to me but having a cigarette is the only thing I do just for myself.

(Graham 1988: 379)

As far as I can see, you can't count on a guy because they are not always there, kids aren't always there . . . I'd say it's [smoking] my security. Because they [cigarettes] are always there.

(Greaves 1996: 65)

That cigarettes should be described in these terms is a powerful indictment of how those living under the yoke of disadvantage experience the health effects of inequality and deprivation. It provides an appropriate set of motifs on which to draw the chapter to a close and move to a few conclusions.

Conclusions

The chapter has highlighted the increase in poverty and income inequality which has occurred across the lifetime of the *HOTN* strategies being pursued in the UK. While a similar trend is evident in other advanced industrialized countries, the rise in poverty, and childhood poverty in particular, has been more pronounced in the UK.

Widening income inequalities are impacting in disproportionate and specific ways on women with children. It is the future generation, and the women who care for them, who are carrying the burden of the upward trend in poverty. One in three mothers in Britain are working to meet their health responsibilities on incomes below the EC poverty line.

The chapter has described the landscapes of risk that come with family poverty. Its central aim has been to point to the ways in which these landscapes, and the wider structures of inequality which frame them, are obscured in current *HOTN* strategies. While the major causes of death display a pronounced class gradient, the *HOTN* checklist of risks to health are not those articulated through surveys of adults and children at the bottom of the class ladder. The risks and barriers are, instead, those flagged up through the analysis of population mortality data.

In epidemiological analyses, the emphasis is more on predictors of future (and premature) mortality, and less on the threats to current physical and emotional health. Within the statistical universe of probabilities and odds ratios, behaviours like eating well and avoiding smoking improve the chances of a long and healthy life. However, those at the sharp end of inequality face more than projected risks. They face immediate dangers, too. In mothers' accounts, behaviours which increase the odds of death in the future can also be identified as integral to their strategies to survive the present.

What conclusions can be drawn from the chapter's review of poverty trends and experiences? What are the implications for policy making and for purchasers and providers working to improve the health of the communities they serve? Two key messages can be highlighted, one relating to the concepts of health and risk underlying *HOTN* strategies, the second relating to the interventions stemming from them.

The first message concerns the need to build health strategies around concepts of health and risk fashioned out of the experience of inequality. While these concepts include the dimensions of health and threats to health on which national health strategies are built, mothers' strategies are tackling a broader and more complex agenda. It is an agenda which, like the WHO definition, embraces psycho-social and emotional well-being as well as physical health. It includes how those one loves feel today as well as how they fare in the future and it includes the financial and emotional welfare of the family unit as well as the physical health of the individuals within it. The risk agenda of mothers in poverty includes behavioural factors but weighs these against the physical barriers and psycho-social dangers which undermine the quality and durability of family relationships, raise levels of stress and threaten the fragile budgetary strategies which keep low-income households together and in a home of their own.

To give an example, a *HOTN* strategy grounded in the health and risk experiences of families in poverty might set different health targets. The objectives could be to improve health expectancy (years living without disability and in good health) and psycho-social well-being as well as (or instead of), the reduction of specific disease risks, like coronary heart disease and cancer. Within this alternative *HOTN* framework, the list of risk factors and risk reduction targets could include not only smoking and diet but low income and environmental risk (poor housing, poor local environment, traffic danger).

There is a second message which comes out of the chapter's review of health and risk. It concerns the need to incorporate the fact and scale of social inequality into strategic approaches to health planning. Positive moves in this direction have been made by a government which seeks to be 'tough on the causes of ill health' (Jowell 1997). The new national health strategy seeks to tackle the material inequalities in income, employment, housing and neighbourhood provision which underlie health inequalities. Thus, there is now official recognition that interventions to tackle the link between poverty and poor health need to improve the material circumstances as well as the health behaviour of those in poverty.

Interventions are required which open up pathways out of poverty, by returning to a policy of uprating benefits in line with average earnings, for example, and through improving access to public housing, to education and training, to day care and to employment. Such measures not only tackle poverty directly, but can also provide parents and children with the material and psycho-social resources to make positive lifestyle changes.

These broader initiatives would complement the range of local projects in the area of food and cigarette smoking which are designed around the domestic health strategies of low-income families. In the area of food, the Department of Health's Low Income Project Team advocates a community development approach (for example, food co-ops, community cafés, transport to shops) resourced by inter-agency partnerships and networked into a national Food and Low Income Network (National Food Alliance 1994; Williams and Dowler 1994; Public Health Alliance 1995; Low Income Project Team 1996). A similar strategy has emerged to support women in making positive changes to their smoking behaviour, again emphasizing community-based inter-agency initiatives and national networks to facilitate the exchange of information and good practice (see Amos, Crossan and Gaunt-Richardson, this volume).

It may be unrealistic to expect *HOTN* strategies to be totally reconstructed around the health needs and risk exposures of low-income households and to be grounded in a wider programme of welfare reform. Nonetheless, a revised strategy could take the first step and incorporate the dimensions and the risks to health which weigh most heavily on those caring for the youngest and most vulnerable members of the community. In a country marked out by increasing social polarization this would carry forward the government's commitment to equalizing health and life chances across the population and take the UK nearer to meeting the WHO objective of *Health for All by the Year 2000*.

Acknowledgements

Earlier versions of this chapter were given at the conference on Researching Women, Gender and Health, University of the West of England, June 1995 and the 3rd international conference on Interdisciplinary Qualitative Health Research, Bournemouth International Centre, October 1996.

References

Ashworth, K., Hill, M. and Walker, R. (1992) *Patterns of Childhood Poverty: New Challenges for Policy*. Loughborough: CRSP, Loughborough University of Technology.

Ben-Shlomo, B., Sheiham, A. and Marmot, M. (1991) Smoking and health. In R. Jowell, L. Brook and A. Taylor (eds) *British Social Attitudes: The Eighth Report*. Aldershot: Dartmouth.

Berthoud, R. and Kempson, E. (1992) *Credit and Debt: The PSI Report*. London: PSI.

Blaxter, M. (1990) *Health and Lifestyles*. London: Routledge.

Cohen, R., Coxall, J., Craig, G. and Sadig-Sangster, A. (1992) *Hardship in Britain: Being Poor in the 1990s*. London: Child Poverty Action Group.

Commission of the European Communities (CEC) (1989) *Interim Report on a Specific Community Action Programme to Combat Poverty*. Brussels: CEC.

Davison, C., Davey-Smith, G. and Frankel, S. (1991) Lay epidemiology and the prevention paradox. *Sociology of Health and Illness*, 13: 1–19.

Denver, F., Whitehead, M. and Roden, M. (1996) Current patterns and trends in male mortality by social class (based on occupation). *Population Trends*, 86: 15–20.

Department of Health (1993) *Working Together for Better Health: A Handbook of Guidance on Forming and Operating Alliances for Health*. London: Department of Health.

Department of Social Security (1996) *Social Security Statistics 1995*. London: HMSO.

Department of Social Security (1997) *Households Below Average Income: A Statistical Analysis 1979–1994/5*. London: HMSO.

Dobson, S., Beardsworth, A., Keil, T. and Walker, K. (1994) *Diet, Choice and Poverty*. London: Family Policy Studies Centre.

Dowler, E. and Calvert, C. (1995) *Nutrition and Diet in Lone Parent Families in London*. London: Family Policy Studies Centre.

Goodman, A. and Webb, S. (1994) *For Richer, For Poorer: The Changing Distribution of Income in the United Kingdom, 1961–91*. London: Institute of Fiscal Studies.

Graham, H. (1988) Women and smoking in the United Kingdom: implications for health promotion. *Health Promotion*, 3 (4): 371–82.

Graham, H. (1993a) *Hardship and Health in Women's Lives*. London: Harvester.

Graham, H. (1993b) *When Life's a Drag: Women, Smoking and Disadvantage*. London: HMSO.

Graham, H. (1996) Researching women's health work: a study of the lifestyles of mothers on income support. In P. Bywaters and E. MacLeod (eds) *Working for Equality in Health*. London: Routledge.

Greaves, L. (1996) *Smoke Screen: Women's Smoking and Social Control*. London: Scarlet Press.

Heady, P. and Smyth, M. (1989) *Living Standards during Unemployment*, vol. 1. London: HMSO.

House of Commons (1993) *Hansard*, 27 July, col. 1010. London: House of Commons.

Jowell, T. (1997) 'Public health strategy launched to tackle root causes of ill-health', Press Release, 7 July. London: Department of Health.

Judge, K. and Benzeval, M. (1993) Health inequalities: new concerns about the children of single mothers. *British Medical Journal*, 306: 677–80.

Kempson, E. (1996) *Life on a Low Income*. York: Joseph Rowntree Foundation.

Kempson, E., Bryson, A. and Rowlingson, K. (1994) *Hard Times? How Poor Families Make Ends Meet*. London: Policy Studies Institute.

Lawson, E. (1993) *The Role of Smoking in the Lives of Low Income Pregnant Adolescents*. Kentucky: Department of Behavioural Science, University of Kentucky.

Lee, P. and Gibney, M. (1985) *Patterns of Food and Nutrition Intake in a Suburb of Dublin with Chronically High Unemployment*. Dublin: Combat Poverty Agency.

Low Income Project Team (1996) *Low Income, Food, Nutrition and Health: Strategies for Improvement*. London: Department of Health.

Lupton, D. (1993) Risk as moral danger: the social and political functions of risk discourse in public health. *International Journal of Health Services*, 23: 425–35.

Macintyre, S. (1994) Socio-economic variations in Scotland's health: a review. *Health Bulletin*, 52 (6): 466–81.

Marsh, A. and McKay, S. (1994) *Poor Smokers*. London: Policy Studies Institute.

Mayall, B. (1986) *Keeping Children Healthy*. London: Allen and Unwin.

Moser, R., Pugh, H. and Goldblatt, P. (1990) Mortality and the social classification of women. In P. Goldblatt (ed.) *Longitudinal Study: Mortality and Social Organisation*. Series LS No. 6. London: OPCS.

National Audit Office (NAO) (1996) *Health of the Nation: A Progress Report*. London: HMSO.

National Food Alliance (1994) *Food and Low Income: A Practical Guide for Advisers and Supporters Working with Families and Young People on Low Incomes*. London: National Food Alliance.

Oldfield, N. and Yu, A.C.S (1993) *The Cost of a Child: Living Standards for the 1990s*. London, Child Poverty Action Group.

Oppenheim, C. and Harker, L. (1996) *Poverty: the Facts*. London: Child Poverty Action Group.

Popay, J. and Williams, G. (1994) Researching the people's health: Dilemmas and opportunities for social scientists. In J. Popay and G. Williams (eds) *Researching the People's Health*. London: Routledge.

Public Health Alliance (1995) *Poverty and Health: Tools for Change*. Birmingham: Public Health Alliance.

Roberts, H., Smith, S.J. and Bryce, C. (1995) *Children at Risk? Safety as a Social Value*. Buckingham: Open University Press.

Secretary of State for Health (1992) *The Health of the Nation: A Strategy for England*. London: HMSO.

Simms, M. and Smith, C. (1986) *Teenage Mothers and their Partners*. London: HMSO.

Wells, N. (1987) *Women's Health Today*. London: Office of Health Economics.

Williams, C. and Dowler, E. (1994) *Identifying Successful Local Projects and Initiatives on Diet and Low Income: A Review of the Issues*, a working paper for the Nutrition Task Force Low Income Project Team. London: Department of Health.

2

•

Reproductive health needs across the lifespan

•

Hilary Thomas

Healthcare related to women's reproductive systems is intimately connected with central aspects of their lives from the teenage years of sexual partners, contraception and safer sex practice, through the longer term relationships of adulthood which sometimes involve pregnancy and childbirth, to the time around the menopause when many women are forging new directions for their lives. Maintaining and promoting the reproductive health of women also represents a unique challenge for healthcare providers. Obstetrics and gynaecology is the only medical specialty devoted to one sex, while obstetrics is unique in being the only area of medicine charged with the simultaneous care of two patients, the woman and her baby.

Women have healthcare requirements additional to those of men both because of their biology and also because of their gender roles. If they cannot control their fertility and give birth safely, their capacity for childbearing can lead to major health problems. Hence their biological potential creates particular needs. Most women also conform to social expectations in taking the major responsibility for the health and healthcare of other people in their household. Yet the resources they need to restore and sustain their own well-being may be in conflict with the needs of those for whom they have responsibility. This can lead to constraints on their access to appropriate and effective healthcare.

Pregnancy, birth and the maintenance of post-natal health have all been absorbed into the domain of professional carers and this has certainly brought considerable benefits for women. However, reproductive health services have also been criticized for medicalizing 'normal' processes at the expense of women's own needs and preferences. Maternity care in particular is said to be organized around a search for pathology without due regard to the experiential and emotional dimensions of pregnancy and childbearing. Similar tensions are evident in the field of fertility control. The development of new technology and the emphasis on female methods of contraception has given women improved technical means and also greater responsibility for control of fertility. Yet inequalities in heterosexual relations continue to limit their capacity to exercise that control.

This chapter will examine women's reproductive healthcare needs from pregnancy prevention through to reproduction and finally to gynaecological problems and the menopause. Using findings from a number of social scientific studies, it will focus on four key areas of tension in reproductive healthcare which need to be acknowledged and addressed by healthcare providers. These are spelled out briefly below and illustrated in subsequent sections of the chapter.

- First there is potential conflict between the medicalization of aspects of reproductive health and the degree of choice and control exercised by women. Choice of contraceptive method for instance is constrained both by the available technology and also by the organization of services in general practice and family planning clinics. Though the medicalization of pregnancy and childbirth was the focus of an extensive literature in the 1970s and 80s, recent policy initiatives have not resolved all the issues raised. In the context of gynaecological services too, unintended effects of cervical screening on women's physical and emotional health, rising rates of hysterectomy and the increased use of HRT during the menopause all give cause for concern.
- The second area of tension in reproductive healthcare is the potential conflict beween the needs of the woman herself and the needs of others. This is potentially at its most stark where there are differences between the medically defined interests of the unborn baby and the desires of the mother. However, it can also be evident in the context of family planning if the needs and/or desires of the woman are displaced by those of her partner. In addition it can be manifest in relation to women's role in the family. If a woman needs gynaecological (or other) surgery for example, with a lengthy period of recuperation, this can be in conflict with the expectation that she is continuously available as a carer (Thomas and Hare 1987).
- Third, there may be a tension between a woman's own wishes and the moral evaluation made of her and her actions by others. This may be apparent in the area of contraceptive choice and also of course in the decision to have (or not to have) a termination of pregnancy. It may also be important in discussions about the suitability of a woman for infertility treatment. Judgements about a woman's sexuality may be especially damaging and appear not only in decisions related directly to reproduction but also in the broader context of procedures such as treatment of cervical abnormalities.

- Finally there is often a tension between health professionals' perceptions of appropriate provision for reproductive healthcare and those of women and their supporters. Reproductive health is a contested area within the National Health Service. It has witnessed a range of changes over recent years, many of them stemming from the campaigns of pressure groups associated with maternity and childbirth. There are further divisions between health professionals, with the tensions between midwives and obstetricians having a long history. The centrality of reproductive healthcare to women's lives means that these areas of actual or potential conflict need careful resolution if the NHS is to meet their needs with greater sensitivity.

Fertility control

Preventing pregnancy

The practice of contraception takes place over much of the fertile span of the life course. It involves most women at some point in their lives with the exception of those who remain celibate, or always choose relationships with other women, and those in a heterosexual relationship where one or both partners are known to be infertile. Public provision through family planning clinics became the responsibility of the NHS in 1974, while general practitioners offered services from 1975 onwards. Following recent concern about the closure of NHS clinics, the Department of Health has emphasized the need for complementarity of services between clinics and GPs (Kenmir 1990; Peckham and Walsh 1996).

There has been much discussion about the relative merits of GP-based and clinic-based services. In a study conducted in three health districts Snowden found that GPs provided a service to more patients but offered less choice of methods while clinics made an important contribution to the training of GPs in family planning work (Snowden 1985). Analyses of consumer preferences showed an important distinction between the two kinds of service. Women who chose clinics tended to prefer the anonymity and non-disease orientation of the setting, and the specialist knowledge available about contraception and related issues such as sexuality. They also welcomed the greater opportunity of seeing a woman doctor. Most women who chose to see a GP preferred the familiar setting of the surgery, the personal attention of someone who knew their medical history, the continuity of care and the absence of an exclusive emphasis on reproductive and sexual health.

Responsibility for contraception now rests predominantly with women. This has given them greater power over their own fertility but has also led to serious concerns about the female methods on offer. Whilst the ideal contraceptive probably could not be devised, existing techniques could certainly be improved if women's interests were more central to the development process (World Health Organisation and International Women's Health Coalition 1991; Hardon 1992). The ideal method would be 100 per cent effective, would carry no risk of adverse health effects and would be acceptable to both women and their partners. Many women would also want a method that was deployed independently of sexual activity though some prefer to make those decisions closer to the time of intercourse itself. The reality, however, is that women use a variety of methods over the life course as relationships, parity and health and bodily processes change. Hence they need accurate information about all available methods. This is now available from a wide range of sources but it is not always presented in an unbiased form or in a way designed to facilitate informed decision making.

In October 1995 the Committee on Safety of Medicines issued a warning about several brands of oral contraceptive pills and this attracted considerable media coverage. Evidence suggests a rise in the number of unplanned conceptions at this time, some of which were followed by abortion (British Pregnancy Advisory Service 1996). A comparison of the reaction to the October 1995 announcement with that of a subsequent report in June 1996 of a link between oral contraceptives and breast cancer indicated that the former was characterized by panic whilst the second remained low-key (Hammond 1996). This reflects the fact that the 1995 story was released to the media in a dramatic way with sufficient references to ensure a scare story while the 1996 evidence was presented in a more factual and thoughtful style.

An additional complication for many women in contraceptive decision making is the overlap with safer sex practice, especially, though not exclusively, in relation to HIV infection. Though use of the condom is the best strategy for preventing various forms of infection it may not be the preferred contraceptive method. Young women face especial difficulties in persuading their partners to adopt safe sex practices (Holland *et al.* 1990). If they try to prepare for sex in advance this may have a ruinous effect on their reputation. Moreover, those who insist on condom use at the beginning of a relationship by invoking fear of pregnancy may have subsequent problems. A woman may, for instance, wish to adopt the pill as a safer method of contraception at a later stage in the relationship, while wanting her partner to continue using the condom as protection against infection. However, this is likely to be rejected if particular methods have already been established.

Thus the technical means now exist for women to control their biological capacity for conception but a number of obstacles limit their ability to achieve this. They continue to be constrained by the gender inequalities inherent in many heterosexual relationships, by limitations in the knowledge available to them and by the organization of care provided by the National Health Service. In some cases this will lead to an unwanted pregnancy and the decision to seek a termination.

Abortion

The 1967 Abortion Act was an important landmark in the provision of services for women's health in Great Britain since it established the possibility of safe, legal abortion up to 28 weeks' gestation. It was amended in 1991 by the Human Fertilisation and Embryology Act which reduced the time limit for abortions in Great Britain from 28 to 24 weeks' gestation but allowed for termination without time limit in specified circumstances. Whilst this legislation was clearly an improvement for those women facing unwanted pregnancy it does not constitute abortion on demand since the signature of two doctors must be obtained to legalize the procedure. Moreover, the access of individual women to the services allowed by the law are crucially dependent on the priority given to the problem of unwanted pregnancy within the NHS.

Abortion rates rose gradually from 1985 onwards, reaching a peak in 1990 since when the trend has been generally downwards, with approximately 162,000 terminations carried out in 1995. The organization of abortion services varies throughout the country with services being provided directly by the NHS, by charities and by private clinics or through NHS funding for terminations in the private sector. In 1992, 50 per cent of abortions in England and Wales were carried out within the NHS, 7 per cent on behalf of the NHS and 43 per cent on non-NHS premises (Family Planning Association 1995). The percentage of terminations carried out in the NHS itself varied dramatically from 45 per cent in the North Western region to 99.7 per cent in the Northern region. While the majority of women would prefer to have an abortion under the NHS only about half actually achieve this (Family Planning Association 1995).

A survey carried out in England and Wales by the Abortion Law Reform Association highlighted a number of practices which prevent women from receiving abortion care under the NHS (Abortion Law Reform Association 1997). These include informal 'means testing' of women by GPs who steer some women towards the private or charitable sector as well as the rationing of services by health authorities. This is done either by specifying, and hence limiting, the criteria for access to abortion or by purchasing only a small number of termination procedures. Some health authorities also appear to employ moral judgements about abortion itself rather than assessing genuine need. The willingness of individual consultant gynaecologists to carry out abortions is also an important factor in determining the availability of services.

Pregnancy and birth

Organization of maternity care

NHS maternity services are currently undergoing a number of changes following the policy initiative *Changing Childbirth* (Expert Maternity Group 1993). The aim is to provide more continuity of care between pregnancy and birth, and to promote greater choice and control for women in the place of birth and in birth practices. The targets for these reforms include: at least 30 per cent of women to have a midwife as the lead professional; 75 per cent of women to be cared for during delivery by someone they have already met; and 30 per cent of women delivered in a maternity unit to be admitted under the management of a midwife. These are important initiatives because they represent a response to the lengthy campaigns of many women and their supporters to 'demedicalize' pregnancy and childbirth where appropriate.

Dissatisfaction with the maternity services has a long history, much of which has been concerned with the immediate circumstances of birth (Garcia 1982). While earlier research had concentrated on some women's under-use of the services (e.g. MacKinlay 1970, 1972) a series of later studies sought to explore the quality of care received, examining women's experiences of both antenatal care and of labour itself (e.g. Graham and McKee 1979; Oakley 1979; Macintyre 1981). Central themes of this research have been the contrast between the perspectives of those who use the services and those who provide them (e.g. Graham and Oakley 1981) or conflicts within the image of pregnancy as presented by healthcare providers (e.g. Comaroff 1977; Graham 1977).

Groups representing the interests of mothers, babies and other recipients of maternity care have campaigned on a number of fronts as well as acting as self-help organizations (Durward and Evans 1990). The National Childbirth Trust (NCT) and the Association for Improvements in the Maternity Services (AIMS) were both founded in the 1950s. During the 1970s and 1980s they were joined by a number of other groups including the Maternity Alliance, and their campaigning work was a major influence on the policies reflected in *Changing Childbirth*.

Innovations in care over this period have had a variety of origins (Thomas *et al.* 1987). Consumer opinion stressed the inconvenient location of services and the impersonal atmosphere experienced in clinics but especially in hospital settings. Medical and midwifery concern, on the other hand, focused more on variations in mortality rates, on confusion over the roles of the various practitioners, on the differing aims and levels of effectiveness of antenatal care, and on unnecessary duplication of services. New developments in service delivery have often involved a change in the physical location of care, and sometimes the integration of hospital and community staff. Other strategies for innovation have included rationalization of the number of antenatal visits and a clearer demarcation of responsibilities between the various practitioners involved.

These changes sometimes ran into unexpected difficulties. For instance, lack of effective communication meant that some women complained about the reduction in the number of antenatal visits under the mistaken impression that this was the result of cuts in health service funding (Hall *et al.* 1985). However, the legacy of such innovations is observable within the new patterns of service delivery. There is now a much stronger emphasis on community rather than hospital-based care, and an enhanced and clearly delineated role for midwives. Most women now hold their own obstetric records which was still a rare and contested phenomenon in the early 1980s.

Ostensibly, women's expectations of the maternity services are now informing the organization and development of care. However, some tensions still remain. Most women define pregnancy and labour as normal processes that are firmly embedded in the wider social context of their lives, yet their experience of maternity care too often continues to be one of a medicalized search for pathology (Graham and Oakley 1981; Schuman and Marteau 1993). One early evaluation of reorganization associated with the *Changing Childbirth* initiative does suggest that with increasing continuity of care this pattern is beginning to change (McCourt and Page 1996). If the relevant lessons are to be learned it is essential that all studies of this kind put women's experiences of service delivery high on their list of research priorities.

Screening and monitoring

During pregnancy, as distinct from birth, there is relatively little that can be done in the way of medical intervention. Pregnant women can be prescribed iron or other supplements and at the other end of the process the baby can be delivered before the onset of labour if the health of mother or baby indicate this. Much antenatal care is therefore devoted to monitoring the progress of the pregnancy and the health of the foetus and an increasing number of monitoring and screening tests are now offered (Birke *et al.* 1990). These may raise difficult ethical questions and pose women and their partners with hard choices (Reid 1990; Faden 1991). There continues to be a drift from the specialized use of tests towards their routine incorporation in antenatal care and this is likely to make adverse news especially difficult to comprehend.

Ultrasound scanning, initially only used when problems were envisaged, has become a familiar feature of virtually all women's antenatal care. Indeed, women who wish to avoid a scan may find this difficult to negotiate with doctors and midwives. The routine scan used for dating the pregnancy and checking the health of the foetus now has a place in the culture of maternity. It is the first time women and their partners 'see' the baby, and often results in a photograph which may take pride of (first) place in the album. Whilst some women report anxiety both about the possible effects of the scan on the baby and about possible bad news, many also find it pleasurable and exciting (Hyde 1986; Rothman 1988). Bad news will always be distressing but the way services are organized will have a significant effect on women's experience of the process itself and on their capacity to use the information generated in positive ways.

Women may not be aware of the purpose and possible outcome of the many tests now carried out routinely during pregnancy. Without realizing it, they can therefore find themselves part way along a series of investigations with major decisions to be made but no prior understanding of the implications (Price 1990). This uncertainty may be exacerbated by the indefinite nature of some test results which require interpretation through complex concepts of thresholds and risk, rather than simply being positive or negative (Parsons and Atkinson 1992). Staff need adequate training so that they are able to understand women's experiences and can also give clear information and explanations.

The result of screening and monitoring sometimes indicates the possibility of major foetal abnormality. In such circumstances termination of pregnancy will be offered. Indeed, willingness to accept it may even be presumed by the practitioners involved, with evidence of some doctors withholding screening if a woman did not agree to termination in advance (Farrant 1985). However, women's wishes and those of their partners may be at odds with those of the professionals. Some may wish to undergo a testing procedure but wait until the result before deciding whether or not to terminate the pregnancy. Others may be clear that they would not wish to have a termination but want to be prepared in advance for a baby that may be damaged.

The techniques now available for screening during pregnancy provide more information in greater detail than was possible previously. However, this information has not necessarily given women more choice. Indeed, it can sometimes cause more problems than it resolves because of the complex decisions which must be made and the failure of some healthcare workers properly to facilitate informed decision making by women and their partners.

Post-natal health

Women's post-natal health is often given little priority in the organization of maternity care. Once the drama of the birth is over and the baby thriving, a woman's own health too often takes second place. The six-week check-up carried out by health visitors is often focused more on the baby than the mother. Yet surveys paint a dismal picture of distress and disability including physical trauma arising from the birth, backache, urinary stress incontinence, continuing gynaecological problems, exhaustion, headaches and mental health problems, particularly post-natal depression (Romito 1990; MacArthur *et al.* 1991). Under these circumstances it is essential that healthcare providers look after both mother and child at all stages of the childbearing process.

Sexual health appears to be especially neglected in the post-natal period. A survey of members of the National Childbirth Trust obtained comments from over 1,000 women (Barrett 1995). This reflects the experiences of a self-selected sample and is unlikely to be representative of the population as a whole. However, it does provide a starting point for understanding this aspect of motherhood. Of the women who required perineal stitching 27 per cent reported that their stitches took seven or more weeks to heal. Sexual intercourse was resumed after less than one month by 20 per cent of respondents, after seven to eight weeks by 66 per cent, and after five to six months by 92 per cent. Intercourse was reported by 67 per cent to be less frequent following the birth, and by 52 per cent to be less good. Whilst the benefits of breastfeeding for the infant are the subject of a large literature its effects on vaginal dryness and loss of libido together with its own potential as a source of sexual stimulation are less well documented (Barrett 1995).

Pregnancy and perinatal loss

Loss of the foetus or baby during pregnancy or at the time of birth raises major issues for women and their partners and families, and for the healthcare practitioners who attend them. The extent to which the pregnancy is wanted, the expectedness of the loss (spontaneous or induced) and the length of gestation are often taken to be indicators of the likely emotional response. However, a woman's experience of a loss can be significantly at variance with the expectations of those around her (Macintyre 1976; Lovell 1983; Oakley *et al.* 1984).

It is often assumed that the degree of loss can be 'read off' from a hierarchy of sadness in which the death of a baby born alive will be worst, a stillbirth or late miscarriage lesser losses and early miscarriage of only passing difficulty (Lovell 1983). However, Lovell suggests that the reality may be very different. Women who miscarry in the first trimester may find it difficult to come to terms with the loss and may not be helped by the claim that it is 'nature's way' of removing a damaged foetus. Even when the loss is deliberate, through termination of pregnancy, many women experience considerable distress. The decision may be taken because the woman is not in a position to keep the baby, engendering complex and sometimes contradictory feelings that need to be understood and respected (Hadley 1996).

These issues raise a number of concerns about the organization of services for women experiencing pregnancy loss. First, the setting may influence the way in which the loss is experienced, so the physical placement of patients needs to be carefully considered. The 'mixed list' in a gynaecological ward or day surgery list may bring women in very different circumstances in close and possibly difficult contact with each other. Women requiring early vaginal termination of pregnancy, for example, or a D and C following a miscarriage, or laparoscopic investigation for fertility problems, may all be accommodated on the same gynaecological ward. Termination for foetal abnormality in close proximity to the maternity ward causes particular difficulties for patients and staff alike.

There are also problems concerning the division of labour on the healthcare team. The consultants who make the medical decisions about termination are not usually involved in the delivery of post-surgical care. If they are not adequately briefed it can be difficult for nursing and midwifery staff to give sensitive and appropriate treatment to women whose circumstances are not properly known to them (Webb 1986). If these problems are to be overcome, services need to reflect the range of different circumstances in which women may suffer loss and the diversity of possible responses needs to be a key concern of healthcare providers.

Infertility and assisted conception

Women and couples who experience infertility can potentially choose from a range of new treatment options but they also face a number of increasingly complex decisions (Stacey 1992; Pfeffer 1993). It is commonly believed that people who have infertility problems must be 'desperate' about their situation, but individuals and couples can respond to this state in a variety of ways. Some replan their lives without children. Others pursue all possible sources of medical assistance but not all of these are offered help. Women who do not fit the expected model of motherhood will face particular problems. Those who are single for instance, lesbian women, or those considered by doctors or the wider society to be too old for motherhood may be denied treatment (Doyal 1994).

For those who choose assisted conception and are accepted as deserving, a wide range of procedures including *in vitro* fertilization and donation of sperm and eggs is now available. However, there is regional variation in the availability of procedures and in the amount of treatment carried out by the National Health Service. This mixed economy of infertility services has proved to be a significant obstacle to infertile women with few financial resources (Doyal 1987; Pfeffer 1993). There have also been major difficulties in establishing success rates (Pfeffer 1993). The criteria used may be diverse, ranging from rates of fertilization without implantation through clinical pregnancy which is not subsequently established to established pregnancy, live births and healthy babies. This makes data from different centres difficult to compare and leaves many women unable to make an informed judgement of their chances of conceiving. This can be extremely stressful, often causing strain on the relationships between women and their partners (Greil *et al.* 1988).

Increasingly complex ethical and social dilemmas are created by the fragmentation of motherhood into egg donor, carrying mother and social mother. This raises profound issues about the nature of kinship, the linking of the biological and social spheres, and the management of knowledge of the origins of children resulting from assisted conception (Stacey 1992; Strathern 1992). If these are to be successfully managed, healthcare workers involved with infertile couples will need to be properly trained both in communication skills and in the facilitation of informed and ethical decision making.

Gynaecological problems and their treatment

In contrast to the extensive literature concerned with pregnancy and birth, relatively little attention has been paid to the needs and experiences of women undergoing gynaecological procedures. However, a number of areas are causing continuing concern. These include the efficacy and impact of cervical screening; rising yet uneven rates of hysterectomy; and the medical management of the menopause.

Screening for cervical cancer has been one of the best publicized stories in preventive medicine. The possibility of intervention at an early stage of the disease has led to a programme of cervical screening being made available to all women via the NHS, and GPs are now paid for recruiting women to the programme. However, there has been little exploration of women's own experiences either of screening or of further investigation and treatment where this is found necessary. One of the few studies of women undergoing diagnostic procedures reported a large amount of unacknowledged morbidity (Posner and Vessey 1988). Most women's reaction to the news of an abnormal smear whether by letter, telephone or in person by a doctor was one of shock. Many did not know what to expect at the colposcopy clinic and reactions to treatment varied, with some women experiencing severe pain. For other women it was not treatment but the after-effects which caused most distress.

Emotional distress often accompanied the physical symptoms, with some women reporting feelings of stigma and difficulties in resumption of sexual relations with their partners. Those who felt that the problem was being blamed on their own sexual activities felt especially distressed. Posner and Vessey noted a difference between those who received laser treatment at an outpatient clinic and those who received surgical treatment as in-patients, with the more minor procedure apparently producing more physical and emotional distress. This unexpected finding highlights the importance of ensuring that women's physical and emotional experience of the services should be a key issue in their evaluation and further development.

Hysterectomy is one of the most commonly performed major surgical procedures and it is estimated that one in five women in the UK will have the operation by the age of seventy-five (Teo 1990). Rates rose during the 1960s but subsequently have remained relatively stable in England and Wales. Few hysterectomies are performed for life-threatening conditions and since the 1970s there has been a significant increase in the proportion performed for menstrual problems (Teo 1990). Teo points out that this could be due to a real increase in menstrual problems themselves, to an increasing reluctance among women to accept such problems or to a greater willingness to use hysterectomy as a treatment. There are also marked regional variations in the frequency with which the procedure is performed (McPherson *et al.* 1981).

The trend towards evidence-based medicine has highlighted the need for further investigation of the effectiveness of this very common procedure and of other ways of treating menstrual problems. The decision to perform a hysterectomy is often based on very imprecise data with few firm indications of likely effects. If this situation is to be improved there is clearly a need for women's experiences of hysterectomy to be taken more seriously by those carrying out evaluations and also for women themselves to be more fully involved in individual decisions about gynaecological surgery (Coulter *et al.* 1988).

One study carried out in the 1980s revealed that following hysterectomy many women still lacked adequate information both about the operation and about the process of recovery (Webb 1986). This raised serious concerns about the extent to which informed consent to surgery had been obtained. Many women had received little support and few had talked about the procedure in detail with friends or family. The great majority of the sample were glad the operation had been performed but many were left with un-answered questions. In response to evidence of this continuing lack of knowledge a book on the topic was produced by the Hysterectomy Support Group (Webb 1989). This charts the varied experiences of a group of 42 women, showing that for some the procedure and its after-effects were traumatic whilst for others it was only a small disruption to their lives.

Finally, it is important to acknowledge the implications of the increasing medical interest in the menopause (Bell 1987). As early as the 1940s, articles on the subject were beginning to appear in the medical journals, while the development of synthetic oestrogen in 1941 marked the beginning of hormone replacement therapy (HRT). This made it possible (and economically profitable) to extend treatment to all women, not only those suffering marked symptoms. MacPherson (1993) has described how the supposed benefits of HRT have shifted from the promise of eternal beauty and femininity, through the possibility of a safe and symptom-free menopause to the current concern with escape from chronic diseases such as osteoporosis and cardiovascular disease. Indeed, some recent advocates of HRT recommend that all women should have at least six months of such therapeutic treatment upon reaching the menopause (Norman and Studd 1994). However, others have pointed out that the proposed benefits are not yet proven and that prescribing on this scale would constitute an unacceptable level of medical intervention in women's lives (Hunt 1994).

Conclusion

This chapter has highlighted current issues in sexual and reproductive healthcare and reviewed recent policy and organizational initiatives. Throughout these debates we have seen that there is a continuing tension between sexual and reproductive experiences as normal, social events and the provision of care framed by professional agendas and often provided in clinical settings. Women's needs for reproductive and gynaecological healthcare are both diverse and complex and the ways in which they are addressed continue to be constrained by professional beliefs about appropriate care and also by the perceived needs of those for whom women have been allocated responsibility. The organization of appropriate and sensitive care requires a recognition of the reality of these constraints and a workable strategy for their removal.

Acknowledgement

I am grateful to Sara Arber for comments on an earlier draft of this chapter.

References

Abortion Law Reform Association (1997) *A Report on NHS Abortion Services*. London: ALRA.

Barrett, G. (1995) 'The National Childbirth Trust "Sex after childbirth" survey: A sociological analysis', unpublished MSc Medical Sociology dissertation. Royal Holloway College, University of London.

Bell, S. (1987) Changing ideas: the medicalisation of the menopause. *Social Science and Medicine*, 24 (6): 535–42.

Birke, L., Himmelweit, S. and Vines G. (1990) *Tomorrow's Child: Reproductive Technologies in the 1990's*. London: Virago.

British Pregnancy Advisory Service (1996) 'Outcome of contraceptive pill announcement', 29 March.

Comaroff, J. (1977) Conflicting paradigms of pregnancy: managing ambiguity in antenatal encounters. In A. Davis and G. Horobin (eds) *Medical Encounters*. London: Croom Helm.

Coulter, A., McPherson, K. and Vessey, M. (1988) Do British women undergo too many or too few hysterectomies? *Social Science and Medicine*, 27 (9): 987–94.

Doyal, L. (1987) Infertility: a life sentence? Women and the National Health Service. In M. Stanworth (ed.) *Reproductive Technologies: Gender, Motherhood and Medicine*. Oxford: Polity Press.

Doyal, L. (1994) Managing conception: self insemination and the limits of reproductive freedom. *Policy and Politics*, 22 (2): 89–93.

Durward, L. and Evans, R. (1990) Pressure groups and maternity care. In J. Garcia, R. Kilpatrick and M. Richards (eds), *The Politics of Maternity Care*. Oxford: Clarendon Press.

Expert Maternity Group (1993) *Changing Childbirth*. London: HMSO.

Faden, R. (1991) Autonomy, choice and the new reproductive technologies: the role of informed consent in prenatal diagnosis. In J. Rodin and A. Collins (eds) *Women and New Reproductive Technologies: Psychosocial, Legal and Ethical Dilemmas*. Hillsdale, NJ: Lawrence Erlbaum Associates.

Family Planning Association (1995) *Abortion: Statistical Trends*. Fact Sheet 6A. London: Family Planning Association.

Farrant, W. (1985) Who's for amniocentesis? The politics of prenatal screening. In Homans, H. (ed.) *The Sexual Politics of Reproduction*. Aldershot: Gower.

Garcia, J. (1982) Women's views of antenatal care. In M. Enkin and I. Chalmers (eds) *Effectiveness and Satisfaction in Antenatal Care*. London: Heinemann Medical.

Graham, H. (1977) Images of pregnancy in antenatal literature. In R. Dingwall, C. Heath, M. Reid and M. Stacey (eds) *Health Care and Health Knowledge*. London: Croom Helm.

Graham, H. and McKee, L. (1979) *The First Months of Motherhood*. Health Education Council.

Graham, H. and Oakley, A. (1981) Competing ideologies of reproduction: medical and maternal perspectives on pregnancy. In H. Roberts (ed.) *Women, Health and Reproduction*. London: Routledge.

Greil, A., Leitko, T. and Porter, K. (1988) Infertility: his and hers. *Gender and Society,* 2 (2): 172–99.

Hadley, J. (1996) *Abortion: Between Freedom and Necessity.* London: Virago.

Hall, M., Macintyre, S. and Porter, M. (1985) *Antenatal Care Assessed.* Aberdeen University Press.

Hammond, P. (1996) *Reporting Pill Panics: A Comparative Analysis of the Media Coverage of Oral Contraceptive Health Scares.* London: Birth Control Trust.

Hardon, A. (1992) Contraceptive research: women's perspectives. In B. Mintzes (ed.) *A Question of Control: Women's Perspectives on the Development and Use of Contraceptive Technology.* Amsterdam: WEMOS.

Holland, J., Ramazonoglou, C., Scott, S., Sharpe, S. and Thompson, R. (1990) *'Don't Die of Ignorance' – I Nearly Died of Embarrassment'.* Women Risk and AIDS, Paper 2. London: Tufnell Press.

Hunt, K. (1994) A cure for all ills? Constructions of the menopause and the chequered fortunes of hormone replacement therapy. In S. Wilkinson and C. Kitzinger (eds) *Women and Health: Feminist Perspectives.* London: Taylor and Francis.

Hyde, B. (1986) An interview study of pregnant women's attitudes to ultrasound scanning. *Social Science and Medicine,* 22 (5): 587–92.

Kenmir, B. (1990) *Family Planning Clinic Cuts: A Survey of NHS Family Planning Clinics in Greater London.* London: Family Planning Association.

Lovell, A. (1983) Some questions of identity: late miscarriage, stillbirth and perinatal loss. *Social Science and Medicine,* 17 (11): 755–61.

MacArthur, C., Lewis, M. and Know, E.G. (1991) *Health After Childbirth.* London: HMSO.

Macintyre, S. (1976) Who wants babies? The social construction of 'instincts'. In D. Barker and S. Allen (eds) *Sexual Divisions and Society: Process and Change.* London: Tavistock.

Macintyre, S. (1981) *Expectations and Experiences of First Pregnancy,* University of Aberdeen Institute of Medical Sociology, Occasional Paper No. 5.

MacKinlay, J.B. (1970) A brief description of a study on the utilisation of maternity and child welfare services by a lower working class subculture. *Social Science and Medicine,* 4: 551–6.

MacKinlay, J.B. (1972) Some approaches and problems in the use of health services – an overview. *Journal of Health and Social Behaviour,* 13: 115–52.

MacPherson, K. (1993) The false promises of hormone replacement therapy and current dilemmas. In J. Callahan (ed.) *Menopause: A Midlife Passage.* Indianapolis: Indianapolis University Press.

McCourt, C. and Page, L. (1996) *Report on the Evaluation of One to One Midwifery.* London: Thames Valley University.

McPherson, K., Strong, P.M., Epstein, A. and Jones, L. (1981) Regional variations in the use of common surgical procedures within and between England and Wales, Canada and the United States. *Social Science and Medicine,* 15A: 273–88.

Norman, S.G. and Studd, J. (1994) A survey of views on hormone replacement therapy. *British Journal of Obstetrics and Gynaecology,* 101: 879–87.

Oakley, A. (1979) *Becoming a Mother.* Oxford: Martin Robertson.

Oakley, A., McPherson, A. and Roberts, H. (1984) *Miscarriage.* London: Fontana.

Parsons, E. and Atkinson, P. (1992) Lay constructions of genetic risk. *Sociology of Health and Illness,* 14 (4): 437–55.

Peckham, S. and Walsh, J. (1996) Provision of complementary services. In J. Walsh and H. Lygo with S. Peckham (eds) *Contraceptive Choices.* London: Family Planning Association.

Pfeffer, N. (1993) *The Stork and the Syringe: A Political History of Reproductive Medicine.* Oxford: Polity Press.

Posner, T. and Vessey, M. (1988) *Prevention of Cervical Cancer: The Patient's View.* London: King Edward's Hospital Fund for London.

Price, F. (1990) The management of uncertainty in obstetric practice: ultrasonography, *in vitro* fertilisation and embryo transfer. In M. McNeil, I. Varcoe and S. Yearley (eds) *The New Reproductive Technologies.* London: Macmillan.

Reid, M. (1990) Prenatal diagnosis and screening: a review. In J. Garcia, R. Kilpatrick and M. Richards (eds) *The Politics of Maternity Care.* Oxford: Clarendon Press.

Romito, P. (1990) Post-partum depression and the experience of motherhood. *Acta Obstetricia and Gynecologica*, Scandinavia, 69, supplement 154: 1–37.

Rothman, B. (1988) *The Tentative Pregnancy: Prenatal Diagnosis and the Future of Motherhood.* London: Pandora.

Schuman, A. and Marteau, T. (1993) Obstetricians' and midwives' contrasting perceptions of pregnancy. *Journal of Reproductive and Infant Psychology*, 11: 115–18.

Snowden, R. (1985) *Consumer Choices in Family Planning.* London: Family Planning Association.

Stacey, M. (1992) (ed.) *Changing Human Reproduction.* London: Sage.

Strathern, M. (1992) *Reproducing the Future: Anthropology, Kinship and the New Reproductive Technologies.* Manchester: Manchester University Press.

Teo, P. (1990) Hysterectomy: a change of heart or a change of trend? In H. Roberts (ed.) *Women's Health Counts.* London: Routledge.

Thomas, H. and Hare, M. (1987) Day case laparoscopic sterilization – time for a rethink? *British Journal of Obstetrics and Gynaecology*, 94: 445–8.

Thomas, H., Draper, J., Field, S. and Hare, M. (1987) The evaluation of an integrated antenatal clinic. *Journal of the Royal College of General Practitioners*, 37: 544–7.

Webb, A. (1989) *Experiences of Hysterectomy.* Channel Islands: Macdonald and Co. Ltd.

Webb, C. (1986) Women as gynaecology patients and nurses. In C. Webb (ed.) *Feminist Practice in Women's Health Care.* London: Wiley.

World Health Organisation and International Women's Health Coalition (1991) *Creating Common Ground: Report of a Meeting between Women's Health Advocates and Scientists.* Geneva: WHO.

3

•

Health, ageing and older women

•

Sara Arber

Older people have traditionally been defined as those above state retirement age. This definition is increasingly problematic, since half of men and women are no longer in paid work by age 61 and 57 respectively. The period after labour force exit therefore spans over 30 years and incorporates great diversity and differentiation, in terms of individuals' social and economic circumstances and their health.

It is surprising, given the richness of work by feminist medical sociologists, that there has been so little work on older women's health. The impact of feminist sociologists has not only been negligible, but has contributed to the pathologization of older women. Countless studies of caring have examined the 'burdens' faced by younger and mid-life women in providing informal care for their ageing parents, focusing on how caring has constrained women's opportunities for paid employment and other activities (Brody 1981; Nissel and Bonnerjea 1982; Lewis and Meredith 1988). Since the majority of older people in need of care are women, these studies have in effect objectified older women as the 'problem', the 'burden' to be cared for, the 'other'.

Within official discourse all elderly people are seen as potentially in need of care. For example, the government's *Informal Carers* survey (Green 1988) identified carers as anyone who 'looks after (or helps) someone who is sick, handicapped or elderly'. This identification of chronological age with needing care fuels ageist images of older people as a burden. It also makes invisible all services, care and unpaid work provided by older people for each other and to the younger generation. Older people's role in voluntary activities, political organizations and community activities is ignored. My own situation illustrates the way the balance of support may differ from conventional assumptions. My 81-year-old father-in-law provides all the required care for his 87-year-old housebound wife, but would not define himself as a carer. He does all our family's gardening, helps with decorating and does our evening 'babysitting' for three children. My neighbour's 82-year-old mother looks after her three children whenever required, including picking them up from school.

Societal attitudes towards older people have varied historically and between countries. Since the nineteenth century and increasingly during the twentieth century, older people have been seen as economically redundant, because of non-participation in paid work (Walker 1980; Phillipson 1982). In the 1990s, older people are often portrayed as socially redundant and a burden on society, both financially through the growing cost of state pensions and healthcare, and on their families, who are expected to provide informal care for them.

The prevalence of these societal attitudes has developed into an alarmist 'moral panic' about what are perceived to be growing numbers of older people in the population. Concern in the media and by policy makers with 'demographic facts' about the size of the elderly population, especially the proportionate increase in the number of people aged over 65 or over 85, reflects contemporary ageism and reinforces stereotypes of older people as a burden and a separate group from the rest of society (Bytheway 1995). This perspective in the US is characterized as 'apocalyptic demography' (Robertson 1991). What are the demographic facts?

The feminization of later life

Women predominate among older people, especially at the oldest ages (Arber and Ginn 1991). In 1994, 19 per cent of women and 13 per cent of men in England and Wales were over age 65 (see Table 3.1). There were 50 per cent more women than men over 65; this numerical predominance has come to be known as the 'feminization of later life'. The gender imbalance is low among the 'young elderly', with only 20 per cent more women than men aged 65–74, but increases to 3 women for every man over 85 (Table 3.1a). Health policy makers and providers cannot neglect the implications of this gender difference.

• The feminization of later life occurs because male mortality exceeds that of females at every age. The expectation of life for women in the United Kingdom is 79 years compared with 74 years for men (CSO 1996). It has increased dramatically this century, and is projected to reach 83 for women and 78 for men by 2021 (see Table 3.2). The female advantage in survival was 3.5 years at the turn of the century. It had increased to 5.8 years by 1961, but has now fallen to 5.3 years.

Table 3.1 Demographic characteristics of women and men aged 65 and over, England and Wales.

	Women	Men	Sex ratio (Women/Men)
(a) *% of population*			
1971			
over 65	16.1	10.6	1.6
over 75	6.4	3.1	2.2
over 85	1.3	0.5	2.9
1994			
over 65	18.6	13.1	1.5
over 75	8.9	4.8	1.9
over 85	2.6	0.9	3.0
(b) *Marital status %*			
1992			
Married	38.4	72.3	0.8
Widowed	49.2	16.8	4.4
Divorced	3.8	3.4	1.6
Never married	8.6	7.5	1.7
N = (millions)	4.88m	3.28m	

Source: OPCS (1995: Tables 6, 7, 12).

Table 3.2 Expectation of life at birth, United Kingdom

Year	Men	Women	Sex differential
1901	45.5	49.0	4.5
1931	57.7	61.6	3.9
1961	67.8	73.6	5.8
1991	73.2	78.7	5.5
1993	73.6	78.9	5.3
2021 (projected)	77.6	82.6	5.0

Source: CSO (1996: Table 7.3).

Despite the alarmist panic about the ageing of the population, since 1981 the proportion aged over 65 has remained constant at 16 per cent. It is projected to fall to 15 per cent by 2001, and rise to 17 per cent by 2011 (CSO 1996). There are varying rates of change within the older population, and the proportion aged over 85 is projected to increase. However, this represents only a very small proportion of the total population (Table 3.1a). Moreover, it is inappropriate to read off a given level of healthcare needs from the number of people of a particular chronological age, since the health status of older people is better now than in the past (Manton *et al.* 1995).

A consequence of men's higher mortality and the cultural norm of men marrying women younger than themselves is that women can expect to be widowed for eight to ten years. Half of women over age 65 are widowed, and most live alone. Nearly three-quarters of older men are married, compared with under two-fifths of women (see Table 3.1b). The feminization of widowhood is particularly pronounced, with 4.4 times more widows than widowers over age 65. The marital status of older people is the principal determinant of their living arrangements, and therefore of whether there are other household members available to undertake informal care should this be needed.

Ageism and the NHS

Ageism refers to structured disadvantages associated with chronological age, and/or negative attitudes associated with advancing age (Bytheway 1995). Ageism may have a differential effect on women and men. For example, mid-life women suffer greater barriers to employment and promotion than men of the same age, a process sometimes referred to as gendered ageism (Bernard *et al.* 1995; Itzin and Phillipson 1995).

Are health providers explicitly or implicitly ageist in their priorities and policies, and does this have a greater adverse effect on older women than on men? Henwood states, 'not only is there widespread discrimination against older people in the provision of health care, but they are also the victims of restricted assumptions about the quality of health care which can be expected in old age' (1990: 43).

How care is rationed and to what extent chronological age is or should be a criterion for provision of medical procedures are matters of increasing urgency, yet they are seldom articulated. Approaches based on Quality Adjusted Life Years (QALYs) are inherently discriminatory because counting extra years as part of the benefit of medical procedures risks shifting resources away from older to younger age groups. Similarly, those judged to have a low quality of life, predominantly older people, will be disadvantaged (Henwood 1990).

Neither *The Health of the Nation* document nor its successor *Our Healthier Nation* provide much comfort for older people (Department of Health 1992 and 1998). The emphasis is on reducing 'premature death', and the main targets specify upper age limits, for example, to reduce rates of CHD and stroke among those under 65 and 65–74, and to reduce lung cancer under the age of 75. Since CHD and stroke are the major causes of death among women and men over 75, it is anomalous and discriminatory that they are excluded from such targets. The only target which specifically mentions older people is to reduce the death rate from accidents among people over 65.

Screening programmes may also have age criteria which are discriminatory. Women aged 65 and over are denied routine screening for cervical
cancer, yet 40 per cent of deaths from cancer of the cervix occur in women
over 65. Similarly, breast screening programmes have a maximum age of 64,
although pilot studies are currently being carried out on women over 65 in
various parts of Britain.

A critical area in which older people have been excluded is epidemiological studies and trials of clinical interventions. One recent study identified a
lack of medical knowledge about the impact of various procedures on older
people because they have largely been excluded from clinical trials. As a
result clinicians may make inappropriate decisions due to lack of available
research evidence. This risk appears to affect older women in particular and
there is now a growing literature on gender bias both in treatment itself and
in the production of medical knowledge (Gurwitz *et al.* 1992; Sharpe 1995;
Sharp, this volume). The Medical Research Council have now recommended
that in future, research studies should have no upper age limit and that chronological age should not be used as a proxy for biological fitness (Medical
Research Council 1994).

The emphasis on clinical problems and medically defined solutions to the
'problems of ageing' tends to neglect many of the genuine concerns of older
people. Health providers need to shift from a focus in which older people are
seen primarily as medical problems to one which sees them as subjects rather
than objects, allowing them to define their own health needs, priorities and
concerns.

The tendency to construct ageing as pathological and to treat ageing as a
medical problem has been termed the 'biomedicalization of aging' (Estes and
Binney 1991). This focuses attention on the diseases of older people, their aetiology, treatment and management from the perspective of doctors. It tends
to neglect the ways in which social, environmental and behavioural factors
influence the process and experience of ageing. It treats older people in an
individualistic way, divorced from their social context and life circumstances.
Older people should be seen in terms of their life course – how their previous roles in the labour force, the family and in childrearing affect them in
later life.

The meanings of age

One of the difficulties in discussing ageing among older women and men is
the lack of conceptual refinement with no clear distinction being made
between the different meanings of 'age'. The simplest measure, *chronological
age*, refers to the individual's age in years. This is the criterion most often
used in making judgements about treatment, and is enshrined in legal restrictions and privileges. In medicine it is usually assumed to be closely
identified with the other meanings of age.

Physiological age refers to the ageing process itself. It is a medically constructed concept associated with the ageing body. Physiological changes occur with ageing in terms of the composition of the bones, the process of degeneration of body tissue and functional impairment and in some important aspects they are clearly different in men and women. However, these changes cannot simply be read off from chronological age. We know that the level of functional impairment of women and men aged 65–69 who were previously in manual jobs is greater than that of upper middle-class people who are over five years older (Arber and Ginn 1993). Thus, physiological age is affected by social and economic influences.

An individual's *social age* is strongly determined by the broader context of his or her life and is profoundly gendered. It has several interrelated meanings. First it can reflect the individual's subjective perception of his or her age. Older people often say they feel the same as they did when they were much younger, but the physiological ageing process means that their physical image has changed. Featherstone and Hepworth (1991) talk of the 'mask of ageing', arguing that the essential identity of the person is concealed beneath the image of an older person. Second, social age may reflect norms about appropriate behaviours for someone perceived to be of a certain chronological (or physiological) age. And third, the age accorded by others to an individual is influenced by that person's appearance and behaviour.

The 'double standard of ageing' particularly affects older women, since women tend to be judged by others in terms of the degree to which they maintain a youthful and sexually attractive appearance (Arber and Ginn 1995). Older women are therefore expected to ward off the signs of ageing, particularly greying hair and wrinkles, and may use surgery to attempt to retain a youthful image, especially in the US.

Gender differences in resources in later life

When considering older women's health, it is essential to distinguish three sets of resources and examine how they interrelate (Arber and Ginn 1991). They are, first, material resources such as income, assets, car ownership, housing and the quality of the home environment; second, the bodily resources of physical health and functional abilities of the individual; and third, access to personal, domestic and health care.

These interlinked sets of resources influence an older person's level of independence, sense of autonomy and personal space for sociability and the development of leisure pursuits. The absence of any one of these resources acts as a constraint on well-being, increasing his or her likelihood of dependency. The ways in which older women are disadvantaged compared to older men will be outlined in relation to each of the three types of resource: income, health and caring.

Income is vital to older women's health. Not only is it necessary to provide the basic health needs of heating, an adequate diet and decent housing, but it is also increasingly important because of the need to pay for social and health care. An adequate income maximizes the likelihood of an older person remaining autonomous and independent within a given level of disability, by allowing the purchase of home aids and adaptations, moving to more suitable accommodation, or paying for private transport when required. Cutbacks in public transport have had particularly adverse effects on older women, because they are less likely to drive. Even if they can drive, most older women have insufficient financial resources to run a car.

Government policies over the last 15 years have had negative consequences for the income of older people, especially women. The state National Insurance pension since 1980 has been uprated in line with prices instead of earnings. This has led to a decline in the real value of the state pension, which is now worth only 16 per cent of average male earnings, and is projected to fall to only 10 per cent by 2021 (Evandrou and Falkingham 1993).

In 1996, the state pension was under £5000 p.a. for a married couple and £3076 p.a. for a single older person. This is below the means-tested Income Support level, so older people who only have a state pension are by definition in poverty. Older women are more adversely affected than men, because most are solely reliant on the state pension. Two-thirds of older men also have an occupational or personal pension, but this is the case for only a quarter of older women (Arber and Ginn 1994).

Research on the personal income of women and men over 65 in 1991 showed the extent of gender inequality (Arber and Ginn 1994). The median income of older men was £106 per week; the top 25 per cent (upper quartile) received over £180 per week, and the top 10 per cent received £300 per week. The lower quarter received £75 and the bottom ten per cent received £60 per week. This showed the very considerable diversity in the incomes of older men. Older women's income falls far below men's, with a median of only £61 and an upper quartile amount of £91. The top 10 per cent of women received under £160 per week.

The major source of gender inequality in personal income is occupational pensions, which are closely linked to previous occupation, employment pattern and lifetime earnings. Older British women are far less likely than men to receive any income from an occupational pension, and the amounts are also less, mainly due to women's unpaid domestic and caring work and the constraints this places on paid employment (Ginn and Arber 1991, 1993, 1994a, forthcoming; Groves 1991).

In spite of formal sex equality and women's increasing employment, the proportion of women belonging to an occupational pension scheme is rising only very slowly (Ginn and Arber 1993); only a quarter of women aged 40–59 in 1988–90 were members of an occupational pension scheme. A substantial gender gap in occupational pension income is likely to persist as long as women shoulder the bulk of society's unpaid caring (Joshi and Davies 1992). Women's disadvantage could be alleviated by redistributive state pensions supported from taxation, as in Denmark (Ginn and Arber 1994b, forthcoming). However, the trend is in the opposite direction: in Britain and in most other OECD countries, concern at the rising cost of public pensions as the population ages has prompted a shift in the balance of pension provision from state to private (OECD 1988; Gillion 1991).

Gender differences in health

Most older women and men are healthy, live independently and provide for their own self-care. Good health is essential to independence, especially the individual's capacity to carry out personal self-care, such as bathing, eating, negotiating stairs and walking outside the home. Chronic illness and disability tend to restrict the individual's independence, as well as generating extra costs for a special diet, additional heating, laundry, or nursing care. People with higher levels of functional disability or cognitive impairment will require more practical support and personal care from either informal carers or the state. Health is a major concern of older people, and their key concern relates to anxiety about the possibility that their health may deteriorate and they may become dependent on others (Braithwaite 1990).

Older women are more likely than older men to suffer from conditions which are non-fatal but result in chronic and disabling illnesses hindering their activities of daily living. In 1985, 7 per cent of men and 14 per cent of women over 65 suffered from disabilities sufficient to require help on a daily basis to remain living in the community (Arber and Ginn 1991).

The 1994 General Household Survey showed that older women were more likely to experience restrictions in mobility, self-care and ability to perform household tasks than older men (Bennett *et al.* 1996) (see Table 3.3). Under a fifth of men over 85 were unable to go out and walk down the road, compared with nearly half of women of this age. Under 10 per cent of men over 85 were unable to go up and downstairs, compared with 29 per cent of women. The levels of mobility restrictions were low for men and women aged 65–74, with the likelihood of a mobility restriction increasing markedly above age 85.

In terms of personal self-care (Table 3.3c) only 10 per cent of women over 65 and 6 per cent of men were unable to bathe, shower or wash all over without assistance. This restriction increased to nearly a quarter of women over 85. Inability to do household shopping largely reflects inability to walk far outside, which was the case for a fifth of older women and a tenth of older men, rising to over half of women over 85.

Therefore, although most older people can live independently, older women are more likely to suffer from disabling conditions which mean they require help from others in the community or from state services.

Table 3.3   Gender differences in percentage unable to perform various activities of daily living by age

	65–69	70–74	75–79	80–84	85+	65+
(a) Going out and walking down road						
Men	4	6	8	18	18	8
Women	9	10	16	23	44	16
(b) Going up and down stairs						
Men	6	4	5	8	9	5
Women	5	9	11	16	29	11
(c) Bathing, washing all over						
Men	3	5	6	12	17	6
Women	5	7	9	15	23	10
(d) Household shopping						
Men	7	7	9	21	26	10
Women	7	14	23	29	55	21

Source: Bennett *et al.* (1996: Tables 6.23, 6.28 and 6.30).

Caring and older women

Changes in community care policies in the early 1990s made it more diffi-cult for older people to obtain local authority-funded residential care and home care (Walker 1993). Although such policies are put forward as gender-neutral, they have had greater adverse effects on older women. Older men have more financial resources to pay for care and are more likely to have a wife who can provide care should they need it, whereas older women tend to live alone.

Older people with severe functional disability need help with activities of daily living or personal self-care on a daily basis. Older disabled women are twice as likely as men with a comparable level of disability to live alone (43 per cent and 21 per cent respectively) and therefore are more reliant on family members living elsewhere, other informal carers in the community and state-provided domiciliary services (Arber and Ginn 1991). The majority of severely disabled older men can rely on support/care provided by their wife (63 per cent). Severely disabled older women are twice as likely as equivalent men to live in the home of an adult child and more share their own home with others.

When older disabled people share their household with others, household members perform virtually all of the necessary personal and domestic care tasks for them, and state services are provided at a very low level (Arber and Ginn 1991). However, care from family members, from different providers in the community and from the state may not be equally acceptable from the older person's point of view in terms of its implications for their self-esteem and degree of autonomy (Arber and Ginn 1991, 1992).

Residential care

The greatest threat to an older person's autonomy and independence is generally considered to be entry into a nursing or residential home. Despite the massive expansion in private residential homes during the 1980s (Higgs and Victor 1993), the 1991 population census showed that only 3 per cent of men and 6.4 per cent of women over 65 lived in communal establishments (OPCS 1993). This increased from 2.5 per cent of men and 4.6 per cent of women in 1981 (Arber and Ginn 1991).

Women over 75 are more likely to be in communal establishments than men, and this gender differential is particularly pronounced for those over 85, among whom 26 per cent of women and 15 per cent of men are residents (see Figure 3.1). The greater number of older women than men living in residential settings primarily reflects their likelihood of being widowed, and not having a partner to care for them should they become disabled. This can be seen from the analysis by marital status and age in Figure 3.2.

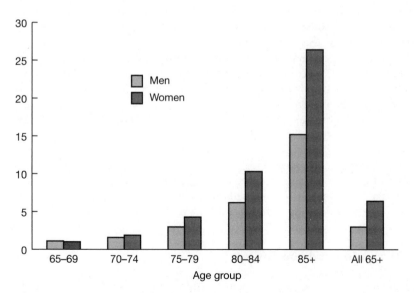

Figure 3.1 Percentage of men and women in communal establishments, 1991
Source: OPCS (1993: Table 2).

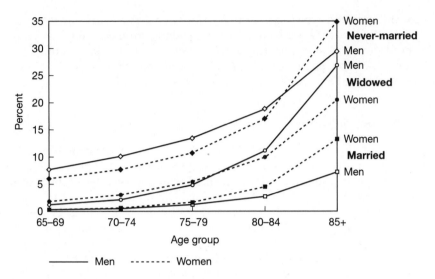

Figure 3.2   Percentage of older men and women resident in communal establishments in 1991 by marital status and age groups
Source: OPCS (1993: Table 2).

Never-married men are most likely and married older people least likely to be in residential care in each age group. This differential is very great, for example, in the 65–69 age group where only 0.2 per cent of the married live in a communal establishment compared with 7.7 per cent of single men and 5.9 per cent of single women. Even among those over 85, 29 per cent of single men are in residential care compared with only 7 per cent of those who are married. The comparable figures for women in residential care are 35 per cent of those who are single and 13 per cent of those who are married. The widowed are in an intermediate position in each age group.

One of the major reasons for these differences is that marital status can be interpreted as a proxy for the availability of family carers. Figure 3.2 demonstrates the very substantial role played by informal carers in supporting older people in the community. Never-married people are least likely to have family carers, the widowed and divorced generally have children as potential carers, while for married older people their partners are likely to be their carers, unless they are too frail or disabled to perform this role.

Discussion and conclusions

Current attitudes discriminate against older people, neglect their socially useful work and see them as an unproductive burden rather than contributors to society. Over a third of informal care for older people is provided by people over age 65 (Arber and Ginn 1991), mainly older spouses caring for their disabled partner, as well as those caring for neighbours and friends. Older people provide the backbone of voluntary support in the health service and innumerable other organizations, without whose unpaid work such organizations would have to recruit additional paid staff or provide poorer quality services. A major source of childcare for the increasing proportion of working mothers is their own mothers or mothers-in-law, many of whom are themselves elderly. To characterize older people as an unproductive burden is not only an inaccurate portrayal, but one which is used to justify cuts in services for older people.

The use of exclusionary terms like 'the elderly' draws an implicit contrast between 'us' (the non-elderly, the normal) and 'them' (the elderly, the 'other'). Such terms reinforce perceptions of older people as a distinctive group, which Bytheway (1995) argues characterize older people as a 'burden en bloc'. The extent to which older people are seen in this negative light is not only ageist but sexist, since later life is dominated by women. Thus, ageist concerns about the burdens of the very old primarily pathologize older women, who form the majority of the very frail and especially those in need of care by the state or informal carers (Arber and Ginn 1991).

The progressively earlier age of exit from paid employment combined with the improving health of the population has meant that women and men spend many more active years not in paid work, both before and after the state pension age, than in the past. The British state pension, which was introduced after the Second World War, has made it possible for older people to live independently of both paid work and of financial support from a spouse or other relatives (Wall 1992). However, current trends in social and economic policy are threatening to reverse these gains, particularly for older women.

The greater the movement towards individual provision for retirement through occupational and personal pensions, the greater will be the income inequality between older women and men and between those with an intermittent, or low-paid employment history and those with an advantaged position in the labour market. Thus the opportunities to enjoy a healthy Third Age of self-development and autonomous action are likely to become increasingly gendered, as well as class-divided, with financial dependency acting as an obstacle to citizenship rights (Arber and Ginn 1995).

Although older women have a longer expectation of life than men, they also have a longer period in which they can expect to be disabled or live in a residential setting. The gender differential in disability means that older women are more likely to require both informal care and state health and welfare services (Arber and Ginn 1991, 1992).

Nearly half of disabled older women live alone. While this promotes independence it also means they are reliant on state domiciliary services, mainly home care services and community nurses. They are also heavily dependent on the unpaid work of relatives and other informal carers, and are more likely to enter residential care. Older women's disadvantage in access to care from family members is compounded by their lower average income; a poor deal for the majority of women who have spent a lifetime of unpaid work looking after children, husband and others, often in addition to waged work.

The NHS is increasingly concerned about rationing health resources, and the danger is that chronological age will become both an overt and covert means of rationing care. Such ageist criteria would have a greater detrimental effect on women, who form the majority of the very old. Policies of community care which have restricted access to state-funded domiciliary and residential care have been particularly disadvantageous for older women because of their longevity and greater chance of being widowed.

The focus in this chapter on older women has neglected other aspects of inequality in later life, especially class and race. Current government policies relating to pensions are leading to growing inequality among older people according to their previous occupation and the continuity of their employment career. Norman (1985) argues that older black women suffer from 'triple jeopardy', because of the interactive disadvantage of old age, being a woman and being black.

Despite the policy scenario for the future looking bleak in Britain, older women have considerable social resources, particularly relating to their wider friendship networks and closer emotional relationships with others (Arber and Ginn 1994). Ageing potentially liberates older women from the restrictions placed upon them by their family and conventional gender roles. Later life may be a time when older women are free to construct more individual gender roles, especially if they are freed from the constraints of marriage and conformity within other institutional contexts. They may develop a more authentic identity and orientation, especially following widowhood, when they are no longer constrained to fulfil gendered role obligations expected within marriage (Wilson 1993; Arber and Ginn 1995).

Health providers need to take on the perspectives of older women, to give them a voice, and provide an opportunity for older people to define the health issues of relevance to them. We need to move their personal concerns and priorities to centre stage, seeing older women as the subjects rather than the objects of healthcare. It is also important to be sensitive to structural inequalities among older people and to understand the ways in which the material and social resources they have in later life have been fashioned by earlier phases of their personal biography. Only then will we be able to meet the healthcare needs of women across the life course.

Acknowledgements

I am grateful to the Office of National Statistics for permission to use data from the General Household Survey and to the Data Archive at University of Essex for supplying the data. I am very grateful to Jay Ginn for her contribution to the research on which the chapter is based, and to Tom Daly for the analysis of residential care.

References

Arber, S. and Ginn, J. (1991) *Gender and Later Life: A Sociological Analysis of Resources and Constraints.* London: Sage.

Arber, S. and Ginn, J. (1992) In sickness and in health: care-giving, gender and independence of elderly people. In C. Marsh and S. Arber (eds) *Families and Households: Divisions and Change.* London: Macmillan.

Arber, S. and Ginn, J. (1993) Gender and inequalities in health in later life. *Social Science and Medicine*, 36 (1): 33–46.

Arber, S. and Ginn, J. (1994) Women and ageing. *Reviews in Clinical Gerontology*, 4: 93–102.

Arber, S. and Ginn, J. (1995) *Connecting Gender and Ageing: A Sociological Approach.* Buckingham: Open University Press.

Bennett, N. *et al.* (1996) *Living in Britain: Results of the 1994 General Household Survey.* London: OPCS/HMSO.

Bernard, M., Phillipson, C., Itzin, C. and Skucha, J. (1995) Gendered Work, Gendered Retirement. In S. Arber and J. Ginn (eds) *Connecting Gender and Ageing: A Sociological Approach.* Buckingham: Open University Press.

Braithwaite, V. (1990) *Bound to Care.* Sydney: Allen and Unwin.

Brody, E. (1981) 'Women in the middle' and family help to older people. *The Gerontologist*, 21 (5): 471–9.

Bytheway, B. (1995) *Ageism.* Buckingham: Open University Press.

Central Statistical Office (1996) *Social Trends, 1996.* London: HMSO.

Department of Health (1992) *The Health of the Nation: A Strategy for Health in England,* Cm 1986. London: HMSO.

Department of Health (1998) *Our Healthier Nation: A Contract for Health,* Cm 3852. London: Stationery Office.

Estes, C. and Binney, E. (1991) The biomedicalization of aging: dangers and dilemmas. In M. Minkler and C. Estes (eds) *Critical Perspectives on Gerontology: The Political and Moral Economy of Growing Old.* New York: Baywood Publishing Co.

Evandrou, M. and Falkingham, J. (1993) Social security and the life course: developing sensitive policy alternatives. In S. Arber and M. Evandrou (eds) *Ageing, Independence and the Life Course.* London: Jessica Kingsley.

Featherstone, M. and Hepworth, M. (1991) The mask of ageing and the postmodern life course. In M. Featherstone, M. Hepworth and B.S. Turner (eds) *The Body: Social Process and Cultural Theory.* London: Sage.

Gillion, C. (1991) Ageing populations: spreading the costs. *Journal of European Social Policy*, 1: 107–28.

Ginn, J. and Arber, S. (1991) Gender, class and income inequalities in later life. *British Journal of Sociology*, 42 (3): 369–96.

Ginn, J. and Arber, S. (1993) Pension penalties: the gendered division of occupational welfare. *Work, Employment and Society*, 7 (1): 47–70.

Ginn, J. and Arber, S. (1994a) Mid-life women's employment and pension entitlements in relation to co-resident children. *Journal of Marriage and the Family*, 56: 813–19.

Ginn, J. and Arber, S. (1994b) Gender and pensions in Europe: current trends in women's pension acquisition. In P. Brown and R. Crompton (eds) *A New Europe: Economic Restructuring and Social Exclusion.* London: UCL Press.

Ginn, J. and Arber, S. (forthcoming) How does part-time work lead to low pension income? In J. O'Reilly and C. Fagan (eds) *Part-time Prospects.* London: Routledge.

Green, H. (1988) *Informal Carers*. OPCS Series GHS, No. 15, Supplement A. London: OPCS/HMSO.

Groves, D. (1991) Occupational pension provision and women's poverty in old age. In C. Glendinning and J. Millar (eds) *Women and Poverty in Britain*. Brighton: Wheatsheaf.

Gurwitz, J., Nanada, F. and Auorn, J. (1992) The exclusion of the elderly and women from clinical trials in acute myocardial infarction. *Journal of the American Medical Association*, 268 (2): 1417–22.

Henwood, M. (1990) No sense of urgency: age discrimination in health care. In E. McEwen (ed.) *Age: The Unrecognised Discrimination*. London: Age Concern.

Higgs, P. and Victor, C. (1993) Institutional care and the life course. In S. Arber and M. Evandrou (eds) *Ageing, Independence and the Life Course*. London: Jessica Kingsley.

Itzin, C. and Phillipson, C. (1995) Gendered ageism: a double jeopardy for women in organizations. In C. Itzin and J. Newman (eds) *Gender, Culture and Organizational Change*. London: Routledge.

Joshi, H. and Davies, H. (1992) *Childcare and mothers' lifetime earnings: some European contrasts*. London: Centre for Economic Policy Research.

Lewis, J. and Meredith, B. (1988) *Daughters Who Care*. London: Routledge.

Manton, K.G., Stallard, E. and Corder, L. (1995) Changes in morbidity and chronic disability in the US elderly population: evidence from the 1982, 1984 and 1989 National Long Term Care Survey. *Journal of Gerontology*, 50B: S104–S204.

Medical Research Council (1994) *The Health of the UK's Elderly People*. London: Medical Research Council.

Nissel, M. and Bonnerjea, L. (1982) *Family Care of the Elderly: Who Pays?* London: Policy Studies Institute.

Norman, A. (1985) *Triple Jeopardy: Growing Old in a Second Homeland*. London: Centre for Policy on Ageing.

OECD (1988) *Reforming Public Pensions*. Social Policy Studies No. 5. Paris: OECD.

OPCS (1993) *Communal Establishments, 1991 Census*. London: HMSO.

OPCS (1995) *Population Trends 82 (winter)*. London: HMSO.

Phillipson, C. (1982) *Capitalism and the Social Construction of Old Age*. London: Macmillan.

Robertson, A. (1991) The politics of Alzheimer's Disease: a case study on apocalyptic demography. In M. Minkler and C. Estes (eds) *Critical Perspectives on Gerontology: The Political and Moral Economy of Growing Old*. New York: Baywood Publishing Co.

Sharpe, P. (1995) Older women and health services: moving from ageism towards empowerment. *Women and Health*, 22 (3): 9–23.

Walker, A. (1980) The social creation of poverty and dependency in old age. *Journal of Social Policy*, 9 (1): 48–75.

Walker, A. (1993) Community care policy: from consensus to conflict. In J. Bornat, C. Pereira, D. Pilgrim and F. Williams (eds) *Community Care: A Reader*. London: Macmillan.

Wall, R. (1992) Relationships between generations in British families past and present. In C. Marsh and S. Arber (eds) *Families and Households: Divisions and Change*. London: Macmillan.

Wilson, G. (1993) Money and independence in old age. In S. Arber and M. Evandrou (eds) *Ageing, Independence and the Life Course*. London: Jessica Kingsley.

4

•

Meeting the health needs of women from black and minority ethnic communities

•

Jenny Douglas

Introduction

The aim of this chapter is to explore similarities and differences in relation to women's health across diverse communities in the UK. It will give an overview of current information available on patterns of health and illness among black and minority ethnic women and will critically review the evidence available on gender, 'race', ethnicity and health. It will examine the experiences of black and minority ethnic women as users (and providers) of health services and identify their current healthcare needs. Finally, the chapter will explore innovative policy developments designed to meet the needs of black and minority ethnic women and will make recommendations for the development of future policies within the NHS to meet the needs of this diverse group of users.

Influences on the health status of black and minority ethnic women

The health status of black and minority ethnic women in the UK is determined to a large extent by the social, economic, environmental and political factors that shape their lives. Put another way, it reflects the interaction between their experiences of race, gender, class and culture. Thus health and well-being are determined in these groups of women as in any other, by a complex mixture of social and psychological influences on the one hand and biological or genetic factors on the other. Black women are often seen by health planners (and others) as a homogeneous group whose needs can be identified and met in some relatively straightforward way. In reality, however, they are extremely diverse. They may be South Asian, Asian, Chinese, Vietnamese, African or African–Caribbean. They may have been born in the UK, may have migrated recently and may be refugees. They may have disabilities, be older, be lesbian. In attempting to examine the need for appropriate health services for black and minority ethnic women the similarities and differences in needs of black women must always be paramount.

In the UK there is still very limited research documenting the lived experiences of black and minority ethnic women (Bryan *et al.* 1985; Wilson 1994; Baxter 1997). In the US on the other hand, a growing number of studies are now providing descriptive accounts of these sections of the population (Adam 1995; Bayne-Smith 1996; Ruzek *et al.* 1997). This reflects the very different traditions of racial politics in the US and the growing recognition of the need to develop more sophisticated identification and classification of health issues relating to different ethnic communities. In a discussion of these developments Bayne-Smith (1996) argues that the health of women from particular black and minority groups cannot be separated from their roles as wives, mothers, grandmothers, daughters, sisters, employees and community participants and that their experiences of morbidity and mortality cannot be understood outside the broader institutions of culture and social structure such as the labour force, the education system, housing provision, health and welfare services, religion, family patterns and the economy itself.

The general links between poverty and health in the UK have been well documented as part of the long-standing exploration of social influences on well-being (Townsend *et al.* 1992; Benzeval *et al.* 1995; Wilkinson 1996*)*. However, the specificity of the experiences of black women have received little attention in this literature. We know that they are more likely than white women to be disadvantaged in a range of identifiable ways (Douglas 1991). They are more likely to live in poor housing, to have low-paid jobs, to be doing part-time or shift work, to be working outside the home while bringing up a family, to be caring for other relatives and to be exposed to occupational health hazards. They are also more likely to be working nights. Many black women also have to bear the major burden of financial responsibility because black men are more likely to be unemployed compared to their white counterparts. Yet they are often employed in more precarious, lower paid jobs than white co-workers (Modood *et al.* 1997). Since employment is a major factor in the determination of life chances, closer examination of patterns of racial and gender inequality in the labour market is central to the development of a better understanding of the health status of black and ethnic minority women.

Thus any attempt to determine the health needs of black women must recognize the complexity of their lives and the reality of their strategies for survival in societies that are characterized by racial and socio-economic inequality. Angela Davis' observations on the United States can be seen to have equal force in the UK.

We have become cognisant of the urgency of contextualising Black women's health in relation to the prevailing political conditions. While our health is undeniably assaulted by natural forces beyond our control, all too often the enemies of our physical and emotional well-being are social and political. This is why we must strive to understand the complex politics of Black women's health.

(Davis 1994)

Understanding the links between race and health

Most health research on black and minority ethnic communities has its roots in the medical paradigm. Hence it is based largely on the assumption that there are biological differences in 'races', leading in turn to variations in patterns of health and illness between different ethnic or racial groups. In much of the early UK literature, definitions of ethnicity itself were unclear, and comparative epidemiological studies have usually employed very crude categories with subject populations divided into 'Asian', African–Caribbean/African and white groups (Douglas 1992). These original classifications themselves are highly problematic. Issues of ethnicity and identity are equally complex and little attention has been paid to factors differentiating those individuals sometimes arbitrarily placed within particular categories. These include important influences such as country of origin, area of residence, socio-economic status, gender and length of residence in Britain. Moreover, categorization of this kind usually ignores the increasing numbers of people of 'mixed parentage' in the UK (Tizard and Phoenix 1993; Camper 1994; Modood *et al.* 1997). Hence the homogenization of groups that are, in reality, diverse may well obscure some of the most important issues under investigation.

Mortality data, for instance, is classified by country of birth so that black people born in Britain are not identifiable as members of ethnic minority groups, making it difficult to assess the impact of race on causes of death. More recently, some researchers have attempted to define ethnic groups more precisely and to recognize their heterogeneity. The category 'South Asian' for example is increasingly being subdivided into Pakistani, Bangladeshi and Indian sub-groups. There is also a growing interest in mapping the social class and gender inequalities within what are defined as the same ethnic groups (Nazroo 1997). However, there are still major weaknesses in the categories used to collect and classify data on the relationship between health, race and ethnicity in the UK.

The available evidence does appear to demonstrate significant differences between ethnic groups in disease patterns. However, there have been few attempts to determine the extent to which these are due to genetic and biological differences and how far they reflect environmental, geographical and cultural influences. These are complex questions. On the one hand it is essential that social and cultural explanations are taken into account where appropriate. However, they should not be used in a way that imposes homogeneity on a group of people while ignoring variations in religion, ethnicity, class and gender. Nor should cultural explanations be used to obscure the importance of material factors. At the same time it is important that genuine biological differences between particular groups are not ignored in an attempt to deny entirely the (limited) explanatory value of certain differences in patterns of genetic inheritance between 'races' (Smaje 1995). More sophisticated research is therefore needed to ascertain the differing influences and effects of biology, genetics, environmental, social, cultural and economic factors on health (Krieger and Zierler 1997).

Black women, health and illness

The sparcity of existing data on the epidemiology of black and minority ethnic communities as a whole is especially evident in the case of women. The information we do have is concentrated on specific diseases, particularly hypertension, diabetes, mental illness, sickle cell disease and thalassaemia. Moreover, this information tends to be narrowly focused and to pay little attention to the experiences of the women themselves. In a recent review of the literature, Smaje (1995) argues that most research on black and minority ethnic women has been concerned with only a small number of topics, including attitudes to health and healthcare, the uptake of specific services particularly obstetric care, the interrelationship between maternal and child health and the mental health problems facing some South Asian women. Overall, there continues to be a dearth of detailed analysis on the general health of women from black and minority ethnic communities and few examples of systematic comparison between the health of women and men in specific groups (Smaje 1995).

Summarizing the relatively limited information available on causes of death among ethnic minority groups, Balarajan and Raleigh (1993) reported that mortality from coronary heart disease was higher in people from the Indian subcontinent and the African Commonwealth than in the UK population as a whole. It was particularly high in women from the Indian subcontinent. Mortality from stroke was higher in people from the Caribbean, the Indian subcontinent and the African Commonwealth, and particularly high in women from the Caribbean. Mortality from hypertension was also higher in these ethnic groups and again was particularly high in African–Caribbean women. Mortality from breast and lung cancer was low in Caribbeans, Africans and people from the Indian subcontinent, but there was some evidence that the incidence of these cancers was rising. Mortality from cervical cancer was raised in Caribbean women (Balarajan and Raleigh 1993).

Turning to reproductive health and morbidity, overall fertility is lower than average among women born in the Caribbean, India and East Africa but relatively high among those born in the rest of Africa, Pakistan and Bangladesh. There is no information available on unwanted pregnancy and conception rates in under-16 year olds for black and minority ethnic communities nor any comparative data on hysterectomies. The incidence of fibroids is said to be higher in black and minority ethnic women – particularly those from Africa and the Caribbean – but again firm data is lacking.

A recent survey compared the health of black and minority ethnic groups with that of the majority white population (Nazroo 1997). The findings demonstrated that while minority ethnic communities as a whole were disadvantaged in terms of both health status and access to services, their experiences were certainly not homogeneous. As far as general health was concerned, members of the Pakistani and Bangladeshi communities were particularly disadvantaged compared to whites, being 50 per cent more likely to report their health as being only fair or poor. Caribbeans too were disadvantaged, though to a lesser extent, being only 30 per cent more likely than whites to report fair or poor health. Only small differences were reported between white respondents and Indian, African–Asian and Chinese groups and these differences were not statistically significant. Nazroo points out, however, that ethnic variations in response to general health questions did not emerge until the age of 35 and above. This could either be because overall health is generally significantly better in the 16–34 age group, or because the key forms of material, cultural or biological disadvantage that are related to poor health do not emerge in most minority ethnic groups until early middle age.

If we look at gender differences in the data, Caribbean men did better than Caribbean women on many of the indicators of health when compared to their white counterparts. For instance, Caribbean women had much higher rates of diagnosed hypertension than white women, whereas Caribbean men had the same rate as white men. Similarly, the Caribbean population as a whole appeared to score better than the white population on various indicators of psycho-social health. However, the difference was due primarily to lower rates among Caribbean men, since Caribbean women generally showed similar patterns to white women. This evidence of differences between men and women in the same ethnic groups demonstrates the importance of placing sex and gender alongside race and class as major determinants of morbidity and mortality. Both the biological differences between men and women and the variations in their daily lives will influence their health as will the social and (and to a lesser extent) the biological variations between different ethnic groups. Untangling this complex mosaic provides both researchers and health planners with a major challenge but it is one which must be met if effective services are to be provided.

Researching black women's health: shortcomings of present practice

Health has rarely been a priority for social researchers documenting the experiences of black and minority ethnic communities. Instead the emphasis has been mainly on education, social welfare and housing issues. Conversely, those researchers who have been primarily concerned with women's health have tended (until recently) to pay little attention to the particular needs of black women. Indeed the research methodologies employed have too often served to render black and minority ethnic women invisible.

Although there is a growing literature on 'race', ethnicity and health, the research on ethnicity has tended to exclude gender, while work on gender and health has paid little attention to ethnic issues. Moreover, white researchers have often failed to address the sensitive issues involved in defining research questions and interviewing black 'subjects'. Instead, black women themselves have been perceived as 'hard to reach and hard to research'. While some researchers have now begun to pay attention to the health problems of South Asian women, there has been much less work on African–Caribbeans and little or none on African, Chinese, Vietnamese and Yemeni women. Moreover, the focus in the case of South Asian women has been predominantly on the influence of culture and religion, with structural factors such as poverty and poor housing receiving almost no attention. In a number of studies this bias has been exacerbated by a negative portrayal of black cultures and lifestyles by comparison with those of the white majority (Lawrence 1982; Parmar 1982).

The lack of research on the health experiences and perceptions of African–Caribbean women reflects in part the fact that the classic 'minority problems' relating to language, diet and cultural resistance to male doctors were not seen to be of relevance to them in the same way that they were for Bangladeshi or Pakistani women. More recently, researchers have begun to take a greater interest in the health of African–Caribbean women. However, the major focus has been on their maternal role, with most researchers viewing them primarily through the problematic lens of the 'lone mother' and/or the 'black superwoman'. In a recent review of the literature Reynolds (1997) has challenged these essentialist representations and the stereotypes inherent in both constructions.

The lesson from this brief literature review is that there is an urgent need both for more quantitative data on the health status of black and minority ethnic women and also for more qualitative information on their health experiences, their own perceptions of their health and their beliefs about the most important influences on their well-being and that of their families.

Health services for black and minority ethnic women

In a recent survey commissioned by the Health Education Authority (Rudat 1994), the results showed that GP consultation was higher amongst African–Caribbeans and South Asians than the UK population at large, but that fewer African–Caribbeans and South Asians felt that the time spent with their GP was adequate. Moreover, fewer people from black and minority ethnic communities reported feeling happy with the outcome of their last visit to the GP. African–Caribbeans and South Asians showed greater dependence on their GP as an individual and lower rates of contact with other member of the primary care team. The use of opticians was lower among black and minority ethnic communities, particularly South Asian women. Use of dental services too was lower amongst black and minority ethnic communities, particularly Bangladeshis. Significant differences were found between African–Caribbeans and South Asian women in relation to screening for cervical cancer. While the figures for African–Caribbean women were similar to the UK average, the figures for South Asian women were significantly lower, particularly amongst Bangladeshi women. Women from all black and minority ethnic communities were less likely than their white counterparts to have been screened for breast cancer.

It is clear that health services cannot be delivered effectively and sensitively in the same way for all women. For many groups of black and minority ethnic women, healthcare continues to be inaccessible and inappropriate and the reasons for this may be geographical, cultural, or linguistic. They may have different ways of thinking about health, illness and healthcare and failure to recognize this will make the care offered inappropriate to their needs. Overtly discriminatory practices (both racist and sexist) may be built into the services themselves and their mode of delivery. All these factors can be exacerbated by poverty and general social deprivation making it more difficult for some women from minority ethnic groups to get optimal care from the NHS.

It is significant that some of the major pieces of legislation and policy documents such as the NHS and Community Care Act (Department of Health 1990) have emphasized the need to make health services more responsive to all sections of the population and to involve local communities in evaluating the effectiveness and accessibility of local services. Although some attempts have been made by health authorities and Trusts to involve black service users in this process they have often been half-hearted and there are few examples of the systematic involvement of black women in new policy initiatives. The previous government's *Health of the Nation* document for instance (Department of Health 1992), did point out the importance of addressing the needs of black and minority ethnic women but made no suggestions for strategies to achieve this, and similar observations can be made about a number of recent initiatives. Hence a preliminary framework does exist for addressing some of these issues but little use has yet been made of it.

Similar observations can be made about the employment of black women within the NHS. Research into the experiences of black women health workers has identified many areas of discrimination (Doyal *et al.* 1980; Baxter 1997). Early studies showed clearly that black women from the Caribbean who migrated to England in the 1950s and 1960s were channelled into ancillary and auxiliary jobs within the NHS. Even when they attempted to undertake nurse training many were offered training opportunities within the lower status State Enrolled Nurse programmes. This reduced career opportunities severely and limited the career development of many black nurses up until the present time. Indeed, recent changes in nurse training and promotion policies have weakened the position of State Enrolled Nurses still further (Beishon *et al.* 1995).

Black nurses were also channelled into the least prestigious areas of work – psychiatric and geriatric nursing in particular. Baxter (1988) argued that black nurses were an endangered species, with discrimination operating in schools and colleges. This, coupled with the knowledge of discrimination and lack of promotion prospects, has meant that fewer and fewer black women are choosing to undertake nurse training. A recent report from the Policy Studies Institute (Beishon *et al.* 1995) highlighted the fact that ethnic minority nursing staff often suspected racial discrimination by their managers, that they identified racism within working relationships and often experienced blatant racial harassment from patients.

There are very few black women senior managers in the NHS. A recent survey of non-executives of health authority and Trust boards (NAHAT and the King's Fund 1993) reported that only 45 out of 1531 non-executive members of regional health authorities, NHS Trusts and special health authorities in March 1993 were from black and minority ethnic communities (3 per cent). Similarly, only four out of 534 chairs of health authorities and Trusts were from black and minority ethnic communities and only one of these was female. This demonstrates the difficulties black and minority women have in relation to both race and gender discrimination.

Black women campaigning for change: examples of good practice

In the UK as in the United States and in most other parts of the world women from many different races and ethnic groups have been actively involved in campaigns for health promotion and healthcare (Doyal 1995: ch. 7). Their priorities, their methods and their strategies have varied depending on their circumstances. However, they have the common thread of striving for equality both between women and men and also between different groups of women. Here in the UK many black women's groups were established in response to inadequate, inappropriate, ethnocentric or racist practice within the NHS, especially in the areas of antenatal and maternity care and family planning. A particular area of concern was the focus of family planning services where the emphasis seemed to be on controlling the size of black families rather than offering women a range of choices with regard to birth control.

Other causes confronted by black women's health groups were the fact that black and minority ethnic women appeared to be more likely than their white contemporaries to be offered hysterectomies (Bryan *et al.* 1985); discriminatory practices in the use of the injectable contraceptive Depo-Provera (Brent Community Health Council 1981); the lack of appropriate provision in relation to mental health services (Wilson 1994); and the paucity of services for sickle cell disorders and thalassaemia (Douglas 1992). One outcome of these campaigns has been the production of black women's health books both in the UK and the US (White 1990; Villarosa 1994; Wilson 1994; Smith 1995).

The chapters in Wilson's book, *Healthy and Wise* cover a range of issues relevant both to black women using the NHS and also to those planning and providing their care. In one of these, Nozipho Patricia January-Bardill puts the position very clearly, stating that black women do not control the institutions that affect their health and well being. On the contrary, the objective social reality of black women is that they are at the bottom of the social pecking order in the eyes of UK governments (January-Bardill 1994).

In a review of NHS services for meeting black women's health needs, Wilson (1996) argues that 'whether the subject is the physical, mental or emotional health of Black women, there is a dearth of culturally relevant mainstream services'. She further argues that black women do not have access to resources to stimulate research into their specific health needs, or entry into the decision-making processes where resource allocation is determined, and services planned, provided and evaluated. In response to this situation black women themselves have developed many self-help initiatives that are culturally relevant, often with very limited resources. The lessons from these initiatives need to be carefully evaluated and where appropriate incorporated into mainstream services.

Two projects in London offer important examples of such initiatives. The London Black Women's Health Action Project aims to promote the general well-being of black women in London and offers advice and counselling on a range of health issues including female genital mutilation (Wilson 1996). This project is an example of a campaigning black women's organization which also offers help to individuals. The Shanti project was set up in 1989 in south London by West Lambeth Health Authority to provide a mental health service for women in a community setting (Stephens 1996; see also Payne, this volume). It was initially funded by an inner city partnership grant and offers a psychotherapy service to women who might traditionally have been denied access to care of this kind. The project runs a number of groups – a black women's group, a group for women who have been sexually abused, a general psychotherapy group and a group for older women. Sixty per cent of Shanti's clients are from ethnic minority backgrounds, with the largest group being of African–Caribbean origin.

The Sandwell Video Project originated from a small-scale study conducted to examine the differences between health experiences of African–Caribbean women who were nurses and those African–Caribbean women who were not nurses. The study concluded that whatever their background, most felt they had received poor treatment from healthcare providers with hysterectomy and menopause highlighted as particular areas of concern. Many black women felt they were more likely to be offered hysterectomies than their white counterparts, and were not offered alternative treatments. The reasons for having hysterectomies were not fully explained to them, and it appeared that they were offered them at an earlier age than white women. Because we have little data on ethnicity it is difficult to determine the truth or otherwise of such fears. However, since it is now mandatory to collect this information for hospital in-patients we should be able to assess it over the next few years.

The Sandwell project also set up focus groups to explore African–Caribbean women's information needs on hysterectomy, menopause and cervical cytology. Although many saw menopause as part of a natural process, others felt they would like more information and more counselling – preferably from African Caribbean women counsellors. Most women felt there was nowhere from which to get appropriate information. HRT was not something that most African–Caribbean women had considered, with much more concern being expressed about the onset of chronic conditions such as hypertension and diabetes. There was poor understanding about screening for cervical cancer. It certainly appeared that health education literature had not reached African–Caribbean women and that they were not aware of the reason for the smear tests or the NHS screening programme. There were also prevalent myths about cervical cancer being linked to uncleanliness.

The information needs identified from the focus groups were used to produce scripts for three videos. Local black women were involved in all aspects of the production of the video from the research to the dissemination. The videos gave information on menopause, hysterectomy and cervical screening but also sought to empower users to ask relevant and challenging questions of service providers and to challenge myths and stereotypes that service providers may have of African–Caribbean women.

New Horizons for Ethnic Women undertook research to document key problems they experienced as black and minority women working within an NHS Trust (1993). They reported the main problems as being shift work and the difficulty of organizing childcare around shifts, concentration in low-paid jobs, lack of access to training and development and lack of gender-sensitive management development courses recognizing the specific issues of black and minority ethnic women. They also commented that white managers had low expectations of black and minority women staff and frequently misjudged them.

In response to this and a number of similar studies, the King's Fund College was funded by the (then) NHS Women's Unit to run a management development programme for senior ethnic minority women managers in the NHS. The first programme held in 1994 was extremely successful with over 100 women applying for 19 places. A further course was run in 1995/6 for 21 women. Manchester Health Services Management Centre have also organized a successful management development course for senior ethnic minority women managers within the NHS. There are now established national and regional networks for ethnic minority women managers within the NHS.

Recommendations for the NHS

In order to develop more sensitive services for black and minority ethnic women, there needs to be greater understanding on the part of purchasers and providers about what is needed. Though there is an increasing literature on black and minority ethnic communities as a whole the lack of attention paid to gender has meant that the information available is often very super-ficial. Moreover, even where needs are well documented as in the case of the provision of interpreters, patient advocates, appropriate dietary informa-tion, or training for health workers on working with diverse communities, Trusts have often failed to act on them.

The interrelationship between ethnicity, 'race', class and gender is com-plex and dynamic. We have very little information on the changing health experience of black and ethnic minority women other than small-scale stud-ies, which often focus on specific groups. While these give detailed informa-tion on the lives of the particular women under review we still have very little baseline information within which to contextualize them. We need to be able to make comparisons across ethnic group, gender and class in order to understand the effect that each has on health while at the same time being able to make sense of their cumulative impact. If this is to be achieved we need to start by developing appropriate research instruments, methodo-logies and sampling frames. In particular we need to develop more rigorous strategies for recording ethnicity in users of community and primary care. More comparative studies are also needed to explore difference and diver-sity cross-culturally and these will need to involve black women themselves in setting the research agenda.

Many health workers – doctors, nurses, managers and other professions allied to medicine – receive little or no information on the healthcare needs of black and minority ethnic communities, in either basic or post-basic train-ing. Hundreds of thousands of other workers such as porters or receptionists may also play a crucial role in an individual's experience of healthcare but receive no training in either race or gender awareness. Baxter (1997) has written extensively on the need for work in this area, particularly within nurse education. She argues that providers of education to caring profes-sions should embrace issues of race equality so that they empower their students to provide the most appropriate and needs-sensitive services. She urges professional and regulatory bodies to provide more specific guidance about incorporating race equality issues in the curriculum and to ensure through their validation and inspection mechanisms that all programmes adopt an anti-racist perspective and equip health workers to practise in this manner.

Overall recommendations

The healthcare needs of women from black and minority ethnic communities need to be addressed strategically and with urgency by policy makers, practitioners and researchers. A change of culture within the NHS is needed to support and implement the policy guidance available and to ensure that purchasers and providers are really addressing the needs of black and minority ethnic women. Their needs must be mainstreamed and integrated into the development of commissioning plans through consultation with black and minority ethnic communities to review, monitor and evaluate services. The voices of black and minority ethnic women, both as service users and service providers, must be listened to and mechanisms developed to work with the relevant voluntary organizations. The provision of sensitive and appropriate services for black and minority ethnic women will improve the health status of their communities as a whole.

Generally speaking the lifestyles of black and minority ethnic women in the UK have many positive characteristics – with lower levels of cigarette smoking for example. However, educational and health promotional materials still have a part to play and if they are to be successful they need to be both linguistically and culturally appropriate and to connect with the realities of black women's lives within the UK. We need to see more translation of research into practice – either into healthcare provision, teaching and education programmes or health promotion materials. Research findings should be disseminated to women from diverse communities and more international exchange of information and good practice is needed, particularly where we can learn from women-centred primary healthcare initiatives which have been developed in other countries (Doyal 1995: ch. 7).

Finally, employment practice cannot be divorced from service provision and health authorities and Trusts have a responsibility to ensure that black and minority women have equal access to training and promotion opportunities. Black and minority ethnic women need to be represented as chairs and non-executive members of health authorities and Trusts and measures should be put in place by NHS organizations actively to recruit them to such posts. Only then can we expect the NHS to optimize the care offered to all its female users and workers.

Acknowledgements

I would like to thank Lesley Doyal for her encouragement, support and helpful comments and changes to drafts of this chapter. Most of all I would like to thank her for reminding me that I had something useful and worthwhile to say and helping to structure the theoretical framework.

References

Adam, D.L. (ed.) (1995) *Health Issues for Women of Colour: A Cultural Diversity Perspective*. Thousand Oaks: Sage.

Balarajan, R. and Soni Raleigh, V. (1993) *The Health of the Nation: Ethnicity and Health*. London: Department of Health.

Baxter, C.V. (1988) *The Black Nurse: An Endangered Species*. Cambridge: National Extension College for Training in Health and Race.

Baxter, C.V. (1997) *Race Equality in Health Care and Education*. London: Ballière Tindall.

Bayne-Smith, M. (ed.) (1996) *Race, Gender and Health*. Thousand Oaks: Sage.

Beishon, S., Virdee, S. and Hagell, A. (1995) *Nursing in a Multi-Ethnic NHS*. London: Policy Studies Institute.

Benzeval, M., Judge, K. and Whitehead, M. (1995) *Tackling Inequalities in Health: An Agenda for Action*. London: King's Fund Institute.

Brent Community Health Council (1981) *Black People and the Health Service*. London: Brent Community Health Council.

Bryan, B., Dadzie, S. and Scafe, S. (1985) *The Heart of the Race: Black Women's Lives in Britain*. London: Virago.

Camper, C. (ed.) (1994) *Miscegenation Blues: Voices of Mixed Race Women*. Toronto: Sister Vision.

Davis, A. (1994) Sick and tired of being sick and tired: the politics of black women's health. In M. Wilson (ed.) *Healthy and Wise: The Essential Health Handbook for Black Women*. London: Virago.

Department of Health (1990) *National Health Service and Community Care Act*. London: HMSO.

Department of Health (1992) *The Health of the Nation: A Strategy for Health in England*. London: HMSO.

Douglas, J. (1991) Black women's health matters. In H. Roberts (ed.) *Women's Health Matters*. London: Routledge.

Douglas, J. (1992) 'Influences on the community development and health movement – a personal view'. Paper delivered at the 'Roots and Branches' Winter School on Community Development and Health, 18–22 March 1990; Ambleside. Milton Keynes: HEA/OU.

Douglas, J. (1995) Developing anti-racist health promotion strategies. In R. Burrows and S. Nettelton (eds) *The Sociology of Health Promotion: Critical Analysis of Consumption, Lifestyle and Risk*. London: Routledge.

Douglas, J. (forthcoming) Health needs assessment: health promotion – the Sandwell experience. In S. Rawaf and V. Bahl (eds) *Assessing the Health Needs of People from Black and Minority Ethnic Communities*. London: Royal College of Physicians.

Doyal, L. (1995) *What Makes Women Sick: Gender and the Political Economy of Health*. London: Macmillan.

Doyal, L., Hunt, G. and Mellor, J. (1980) *Migrant Workers in the NHS. A Report to the Social Science Research Council*. London: Department of Sociology, Polytechnic of North London.

January-Bardill, N.P. (1994) Black women and HIV/AIDS. In M. Wilson (ed.) *Healthy and Wise: The Essential Health Handbook for Black Women.*

Krieger, N. and Zierler, S. (1997) Accounting for the health of women. *Critical Public Health*, 7 (1/2): 38–49.

Lawrence, E. (1982) In the abundance of water the fool is thirsty. In Centre for Contemporary Cultural Studies, *The Empire Strikes Back*. London: Hutchinson.

Modood, T., Berthoud, R., Lakey, J., Nazroo, J., Smith, P., Virdee, S. *et al.* (1997) *Ethnic Minorities in Britain: Diversity and Disadvantage*. London: Policy Studies Institute.

National Association of Health Authorities and Trusts and the King's Fund Centre (1993) *Equality Across the Board*. London: King's Fund Centre.

Nazroo, J. (1997) *The Health of Britain's Ethnic Minorities: Findings from a National Survey*. London: Policy Studies Institute.

New Horizons for Ethnic Women (NHS for Ethnic Women) (1993) *The Experiences of Black and Minority Ethnic Women in the Guy's and St Thomas' Hospital Trust*. London: NHS FEW.

Parmar, P. (1982) Gender, race and class: Asian women in resistance. In Centre for Contemporary Cultural Studies, *The Empire Strikes Back*. London: Hutchinson.

Reynolds, T. (1997) (Mis) representing the black (super) woman. In H. Mirza (ed.) Black British Feminism. London: Routledge.

Rudat, K. (1994) *Black and Minority Ethnic Groups in England: Health and Lifestyles*. London: Health Education Authority.

Ruzek, S.B., Olesen, V.L. and Clarke, A.E. (1997) *Women's Health: Complexities and Differences*. Columbus, OH: Ohio State University Press.

Smaje, C. (1995) *Health, 'Race' and Ethnicity: Making Sense of the Evidence*. London: King's Fund Institute/Share.

Smith, S. (1995) *Sick and Tired of Being Sick and Tired: Black Women's Health Activism in America 1890–1950*. Philadelphia: University of Pennsylvania Press.

Stephens, S. (1996) Therapy with attitude. *Share Newsletter*, 14: 7–8.

Tizard, B. and Phoenix, A. (1993) *Black, White or Mixed Race – Race and Racism in the Lives of Young People of Mixed Parentage*. London: Routledge.

Townsend, P., Davidson, N. and Whitehead, M. (1992) *Inequalities in Health/The Health Divide*. Harmondsworth: Penguin.

Villarosa, L. (ed.) (1994) *Body and Soul: The Black Women's Guide to Physical Health and Emotional Well-Being – A National Black Women's Health Project Book*. New York: Harper Perennial.

White, E. (1990) *The Black Women's Health Book – Speaking for Ourselves*. Washington, DC: Seal Press.

Wilkinson, R. (1996) *Unhealthy Societies*. London: Routledge.

Wilson, M. (1994) *Healthy and Wise: The Essential Health Handbook for Black Women*. London: Virago.

Wilson, M. (1996) Black women's health. *Share Newsletter*, 14: 2–4.

5

•

'Hit and miss': the success and failure of psychiatric services for women

•

Sarah Payne

In Britain, as in other developed countries, women are more likely than men to be admitted to hospital for psychiatric treatment at some point in their lives, and both first-time and total admissions to psychiatric hospital are dominated by women (Miles 1988; Department of Health 1995; Payne 1995). In addition, more women than men are treated by general practitioners and community psychiatric teams for mental health problems (Wooff *et al.* 1986; Miles 1988; OPCS 1995). Women, particularly those in older age groups, continue to be prescribed tranquillizers more often than men, and more women in the general population report psychiatric symptoms. A recent survey of psychiatric morbidity in private households found that nearly a quarter of women aged 20–54 were experiencing a significant number of psychiatric symptoms, compared with a tenth of men in that age group (Meltzer *et al.* 1994).

However, the degree to which women are over-represented among users of psychiatric services varies between different types of care. In 1991–2 female admissions to hospital were about 20 per cent higher than male admissions, whilst in general practice women received psychiatric treatment twice as often as men (DOH 1995; OPCS 1995). Admissions patterns also vary by age and by marital status. The greatest proportion of female in-patients is found in older age groups, and single (never-married) people make up 40 per cent of male admissions compared with 23 per cent of female admissions (DOH 1995).

Patterns of mental health treatment for each sex also differ by diagnosis. Nearly twice as many women as men are hospitalized for depression and anxiety each year, but women and men are more equally represented amongst psychiatric admissions for those diagnosed as suffering from schizophrenia (DOH 1995; Payne 1995). In general practice women are more than twice as likely as men to be consulting for depression or neurotic disorders (OPCS 1995). In community surveys, more women have symptoms of anxiety, depression, phobias and compulsive disorders, whilst men have more symptoms of alcohol and drug-related illness.

Although statistics broken down by ethnicity are more difficult to obtain, figures suggest that both women and men from minority ethnic groups have higher rates of treatment than the general population for some psychiatric conditions. However, this varies across age range and treatment type, as well as ethnic group (Littlewood and Lipsedge 1988; Cochrane and Bal 1989; Knowles 1991). Young African–Caribbean women and men have higher risks than young white people of being admitted to psychiatric hospital for schizophrenia. For African–Caribbean women the risk is 13 times higher than that for white women (Littlewood and Lipsedge 1988). Similarly, the recent OPCS psychiatric morbidity survey found higher levels of psychiatric symptoms amongst both men and women in West Indian and African minority groups, and Asian and Oriental groups, compared with the white population. Women were more likely than men, in every ethnic group, to have higher psychiatric morbidity scores.

Men and women also experience different degrees of coercion in the psychiatric system. Until very recently women have been more likely than men to be compulsorily admitted to hospital under the 1983 Mental Health Act, although figures now show slightly higher rates for men than for women (DOH 1995). Again, both women and men from minority ethnic groups are more likely to be compulsorily admitted in comparison with members of the white population, and are more likely to be treated coercively when in hospital (Lloyd and Moodley 1992).

In sum, the picture of treatment for psychiatric ill-health suggests that women are more likely than men to be treated both in hospital and in the community for psychiatric illness, particularly for depression and anxiety, and that older women and women from minority ethnic groups are the most likely of all to be given a psychiatric diagnosis and to receive treatment for such a condition.

Explanations of women's use of mental health services

Two explanations have been put forward for women's more frequent appearance in mental health statistics. The first is that particular pressures in women's lives put them at greater risk of mental distress, whilst the second argues that women's apparent vulnerability to psychiatric illness is the result of misogynist medical practice (Chesler 1974; Ussher 1991). This second argument suggests that women's over-representation in figures for mental health treatment is explained by a bias in the medical profession towards seeing women as mentally ill, and that mental health statistics should therefore be treated with caution.

It is undoubtedly the case that – like health statistics in general – figures for mental health are subject to methodological problems and it is hard to determine whether the primary explanation for women's mental health difficulties is stress, misogyny or a more complex model which involves both of these (Ussher 1991). However, the fact remains that figures for psychiatric treatment show that the majority of users within the mental health system are women and that psychiatric services are a central part of many women's experiences of the healthcare system. This chapter explores the delivery of these services, asking how well they meet the needs of their women patients.

Gender and mental health policy

What determines the treatment men and women get inside the mental health system? Government policy is a major factor shaping psychiatric services and it is influenced by a number of pressures, including the costs of existing services, competing demands on resources and public pressure for change. The public outcry in the early 1990s, for example, over highly publicized acts of violence by a few people diagnosed as suffering severe mental disorders led to increasing pressure for greater regulation of discharged patients. This was a major factor in creating the 1996 Mental Health (Care in the Community) Act.

However, individual clinicians and their representative body, the Royal College of Psychiatrists, have also played a significant part in policy formation. Though their power has been reduced in comparison with earlier years (Day and Klein 1991), doctors are still able to exert pressure on central government, and on public opinion, which in turn affects policy.

Within this process women are not well represented. The medical profession remains male-dominated despite increasing numbers of women in training and in the lower levels of the medical hierarchy. Only a minority of consultants are female, and women are more likely to be concentrated in the 'female' specialites (Doyal 1994). Child psychiatry is one of the specialties with a slightly higher proportion of women consultants (although even here women remain the minority), but adult psychiatry remains an overwhelmingly male specialty. The ratio of women to men at registrar level has increased over the past decade, but the key professional bodies in the medical profession are largely made up of men (Doyal 1994).

In recent years the challenge to the autonomy of the medical profession in everyday practice and in policy making has come mainly from the increasing power of managers within the NHS (Day and Klein 1991; Mohan 1995). But here too women remain under-represented (Doyal 1994). The

1990 NHS and Community Care Act removed locally elected representatives from the decision-making bodies of health authorities. This denied women who had been elected at local authority level the opportunity to participate in decisions about local health policy and also removed one route through which women's groups could lobby local representatives.

Whilst it would be overly simplistic to suggest that healthcare services for women would automatically improve if they were more equally represented in the decision-making process, it is clear that without women's voices many of the specific issues which affect them are less likely to be raised. The structural barriers to women's use of services – childcare responsibilities and the lack of local transport, for example – have often been ignored by the statutory services, though some groups in the voluntary sector have attempted to put them on the agenda (MIND 1988; Abel *et al.* 1996).

Perceptions of gender in psychiatric treatment

The second major element which helps to shape psychiatric treatment for men and women is the attitudes of the doctors themselves. Feminists have long argued that the medical profession holds a stereotypical view of women (Fee 1975; Oakley and Mitchell 1976), and that this is particularly evident in psychiatry (Chesler 1974; Busfield 1989, 1996). One well-known study (Broverman *et al.* 1970) found that clinicians held a different model of mental health for women and for men, and that women were trapped within a 'double bind'. On the one hand, those who were independent, objective and confident were viewed as abnormal and unhealthy, because they did not fit the feminine stereotype. On the other, women who did conform were also viewed as unhealthy, because the model of good mental health was a male one: 'Either way, the woman loses' (Johnstone 1989). Writers in the UK have concurred in this view that the medical profession is likely to view 'feminine' characteristics as closer to mental illness (Corob 1987; Ussher 1991), and that women who are seen as different are also subject to discrimination and pressures to conform (Johnstone 1989).

There is little evidence that this belief in the instability of women's mental health has changed substantially (Corob 1987; Ussher 1991). Medical stereotyping has long been visible, for example, in the representation of women in advertisements for tranquillizers and other psychotropic drugs – as the harassed housewife who needed her valium to get her through the day (Elston and Doyal 1983). In recent advertisements pharmaceutical companies have shown women more often in paid work, but advertisements for psychotropic drugs continue to show women more often than men. Women are also portrayed in settings which remain linked with ideas about normal or appropriate feminine behaviour (Ashton 1991; Ettore and Riska 1995).

The impact of this perception of gender-appropriate behaviour on individual patients varies. Chesler (1974) described the ways in which women who behaved in approved female ways – paying attention to their hair and appearance, for example, and helping to clean the ward – were more readily discharged from in-patient treatment. More recent accounts of hospital treatment suggest that much of this remains, and that female patients continue to be judged against 'normal' female behaviour (MIND 1995). This is particularly evident in the treatment of lesbian patients (Nettle and Phillips 1996; Perkins 1996).

Perkins (1996) identifies a number of ways in which mental health treatment and medical responses to lesbian patients fail to meet their needs (see also Wilton, this volume). This is most apparent when the objective of treatment appears to change the woman's sexuality, but other problems are also caused by assumptions of heterosexuality, or by silence on the part of the doctor or therapist about the woman's sexuality. There can also be problems when the doctor expressly accepts the woman's sexuality but then becomes 'sexuality-blind', arguing that all women should be treated in the same way. Each of these approaches invalidates the woman's sexual identity.

Whilst women's mental health is constituted within a set of prescriptive assumptions such as the norm of heterosexuality, studies also suggest that women and men are treated differently within the mental health system, and that the mental health problems of men are often taken more seriously than those of women. This is particularly evident in the path to specialist treatment, where men are more readily referred by general practitioners to specialist psychiatric services, despite the fact that more women present in primary healthcare with symptoms of mental disorder (Goldberg and Huxley 1980). In addition, white people are referred more readily to psychiatric specialist care than people from minority ethnic groups (Mills 1996). Thus women from minority ethnic groups are the least likely of all to be referred to such specialist treatment – and this is related to their increased risk of admission via the emergency services, often formally under a section of the 1983 Mental Health Act (Knowles 1991).

Whilst men are more readily referred to specialist care, women are more likely to be seen as in need of coercive treatment, in the shape of compulsory admission to psychiatric hospital. In one recent study women were referred by their GPs for assessment for formal admission more often than men with the same level of symptoms. The women who were referred were also more likely than men to be experiencing social problems, including marital difficulties, loss and separation: 'GPs seemed to be seeking a medical solution to these women's problems' (Sheppard 1991: 672). The inappropriateness of many of the GP referrals of their women patients is suggested by the fact that a much higher proportion of the men than the women were formally admitted after assessment (Sheppard 1991).

Gendered perceptions of mental health also help to maintain a system in which certain types of mental illness are not recognized in women. Services for alcohol and drug-related illness, for example, are primarily planned around the needs of male users, whilst women remain largely invisible, despite increasing levels of problem drinking among women and the greater impact of drinking on women's health (Davison and Marshall 1996). In the United States women have a higher mortality rate from alcoholism compared with men (Ettore and Riska 1995), whilst in Britain women with alcohol problems have higher suicide rates than men who misuse alcohol (Harris and Barraclough 1997).

Research suggests that women are more likely to become heavy drinkers in response to stress, but the focus in alcohol research has been almost entirely on men. Women are seen primarily as appendages of male alcoholics, and the underlying causes of women's drinking behaviour – including stress in relationships, in the home and the experience of domestic violence – remain unexplored (Ettore and Riska 1995). Despite a recommendation by the Royal College of Psychiatrists in 1986 that services specifically targeted at women with alcohol problems should be based locally and provide childcare, few such services exist (Ettore and Riska 1995).[1]

Thus gendered notions of mental health persist within a system which is ostensibly gender neutral. Stereotypes about the mental health of each sex continue to affect whether women and men are seen as psychologically frail or robust, how seriously their mental distress is taken, and what they are offered within the mental health system.

Women in the mental health system

In the UK mental health is one of the few areas of healthcare where women have been actively creating alternatives outside the state sector (MIND 1988; Doyal 1994; Abel *et al.* 1996) and this is largely the result of the failure of the public sector to meet women's needs. At every level – from hospital inpatient treatment through to the primary healthcare sector – women users have expressed concern over the way services are delivered.

Hospital admission and in-patient treatment

In-patient treatment for psychiatric illness is on the whole rare – the vast majority of people who receive a psychiatric diagnosis will receive their treatment and care in the primary healthcare system, usually from the general practitioner. However, the hospital-based services are still significant in mental health policy, not least because this sector remains the major consumer of mental healthcare resources, currently taking up between 85 per cent and 90 per cent of all funding in this area (Pilgrim 1992; Lelliott *et al.* 1993).

An excess of female psychiatric in-patients has persisted throughout the twentieth century, although recently women's over-representation in hospital figures has begun to decline. However, in the latter half of this century the structure of psychiatric services changed. Between the mid-1950s and the early 1990s the in-patient population of the psychiatric hospitals decreased by nearly 300 per cent (House of Commons Health Committee 1994), as care was transferred to smaller units, often located within the district general hospital (Pilgrim 1992).

Despite this reduction in the number of psychiatric beds, the number of psychiatric admissions each year actually increased over this period – by more than 21 per cent between 1964 and 1991–2 (Department of Health 1969, 1995). This increase in in-patient treatment was achieved by shorter in-patient stays and earlier discharge. Figures for first-time admissions decreased during this period, but there was a marked increase in figures for readmissions of those who had already been treated as an in-patient in the psychiatric sector, who were more likely to experience the 'revolving door' of in-patient treatment, discharge, followed by readmission and so on.

In a situation where the demand for medical treatment or care exceeds its availability, rationing of some form or another is inevitable, and this appears to have affected women and men differently. In the mental health services it is the general practitioner and the psychiatrist who decide who is to be diagnosed as mentally ill, and who is in need of different forms of treatment. Assumptions about the nature of illness amongst men and women and about the likely effects and outcomes of that illness – including the danger that patients pose to themselves or to the community – help to determine each patient's diversion into a particular kind of service or form of treatment. In many areas this has meant that only those deemed to be a risk to themselves or to others will be admitted (see Payne, 1996). This process also extends to discharge policy, where those who seem to present the least threat to themselves or others are discharged when a bed is urgently needed, for example to accommodate a patient who has been sectioned under the 1983 Mental Health Act (House of Commons Health Committee 1994).

The recent increase in male admissions compared with female admissions, particularly in the younger age groups (Payne 1995), may reflect this rationing process. Young women are less likely than in earlier years to receive treatment as a hospital in-patient at the same level of illness. Whilst the adequacy and appropriateness of institutional treatment has been rightly criticized (Pilgrim 1992), there are some women who want in-patient treatment as a respite from a difficult situation, as 'asylum' when they feel unsafe in the world outside (Chesler 1974; Ussher 1991; Perkins 1996). Such an option is no longer available in many areas, particularly in the inner city where there is the greatest demand for in-patient treatment (House of Commons Health Committee 1994).

In addition, the severity of illness amongst those who are admitted to hospital is now such that the experience of in-patient treatment may be harmful in new ways. Community psychiatric workers describe hospital services as 'an exercise in containment' (Payne 1996). In such circumstances the hospital is unlikely to be able to offer 'asylum', let alone a therapeutic environment.

Mental health policy in recent years has introduced mixed-sex wards in psychiatric hospitals, as part of a generalized process within hospital treatment, and this trend has had further adverse effects on women's experiences as in-patients. The justification put forward for mixed-sex wards is that they more closely represent the world outside the hospital and that both women and men recover better in such a situation. However, mixed-sex wards reflect only too well the world outside for those women who have suffered abuse either in childhood or as adults and who feel threatened in such a situation.

As MIND have pointed out, to place female patients in such an unsafe situation precisely at the time that they feel most vulnerable is hardly good sense, or good therapy (MIND 1994). This is particularly relevant for female patients as there is increasing evidence that childhood experience of sexual and other abuse has a major link with poor mental health as an adult (Brown 1992; Palmer *et al.* 1993) and many of those women who are admitted as in-patients will have a history of childhood sexual abuse.

In January 1997 the Department of Health announced plans to secure 'acceptable standards of segregated hospital accommodation', including 'safe facilities for patients in hospital who are mentally ill, while safeguarding their privacy and dignity', and later that year the new Labour government announced plans to speed up the process of segregating hospital accommodation (DoH 1997). This return to separate wards should lead to a significant improvement in the experience of many women in the psychiatric system. However, there is a continuing need to consider safety measures within hospitals, particularly in day wards.

The recent MIND campaign, 'Stress on Women', argued that women within the mental health system, and in the hospital itself, were particularly vulnerable to sexual harassment and sexual assault, both from other patients and from staff (MIND 1995; Sayce 1996). This too has gone largely unrecognized in decision making by either purchasers or providers. Overall, then, one of the major issues for women as patients is the extent to which the hospital offers protection, both from actual harm from others, and from their fear of harm.

Another issue rarely considered is the sex of the professionals involved with the patient. Whilst many patients would prefer to have greater choice over their therapist or doctor, women whose difficulties relate to the experience of sexual abuse in childhood may have a particular need for a woman doctor or therapist. Despite this, there are as yet no agreed policy guidelines which guarantee that this option is made available to patients.

Female psychiatric in-patients are also vulnerable to the disproportionate use of certain forms of treatment within the hospital system. In particular, they are more likely to receive electroconvulsive therapy (ECT), both on a 'voluntary' basis and as compulsory treatment under the 1983 Mental Health Act (Showalter 1987; Ussher 1991). Ussher suggests that the main impact of ECT, and other physical treatments, is to reduce women to a childlike dependent state, 'as well as having the added benefits of resulting in more stereotypically acceptable feminine behaviour' (1991: 174). It is not surprising that women who are users and survivors of the psychiatric system talk of their fear of such treatments, and their desire to avoid them (MIND 1995). Women have likewise been critical of other 'treatments' received as in-patients: force-feeding for eating disorders; seclusion in order to intimidate; forceful administration of medication; and removal of clothing (MIND 1995).

Hospitals have also been criticized for their insensitivity to the needs of specific groups. Women who are lesbians have described the ways in which they have been denied contact with their lovers whilst in hospital, whilst their sexuality is pathologized as part of the problem (MIND 1994; Perkins 1996). Similarly, black women have described suffering from racial harassment whilst in hospital. Hospitals have also failed to provide an interpreter for women whose first language is not English (MIND 1994; Ismail 1996). Whilst such insensitivity may be found in other parts of the mental health services, the effect inside psychiatric hospital is more devastating because of the woman's isolation from her usual support system.

Discharge from hospital

Under the 1990 NHS and Community Care Act and with the introduction of care programmes, local authorities now have the major responsibility for the development of community care services for the mentally ill. Since 1993 health authorities have been obliged to assess patients being considered for discharge from psychiatric hospital, and patients accepted into specialist psychiatric services, to ascertain their needs for care. Whilst an assessment of need does not guarantee that care will be provided, a lack of funding has meant that at times patients cannot be discharged, as the services they need are unavailable. In addition, local authorities are required to spend the major part of this funding in the independent sector and in many areas this has meant a concentration of resources on residential services. Thus for discharged patients, services in the community may simply mean another form of institutional care. Whilst care managers are now required to assess need without reference to the availability of services to meet that need, operational guidelines have explicitly linked care assessment with the need to ration resources (Lewis 1994).

In terms of the likely effect of this policy on men and women, there is some reason to suppose that women may be more able than men to find a place in the community in comparison with men, particularly in younger age groups, since most residential care in the private sector has been provided for 'less difficult-to-manage' patients (Payne 1996). However, gendered perceptions about mental health and appropriate behaviour for each sex remain significant. Where women are perceived as failing to conform to 'normal' femininity, and are seen as difficult to manage, they may in fact be less likely to get accommodation than men. Moreover, there is some doubt as to whether these services are the ones most appropriate for either sex. To date, the independent sector has largely provided what is most profitable: residential care for people with less serious or challenging mental health problems (Payne 1996).

Treatment in the community

Just as the term 'community' might refer to a range of concepts, so the term 'community psychiatric care' encompasses a range of services. Some of these services are heavily medicalized and could be seen as simply a shift in the location of the power of psychiatry 'over the walls of the institution' (Pilgrim 1992). The move from the psychiatric hospital towards community care might have been an opportunity to move away from a medically dominated model of psychiatric care (Pilgrim 1993). However, the profession has demonstrated its desire to retain a central position in the structure (Busfield 1993; Tyrer *et al.* 1993) and services have continued to be dominated by doctors, and in particular, by the psychiatrist (*Open Mind* 1994). This in turn means that medical ideas in relation to gendered differences in mental health retain their importance in the treatment of mental ill-health for each sex.

Research shows that users of the mental health system overwhelmingly prefer to be treated outside the psychiatric hospital (Pilgrim 1992; Pilgrim and Rogers 1993), and most psychiatric care in the community is provided by the primary healthcare system. General practitioners, for example, treat a hundred mentally ill patients for every one who is transferred to the hospital for treatment (Strathdee 1992). Some services are provided within the 'mixed economy' of welfare that has developed since the 1980s – the referral within general practice of patients to voluntary services, private therapists or self-help networks, for example. Most community psychiatric teams have both social workers and health professionals – although the division of labour and of control within the team will vary. How well does this range of services meet the needs of women for care in times of mental distress?

As community psychiatric teams have become more numerous and as their workload has increased, there has been concern over who receives treatment from such services. Studies have shown that community psychiatric nurses, for example, have decreased the number of patients with severe mental health problems in their caseload, and have decreased the amount of time they spend with such patients, whilst their caseload and time has been increasingly absorbed by those with less severe illness (Wooff *et al.* 1986; Goldberg 1991). This has led to the criticism – particularly from the psychiatric profession – that the community services are reaching what have been termed 'the worried well' at the expense of those suffering from long-term and chronic illness (Kendrick *et al.* 1993).

However, the concept of the 'worried well' disguises a number of gender issues, for the majority of depressed and anxious patients now being referred by GPs to their colleagues in community psychiatric work are in fact women (Goldberg 1991). The underlying implication is that it is men with more serious illness who are being displaced from the services they need and deserve but there is little evidence to confirm this. A recent study of services for long-term psychiatric patients – the chronic mentally ill – shows that it is women whose needs for both care and support are not being met (Perkins and Rowland 1991).

Home-based care – treatment designed to help those who would otherwise be admitted as in-patients – has recently been added to the range of psychiatric services outside the hospital (Dean and Gadd 1990; Burns *et al.* 1993). This way of organizing treatment is said to be preferred by both users and carers (Dean and Gadd 1990; Muijen *et al.* 1992). However, it is not safe to assume that this is true of all potential patients. Home-based care is not appropriate for those whose domestic environment is unsafe, as a result of domestic violence, emotional or sexual abuse. Some women need to get out of their home before they can hope to recover (Williams *et al.* 1993).

Similarly, one survey at least has suggested that many carers do not favour home-based treatment as a substitute for in-patient admission (Burns *et al.* 1993). Most people diagnosed with a psychiatric illness provide their own care or do not need care, and even amongst those with more severe illness a large proportion will be living alone (Pilgrim 1992). Where care is needed, it is more often emotional rather than physical support and may be provided by either men or women (Pilgrim 1992). However, more women than men are involved in caring for someone with mental illness, particularly for those diagnosed as having early onset schizophrenia (Parker 1996). Whilst most studies of the value of home-based treatment do assess the preference of carers, there has been little exploration of the impact of this treatment on the carers' lives – on paid employment or social contacts, for example. Most researchers remain gender-neutral in the reporting of their findings. Hence we have no way of knowing whether there is a difference in the views of women and men carers.

Good practice in mental health

In this final section we consider services which have been developed to meet the specific needs of women. There are a number of examples, mostly small-scale and highly localized, and also largely dependent on a mixture of paid staff and volunteers. Some receive funding from health and social services but many also rely on charitable support. What unites them is the emphasis they have placed on women identifying their own needs. Whilst most services recognize that there will be some women whose illness is so severe that they cannot make such choices, there is also a commitment to developing the skills necessary to enable effective consultation with women in the mental health system and a commitment to act on their proposals and ideas.

One example of such a service is a 'women only' crisis centre which has recently opened in Islington, with the support of the local mental health trust. It operates within a model which is not itself medical, although women on medication are allowed to stay. What the new crisis centre illustrates in particular is the significant role played in the development of alternatives by pressure groups and by user and survivor groups. The women's centre in Islington has been developed by – not merely in consultation with – users, and has been shaped by the demands and ideas of women themselves. It is an illustration of the way in which alternatives to traditional psychiatry can be created.

Similarly, Shanti, an 'intercultural, psychodynamic psychotherapy centre' in inner-city Brixton, was created as a service for women in mental distress (Williams *et al.* 1993; Mills 1996). It began by canvassing women in a wide variety of places, both informal and formal, and the services were planned in response to the needs identified by women in this process: 'Shanti's first task was to build a centre for women's mental health that at least did not alienate clients' (Mills 1996: 220). The centre is funded with NHS money but is set up outside the conventional care system, and the women using the centre see it as separate from mainstream mental health services.

Shanti operates on a system of self-referral, although GPs and other health professionals may suggest to a woman that she considers contacting them. Within the centre women work in a range of different settings with female therapists, and Shanti's aim is to provide women with workers who share their ethnic background if this is desired. Where this is not possible, women 'should always be entitled to expect a sensitivity to the issues of intercultural work, even where their therapist has a different ethnic background from their own' (Mills 1996: 226).

Other examples of mental health services set up to meet women's needs include NEWPIN and HOME-START, both created for mothers suffering from mental distress. These are primarily voluntary organizations working in a variety of ways with women with young children. The Women's Therapy Centre in London is another well-known initiative which aims to offer a range of therapies to women in distress, and also offers training courses. Many of these mental health services for women are locally based. Since it has often been easier to create a service which is unconnected with conventional healthcare systems, many of the services are 'self-help' and unfunded. They may be organized by survivors' groups for example, or financed through the voluntary sector.

More recently, a number of initiatives have been developed in partnership with local statutory agencies, to offer a wider range of services. At the same time a number of groups have elaborated the kind of care they would like to see provided within mainstream services. Recent developments in the structure of both the NHS and the local authority social services, in particular the introduction of the purchaser/provider split, may mean that more of these ideas can in future be built into the commissioning of services.

These ideas about what women want from mental health services come from a variety of sources, from organizations working with and set up by women, and they represent a number of different groups in the community. Not all of the needs identified by women in this way are the same, as different issues will be highlighted by diverse groups. However, certain key themes can be identified that run through these recommendations for good practice.

The most important shared recommendation is perhaps the most obvious, though it is one that is not always followed. There needs to be wide consultation with women in the prospective user population before beginning to plan services, at every stage in the planning process and after the service has been set up. Consulting widely means asking questions of women in a range of informal locations – in sandwich queues, bingo clubs and other places where women can be found – as well as consulting with existing organized groups (Mills 1996).

Mental health services – whether in the community or in hospital – need to respect and support women's difference, without making unwarranted assumptions about their requirements, their objectives, their sexuality or their sameness. In addition, the more practical needs of some users of mental health services need to be acknowledged and provided for. Crèche facilities, the provision of safe transport, and the availability of treatment at different hours, for example, may make it possible for women to access the care they need.

Some of this requires better planning in how and where services are located, in the recruitment and training of staff, and in the provision of specific resources which are built into the service plan. Some of it requires the development of specific policy measures or guidelines to ensure good practice – in ensuring the safety of both women users and staff workers, for example, and in equal opportunities for both workers and users.

One of the most important yet difficult aspects of planning mental health policy which is gendered in a positive way will be the development of appropriate outcome measures and a reflexivity which ensures that services are acting on these recommendations, whilst engaging in a continuous dialogue with users to prevent current ideas becoming set in stone. Mills, in describing the creation of Shanti, outlines one of their objectives which should be shared by any mental health service for women: the therapeutic environment should reflect as little as possible the conditions in society that demoralise women' (1996: 223). How many of our existing psychiatric services could claim to do this – or even to have articulated it as an objective?

Conclusion

Women's experience of mental health treatment both in and out of hospital is, therefore, mixed. It is impossible to prescribe a simple solution for the problems women experience in their mental well-being or an ideal treatment they should receive when suffering from mental distress. Indeed, the underlying causes of that distress will vary from woman to woman. However, there are similarities amongst groups of women – sufficient to begin to articulate the kinds of policies which might open up new directions in mental health policy for women. Of course, many of women's needs are shared with male patients, and this strand of the collective experience shared by women and men also has to be considered alongside the experience of women alone. A mental health policy which was positively gendered would recognize both female and male users of the mental health system in ways which identify and support differences – both those between men and women and those between women themselves.

Currently, few mental health facilities deliver this kind of service. A number of problems remain and these are often because mental health policies are discriminatory or gender-blind. Recent changes have created a system with greater coercion and control for one small group of mental health users, whilst years of underfunding leaves a serious shortfall in the availability of appropriate rates for the vast majority of mental health service users. However, there are also new opportunities for user groups to become involved in the planning process and in the delivery of services. It is possible, therefore, to move towards a situation in which mental health services are both gender-specific and gender-sensitive, and in this way to develop a mental health system which meets the needs of both women and men.

Note

1 Typically, medical research has focused increasingly on the effects of alcohol on the unborn children of women who drink, and as with the pressure on women who smoke or take non-prescribed drugs during their pregnancy, the emphasis in the health services has been on getting women to change their behaviour for the sake of the child (Ettore and Riska 1995).

References

Abel, K., Buscewicz, M., Davison, S., Johnson, S. and Staples, E. (1996) (eds) *Planning Mental Health Services for Women: A Multiprofessional Handbook.* London: Routledge.

Ashton, H. (1991) Psychotropic drug prescribing in women. *British Journal of Psychiatry,* 158 (Supplement 10): 30–35.

Broverman, I.K., Broverman, D., Clarkson, F., Rosencrantz, P. and Vogel, S. (1970) Sex role stereotypes and clinical judgements of mental health. *Journal of Consulting and Clinical Psychology,* 34: 1–7.

Brown, G. (1992) Life events and social support: possibilities for primary prevention. In R. Jenkins, J. Newton and R. Young (eds) *The Prevention of Depression and Anxiety: The Role of the Primary Health Care Team.* London: HMSO.

Burns, T., Beadsmoore, A., Bhat, A.V., Oliver, A. and Mathers, C. (1993) A controlled trial of home-based acute psychiatric services: 1. Clinical and social outcomes. *British Journal of Psychiatry*, 163: 49–54.

Busfield, J. (1989) Sexism and Psychiatry. *Sociology*, 23 (3): 343–64.

Busfield, J. (1993) Managing madness: changing ideas and practice. In J. Bornat, C. Pereira, D. Pilgrim and F. Williams (eds) *Community Care: A Reader*. Buckingham: Open University Press/Macmillan.

Busfield, J. (1996) *Men, Women and Madness*. London: Routledge.

Chesler, P. (1974) *Women and Madness*. London: Allen Lane.

Cochrane, R. and Bal, S. (1989) Mental hospital admission rates of immigrants to England: a comparison of 1971 and 1981. *Social Psychiatry and Psychiatric Epidemiology*, 24: 2–11.

Corob, A. (1987) *Working with Depressed Women: A Feminist Approach*. Aldershot: Gower.

Davison, S. and Marshall, J. (1996) Women with drug and alcohol problems. In K. Abel, M. Buscewicz, S. Davison *et al.* (eds) *Planning Mental Health Services for Women: A Multiprofessional Handbook*. London: Routledge.

Day, P. and Klein, R. (1991) Britain's health care experiment. *Health Affairs*, 1: 39–59.

Dean, C. and Gadd, E. (1990) Home treatment for acute psychiatric illness. *British Medical Journal*, 301: 1021–23.

Department of Health (1969) *Digest of Health Statistics for England and Wales*. London: Department of Health.

Department of Health (1995) *Mental Health in England (from Calendar Year 1982 to Financial Year Ending March 1992)*. London: Government Statistical Service.

Department of Health (1997) *New drive to rid NHS of mixed sex hospital accommodation*. Press release, 6 August. London: Department of Health.

Doyal, L. (1994) Changing medicine? Gender and the politics of health care. In J. Gabe *et al.* (eds) *Challenging Medicine*, London: Routledge.

Elston, M.A. and Doyal, L. (1983) *The Changing Experience of Women. Unit 14: Health and Medicine*. Milton Keynes: Open University.

Ettore, E. and Riska, E. (1995) *Gendered Moods: Psychotropics and Society*. London: Routledge.

Fee, E. (1975) Women and health care: a comparison of theories. *International Journal of Health Services*, 5 (3): 397–415.

Goldberg, D.P. (1991) Integrating mental health in primary care. In H. Freeman and J. Henderson (eds) *Evaluation of Comprehensive Care of the Mentally Ill*. London: Gaskell.

Goldberg, D.P. and Huxley, P. (1980) *Mental Illness in the Community: The Pathway to Psychiatric Care*. London: Tavistock.

Harris, E.C. and Barraclough, B. (1997) Suicide as an outcome for mental disorders. *British Journal of Psychiatry*, 170: 205–28.

House of Commons Health Committee (1994) *Better Off in the Community? The Care of People Who Are Seriously Mentally Ill*. First Report. London: HMSO.

Ismail, K. (1996) Planning services for black women. In K. Abel, M. Buscewicz, S. Davison, S. Johnson and E. Staples (eds) *Planning Community Mental Health Services for Women*. London: Routledge.

Johnstone, L. (1989) *Users and Abusers of Psychiatry: A Critical Look at Psychiatric Practice*. London: Routledge.

Kendrick, T., Sibbald, B. and Addington-Hall, J. (1993) General practice: distribution of mental health professionals working on site in English and Welsh general practices. *British Medical Journal*, 307: 544–6.

Knowles, C. (1991) Afro-Caribbeans and schizophrenia: how does psychiatry deal with issues of race, culture and ethnicity? *Journal of Social Policy*, 20 (2): 173–90.

Lelliott, P., Sims, A. and Wing, J. (1993) Who pays for community care? The same old question. *British Medical Journal*, 307: 991–4.

Lewis, J. (1994) Choice, needs and enabling: the new community care. In A. Oakley and Susan Williams (eds) *The Politics of the Welfare State*. London: UCL Press.

Littlewood, R. and Lipsedge, M. (1988) Psychiatric illness amongst British Afro-Caribbeans. *British Medical Journal*, 296: 950–1.

Lloyd, K. and Moodley, P. (1992) Psychotropic medication and ethnicity: an inpatient survey. *Social Psychiatry and Psychiatric Epidemiology*, 27: 95–101.

Meltzer, H., Gill, B. and Pettigrew, M. (1994) *The Prevalence of Psychiatric Morbidity among Adults Aged 16–64, Living in Private Households, in Great Britain*. OPCS Surveys of Psychiatric Morbidity in Great Britain Bulletin No 1. London: OPCS.

Miles, A. (1988) *Women and Mental Illness*. Hemel Hempstead: Harvester Wheatsheaf.

Mills, M. (1996) Shanti: an intercultural psychotherapy centre for women in the community. In K. Abel, M. Buscewicz, S. Davison, S. Johnson and E. Staples (eds) *Planning Community Mental Health Services for Women*. London: Routledge.

MIND (1988) *Finding our own solutions*. London: MIND.

MIND (1994) *Eve Fights Back: Successes of the 'Stress on Women' Campaign*. London: Mind.

MIND (1995) *Stress on Women: Policy Paper on Women and Mental Health*, 2nd edn, London: MIND.

Mohan, J. (1995) *A National Health Service? The Restructuring of Health Care in Britain since 1979*. Basingstoke: Macmillan Press.

Muijen, M., Marks, I., Connolly, J. and Audini, B. (1992) Home based care and standard hospital care for patients with severe mental illness: a randomised controlled trial. *British Medical Journal*, 304: 749–54.

Nettle, M. and Phillips, A. (1996) The user's perspective: our experiences and recommendations. In K. Abel, M. Buscewicz, S. Davison, S. Johnson and E. Staples (eds) *Planning Community Mental Health Services for Women*. London: Routledge.

Oakley, A. and Mitchell, J. (1976) Wise women and medicine men. In J. Mitchell and A. Oakley (eds) *The Rights and Wrongs of Women*. Penguin: Harmondsworth.

OPCS (1995) *Morbidity Statistics from General Practice 1991–2*. London: HMSO.

Open Mind (1994) Crisis services: where are they? *Open Mind* 66: 14–17.

Palmer, R.L., Coleman, L., Chaloner, D., Oppenheimer, R. and Smith, J. (1993) Childhood sexual experiences with adults: a comparison of reports by women psychiatric patients and general practice attenders. *British Journal of Psychiatry*, 163: 499–504.

Parker, G. (1996) Carers and the development of community mental health policy. In K. Abel, M. Buscewicz, S. Davison, S. Johnson and E. Staples (eds) *Planning Community Mental Health Services for Women*. London: Routledge.

Payne, S. (1995) The rationing of psychiatric beds: changing trends in sex-ratios in admission to psychiatric hospital. *Health and Social Care in the Community*, 3 (5): 289–300.

Payne, S. (1996) Psychiatric care in the community: does it fail young men? *Policy and Politics*, 24 (2): 193–205.

Perkins, R.E. (1996) Women, lesbians and community care. In K. Abel, M. Buscewicz, S. Davison, S. Johnson and E. Staples (eds) *Planning Community Mental Health Services for Women*. London: Routledge.

Perkins, R.E. and Rowland, L.A. (1991) Sex differences in service usage in long-term psychiatric care – are women adequately served? *British Journal of Psychiatry*, 158 (Suppl 10): 75–9.

Pilgrim, D. (1992) Rhetoric and nihilism in mental health policy: a reply to Chapman *et al. Critical Social Policy*, 34: 106–13.

Pilgrim, D. (1993) Mental health services in the twenty-first century: the user–professional divide. In J. Bornea, C. Pereira, D. Pilgrim and F. Williams (eds) *Community Care: A Reader*. Basingstoke: Open University/Macmillan.

Pilgrim, D. and Rogers, A. (1993) *A sociology of mental health and illness*. Buckingham: Open University Press.

Sayce, L. (1996) Campaigning for change. In K. Abel, M. Buscewicz, S. Davison, S. Johnson and E. Staples (eds) *Planning Community Mental Health Services for Women*. London: Routledge.

Sheppard, M. (1991) General practice, social work and mental health sections: the social control of women. *British Journal of Social Work*, 21: 663–83.

Showalter, E. (1987) *The Female Malady*. London: Virago.

Strathdee, G. (1992) Liaison between primary and secondary care teams towards early intervention: a general approach. In R. Jenkins, J. Newton and R. Young (eds) *The Prevention of Depression and Anxiety: The Role of the Primary Health Care Team*. London: HMSO.

Tyrer, P., Merson, S. and Ghandi, N. (1993) Home treatment for psychiatric disorder (Letters). *British Medical Journal*, 307: 200–1.

Ussher, J. (1991) *Women's Madness: Misogyny or Mental Illness?* Hemel Hempstead: Harvester Wheatsheaf.

Williams, J., Watson, G., Smith, H. and Wood, D. (1993) *Purchasing Effective Mental Health Services for Women: A Framework for Action*. London: MIND.

Wooff, K., Goldberg, D.P. and Fryers, T. (1986) Patients in receipt of community psychiatric nursing care in Salford 1976–82. *Psychological Medicine*, 16: 407–14.

6

•

Gender issues in the prevention and treatment of coronary heart disease

•

Imogen Sharp

Coronary heart disease is the leading single cause of death among women in the UK. However, 'the captain of the men of death' is seen primarily as a man's disease, by both the public and health professionals. This male image is reinforced by the media, health education, research and the medical press, with major implications for women's health.

Rates of coronary heart disease in women

Coronary heart disease (CHD) kills some 70,000 women in the UK each year (Kaduskar *et al.* 1997). Although most of these deaths are in older women, CHD is also the single most common cause of death at younger ages, accounting for 18 per cent of all deaths in women under 75 years. In 1995, 18,630 women under the age of 75 died from CHD in the UK. By comparison, there were 14,080 female deaths from breast cancer, a disease which attracts far more attention and earmarked resources.

The disease also causes considerable illness and disability among women. Although women have fewer heart attacks than men the difference is much smaller for angina, the main presenting complaint of CHD among women. Partly because they get heart disease later than men, it is less visible among women but the reality is that their extra years of life are often marred by disablity and dependency with cardiovascular disease (CHD and stroke) a major contributor. With an ageing population, these numbers are likely to increase in the future.

Death rates from CHD among both women and men in the UK are among the highest in the world with Scotland and Northern Ireland having particularly high rates (though they are now being overtaken by countries in Eastern Europe). A woman aged between 35 and 74 in Scotland has more than 10 times the risk of dying of heart disease as a woman of the same age in Japan. Even more surprisingly perhaps, she also has a four and a half times greater risk than a man of similar age in Japan. Women in countries with high rates of the disease, such as the UK, have far higher rates than men in countries with low rates, such as Japan, France, Spain and Italy (see Sharp 1994).

The international league table is similar among women and men – countries with high CHD rates in women also have high CHD rates among men – indicating that the influence of environmental factors outweighs the influence of sex and gender differences. However, while death rates in the UK are falling, they are not falling as fast as in other developed countries such as the US and Australia. Furthermore, death rates seem to be falling more slowly among women than among men: for example, between 1981 and 1991, death rates among women in England fell by only 17 per cent among women but by 25 per cent among men (Kaduskar *et al.* 1997).

There are also important social class and ethnic differences in CHD rates within the UK (Kaduskar *et al.* 1997). While the stereotypical image of the heart disease victim is a stressed middle-class (male) business executive, it is those in manual social groups who are most likely to get heart disease. Thus, a women aged 20–59 in social class V has up to four times the risk of heart disease of a woman in social class I and this gap is widening. Ethnic differences too are apparent. Heart disease rates are highest among South Asians living in the UK: a South Asian woman has a risk that is almost 50 per cent higher than the indigenous population. These inequalities in heart disease, among women as well as men, have important resource implications and need to be taken into account in any strategy to tackle coronary heart disease.

Stereotypes of the heart disease victim

Over 100 years ago, in 1892, Osler described the person prone to CHD as '. . . not the delicate, neurotic person . . . but the robust, the vigorous in mind and body, the keen and ambitious man, the indicator of whose engine is always at full speed ahead' (Osler 1892). Almost 70 years later, in the late 1950s, Friedman and Rosenman (1959) described the Type-A or coronary-prone personality as one of 'intense striving for achievement, competitiveness, easily provoked impatience, time urgency, abruptness of gesture and speech, overcommitment to vocation or profession, and an excess of drive and hostility'. This view of coronary heart disease as primarily a (middle-class) man's disease has influenced the research community, health education, and health professionals in very profound ways.

Until recently, most research into the causes, prevention, diagnosis, treatment and rehabilitation of CHD had been carried out among men. Hence the knowledge which has shaped most interventions to prevent and treat heart disease has been conducted in exclusively male populations (Marmot *et al.* 1978; WHO European Collaborative Group 1980; Hjerman *et al.* 1981; MRFIT Research Group 1982; Shaper *et al.* 1982; Lipid Research Clinics Program 1984). While some of this can be justified by the excess of CHD among men in younger age groups, the dearth of research data on women is a real cause for concern.

The view of CHD as primarily a man's disease has also influenced health education. Traditionally, most images of heart disease victims in health education have been male, and men have been the main target audience for many publications. Rarely has health education on CHD shown women as victims. If they have been portrayed, women have usually been targeted as a means of reaching their partners, for example by influencing their diet (Amos 1993). The medical profession too has been exposed to predominantly male images through pharmaceutical advertising. Though this pattern is gradually changing, the image of the heart disease victim is still predominantly male and this exerts a significant influence both on the behaviour of women themselves and also on that of health professionals (Sharp 1994; British Heart Foundation 1995).

Women's response to health messages

Because of the belief that heart disease is primarily a man's problem, women may be less likely to respond to 'messages' about CHD. National surveys show that women are less likely than men to see heart disease as a risk to their own health. In one Health Education Authority survey (Health Education Authority 1990), for example, 52 per cent of women and 65 per cent of men picked out heart disease as a possible danger to their own health, although equal proportions recognized CHD as the leading cause of death in Britain today (HEA 1990).

The differences in coronary heart disease between men and women are due to a combination of biological differences and gender variations in behavioural or lifestyle factors. The risk factors for heart disease among women and men are the same and the classic risk factors – smoking, raised blood cholesterol and high blood pressure – confer the same level of relative risk (Sharp 1994). Thus the messages for prevention – on smoking, diet and physical activity, for example – are the same, and it is important that they influence women as well as men.

While there is a lower risk of CHD for women before the age of the meno-pause, which may be associated with oestrogen levels, much of women's lower risk of CHD overall is due to traditionally healthier lifestyles in women. However, these gender differences in behavioural risk factors are now beginning to change.

Smoking is the main preventable cause of heart disease. Since the early 1970s, smoking rates have been declining among all adults. However, smoking among women has been declining more slowly than rates among men: the gender difference in adult smoking has been steadily narrowing and has now virtually disappeared. In 1994, 28 per cent of men and 26 per cent of women were still regular smokers (Kaduskar 1997). Furthermore, smoking rates are higher among girls than boys, and rates among younger teenagers are increasing. By 1996, 15 per cent of girls aged 11–15 in England were regular smokers, compared to 11 per cent of boys (Office of National Statistics 1996) (see also Woodhouse, this volume).

Smoking is also increasingly associated with disadvantage, among women as well as men, reflecting social class differences in rates of heart disease (see also Graham; Amos *et al.*, this volume). By 1994, 13 per cent of women in professional groups (social class I) were smokers, compared to 32 per cent of women in social class V (unskilled) (Kaduskar 1997). Smoking rates do not seem to be decreasing among manual groups. Current trends could have an important effect on women's risk of heart disease, as well as other diseases, in the future.

Some population interventions to reduce heart disease risk can be used to influence both men and women simultaneously but others need to be more gender-sensitive in their approach. Similarly, strategies for changing the behaviour of individual women (or men) will need to take the differences in their lives into account. Women and men often experience health-related concerns very differently and their behaviour may be influenced by very different factors. Women are likely to be more conscious of what they eat, for example, though their diets will not necessarily be healthier; for physical activity, their major concern is weight loss (Activity and Health Research 1992; Dowler 1994). If strategies for change are to be effective they need to recognize these differences and target advice accordingly.

If women do develop CHD they may be less likely to recognize the symptoms and to delay longer in seeking help after the onset. When they have a heart attack, for example, they are more likely to call their GP rather than the emergency services, thus increasing the time taken to reach hospital (Clarke *et al.* 1994). Consistent with this, data from the Framingham study in the US showed that women were more likely to have electrocardiogram (ECG) evidence of previously unrecognized heart attacks in routine follow-up visits. Excessive pre-hospital delay of this kind can reduce both treatment options and survival chances (Hsia 1993; Clarke *et al.* 1994). There is therefore a clear need for public education to increase women's awareness of their risk of heart disease, of what they can do to prevent it, and of the possible symptoms.

Professional attitudes to CHD in women

The male image of heart disease may also have major implications for women's health, by influencing the decisions of health professionals. If they do not consider women to be at high risk of CHD, health professionals are less likely to give preventive advice and to offer women risk assessment. They may also be less likely to diagnose symptoms in women as CHD and to refer women for relevant tests and treatment.

Primary care teams in particular have the opportunity to make women aware of their risk of CHD. However, well woman clinics have traditionally focused on the risk of breast and cervical cancer, while heart disease clinics have tended to be directed at men (Calnan and Williams 1992; *Nursing Times* 1994). Though this pattern is beginning to change, much more work is needed to alter these long-standing and highly gendered practices.

It is also important that primary care professionals understand about CHD risk and take both age and sex into account when doing an overall assessment. For example, simple cut-off points for treatment of blood cholesterol levels are often inappropriate and have been based on research among men. The majority of older women have total cholesterol levels that are higher than the recommended level for treatment among men (for example 75 per cent of women aged 55 to 64 have levels over 6.5 mmol/l) but much of this is accounted for by their higher levels of HDL cholesterol – the 'protective' cholesterol. For any given cholesterol level, women have a lower risk of heart disease than men at all ages, so that decisions about whether or not to refer for treatment must be taken carefully with the sex of the individual patient in mind (Tunstall-Pedoe 1994).

Referral for diagnostic tests

The diagnosis and long-term management of CHD have become increasingly dependent on diagnostic tests and invasive procedures. However, several studies have found that doctors are less likely to refer women for such tests, and that CHD in women is likely to be diagnosed at a later stage. Diagnostic tests for heart disease include exercise testing, nuclear imaging and cardiac catheterization with coronary angiography. However, several studies have shown that women with angina or heart attack are less likely than men to be referred for some of these procedures despite the presence of more disabling symptoms. Even when the tests indicate a high likelihood of heart disease, fewer women are referred for arteriography and bypass surgery, and such referrals tend to be later in the course of their illness.

Coronary angiography – which involves catheterization – is the gold standard for establishing a diagnosis of CHD, on the basis of chest pain or angina. However, women are less likely to be referred for angiography than are men with the same diagnosis (Tobin *et al.* 1987; Ayanian and Epstein 1991;

Hsia 1993). Tobin *et al.* in the US found that of patients who were positive for CHD on nuclear exercise testing (i.e. had an abnormal nuclear scan result), women were six times less likely than men to be referred for cardiac catheterization, even after controlling for age, previous heart attack, the presence of angina, and abnormal test results. Furthermore, although women in this study tended to have more chest pain than men, doctors were twice as likely to attribute their symptoms to non-cardiac causes (Tobin *et al.* 1987).

UK findings have confirmed a similar pattern of gender bias in the ordering of investigations. One Northern Ireland study found that women were only half as likely to be referred for coronary angiography as men, even after controlling for age and admission rates for CHD (Kee *et al.* 1993). Another UK study found that women comprised less than a quarter (23 per cent) of patients who were referred with a clinical diagnosis of angina for further investigation by coronary angiography, indicating again that the threshold for referral is higher in women than in men (Sullivan *et al.* 1994).

Referral for treatment

A number of studies have found that gender differences in referral for diagnostic tests are also found in referral rates for treatment for heart disease. Indeed, research in both the US and the UK has found that women do not have as good access to treatment as men. Ayanian and Epstein, using data on over 80,000 discharges in Massachussetts and Maryland in the United States, found that women who were hospitalized for CHD underwent fewer major diagnostic and therapeutic procedures than men (Ayanian and Epstein 1991). In both states, men were about twice as likely as women to undergo some type of surgical revascularization procedure.

Steingart *et al.* (1991) also compared the coronary care received by men and women in the United States and found that, although women had angina before their heart attack as frequently as men, and reported greater disability from their symptoms, men were twice as likely as women to undergo cardiac catheterization and bypass surgery. Despite their greater disability from angina symptoms, only 15.4 per cent of women were referred for cardiac catheterization, compared to 27.3 per cent of men, and only 5.9 per cent of women were referred for coronary artery bypass surgery (CABG), compared to 12.7 per cent of men. Significantly, women were less likely than men to undergo these procedures whether or not they had a previous history of heart disease.

The twofold difference in the use of cardiac catheterization and bypass surgery (CABG) in men and women could not be explained by differences in coronary risk factors or cardiovascular medications, and persisted even after controlling for other relevant variables such as smoking, education, previous history of diabetes, hypertension and angina. However, bypass surgery was as likely in women as in men once they had undergone cardiac catheterization.

Research indicates that similar differences exist in the management of CHD in the UK. One study examining data on over 23,000 hospital discharges from two London health authorities revealed that in all age groups, and among all patients with a main diagnosis of angina or chronic ischaemia, men were 50 to 60 per cent more likely than women to receive surgical treatment, including angioplasty or CABG (Pettigrew *et al.* 1993). In North West Thames, where numbers were larger, men with a principal diagnosis of myocardial infarction were also significantly more likely than women to undergo revascularization.

Thus women are less likely to undergo procedures that are known, at least in men, to lessen symptoms and improve the capacity to function. However, once a diagnosis of heart disease has been established by an invasive diagnostic test, such as angiography, the sex difference in treatment for CHD may disappear: a phenomenon which has been labelled the Yentl syndrome (Healy 1991).

Explaining the sex differences in patient care

Several hypotheses have been proposed to explain the sex differences in patient care for CHD, and lower rates of diagnostic tests and treatment procedures among women. One explanation may be that heart disease is more severe in men. That is to say there may be sound clinical reasons for these differences in rates of investigation and treatment. However, women tend to have more severe CHD at presentation, and more severe heart attacks than men, and the prognosis for women is at least as severe as that in men (Wiklund *et al.* 1993; Clarke *et al.* 1994). Hence while doctors may define CHD as more severe in men because of their higher incidences of the disease, the evidence does not support sex differences in severity.

A second possibility is that women with cardiac symptoms may be less likely to have true CHD. Angina in women is often associated with normal coronary arteries leading many doctors to believe that angina is less likely to be followed by serious cardiovascular events (Wenger 1990). For example, the Coronary Artery Surgery Study (CASS) found that 50 per cent of women referred with chest pain for angiography had normal coronary arteries or minimal narrowing, compared to 17 per cent of men (Kennedy *et al.* 1982). However, this is based predominantly on findings in younger women, and may not be valid among those who are older (Steingart *et al.* 1991). Furthermore, the sex difference in the use of cardiac tests and treatment is also found among those who have had a heart attack – a well-defined diagnosis – not simply among those with angina.

It is also argued that the less frequent referral of women for diagnostic tests is because doctors believe them to be less accurate in women than in men. This is certainly true in the case of exercise testing where its limitations in predicting CHD in women are well documented (26,32). The Rose angina questionnaire (a standard diagnostic tool) may well have similar problems since it has not been validated among women. However, gender differences in referral decisions cannot be explained only by reference to the performance of the tests themselves. The diagnostic accuracy of nuclear exercise testing, for example, is similar in women and men when anatomical differences are taken into account (Sketch *et al.* 1975; Tobin *et al.* 1987).

In the same way that some doctors are suspicious of the use of diagnostic procedures in women they may also view particular treatments as either less effective or more risky for women. In this case they may be more reluctant to carry them out. This was supported by some studies in the 1970s and early 1980s, which found that women had higher operative mortality and less relief from symptoms – though their long-term survival was equivalent to that of men (Ayanian and Epstein 1991; Pettigrew *et al.* 1993). Early studies explained this by women's smaller arteries, but improvements in surgical techniques are likely to have eliminated this problem. Moreover, recent research indicates that this higher operative mortality could be the result, rather than the cause, of a referral bias, since women have more advanced disease at the time of treatment.

Overall, there seems to be little evidence that scientific or clinical criteria can fully explain gender differences in the use of tests or treatment for CHD. It seems likely therefore that there is a systematic bias in the delivery of services which is itself related to the widely held perception that CHD is primarily a man's disease. This gives rise to serious concern that the clinical outcomes in seriously ill women may be compromised if their diagnosis is delayed and they undergo procedures at a later stage of disease.

Recovery and rehabilitation from coronary heart disease

Research shows that women take longer to recover from CHD and the prognosis is worse for women than for men. This has implications both for women themselves, and also for the organization of health services. Hospital in-patient data indicate that, on average, women with CHD stay in hospital longer than men at all ages over 65 with obvious economic implications for both purchasers and providers (Information and Statistics Division, NHS in Scotland 1994).

It is well established that women have a worse prognosis after a heart attack than men, with greater morbidity, and a greater chance of dying. Once CHD is clinically manifest, the case fatality rate is greater among women, who also seem to be at increased risk of re-infarction and death after a heart attack (Hsia 1993). For example, one UK study found that one-third of women admitted to hospital with a heart attack had died within six months, compared to one-sixth of men (Wilkinson *et al.* 1994). Only part of this excess risk can be explained by older age, greater prevalence of risk factors such as hypertension and diabetes, and greater severity of heart attacks among women.

Women may also have less relief from symptoms and a higher risk of death after clinical procedures such as bypass surgery (CABG) and angioplasty, a consistent finding for over 15 years (Hsia 1993; Rahimtoola *et al.* 1993; Weintraub *et al.* 1993; National Health Service in Scotland 1994). This includes both short-term operative mortality, and long-term survival. The higher mortality after CABG may relate partly to women's higher likelihood of being older, of having diabetes or hypertension, and of having a smaller body size and smaller coronary arteries, all of which increase the risk of death (Rahimtoola *et al.* 1993; Weintraub *et al.* 1993).

But as we have seen, women's prognosis may also be worsened by the fact that they are referred for procedures at a more advanced stage of CHD (Khan *et al.* 1990; Kornfield 1991). Women in studies of cardiac surgery tend to be older and sicker than the men, and may have had surgery with more advanced CHD. However, further research is needed to determine whether it is the clinical features of the disease in women, or gender bias in the healthcare delivery system that plays the key part in giving women a worse prognosis (Weintraub *et al.* 1993).

Rehabilitation after CHD, including psychosocial adjustment, also seems to be slower for women and this may lead to longer stays in hospital. If women's heart attacks are perceived as being more serious by the health professionals, they may get treated more cautiously and may recover more slowly. Furthermore, women themselves may be more anxious, and less keen to be discharged from hospital. Cardiac rehabilitation programmes can aid recovery and provide valuable secondary prevention after a heart attack. However, women are less likely than men to take part in a structured rehabilitation programme, particularly those involving vigorous exercise (McGee and Horgan 1992). They are also more likely to drop out of such a programme prematurely. One study found a one-year drop-out rate of 64 per cent among women, compared to 42 per cent among men patients after a heart attack or surgery (Oldridge *et al.* 1980).

There has been little research on physical and social rehabilitation among women, and in particular on the psychological effect of having a heart attack. However, the small-scale studies that have included women indicate that women suffer more distress and psychological disturbance than men following heart attack, and more difficulty in rehabilitation, in both the short and long term (Stern *et al.* 1977; Shaw 1990; Sharpe *et al.* 1991).

It is well recognized that stress is an important factor in determining the success of rehabilitation in CHD (Julian and Marley 1991). Psychological rehabilitation problems may be more related to patients' attitudes and psychological status than to severity of heart attack (Shaw 1990). For example, one study found that, four days after a heart attack, women were more likely than men to report depression, negative self-image, and poor coping mechanisms (Guiry *et al.* 1987). Another study showed significantly higher levels of anxiety in women than in men admitted to a British coronary care unit. High anxiety levels were linked in turn with fatal cardiac arrests prior to discharge (Vetter *et al.* 1977).

In the longer term, women heart attack patients also experience more limited social functioning, and more psychological, emotional and physical complications than men, after controlling for age and morbidity (Wiklund *et al.* 1993). Women also return to work later than men following a heart attack (Shaw 1990).

It would appear therefore that women with CHD adapt less well than men, have more difficulty in rehabilitation and have different needs and problems than men. Health professionals may be badly equipped to meet these needs.

One further reason for longer stays in hospital – and slower rehabilitation – among older women may be that they are less likely to have a caring partner at home to look after them. Men's life expectancy is lower, and thus women are more likely than men to be widowed and alone when they have heart disease. As a result, they may be discharged from hospital later: the hospital providing care as well as cure.

Conclusions

The male image of CHD may have an important impact on women's health by affecting the way CHD risk and symptoms are perceived and dealt with, both by women themselves and by health professionals. There is a potential impact at every stage, from prevention, to diagnosis, to treatment, to rehabilitation.

There is a clear need for public and professional education, to increase awareness that heart disease is the leading single cause of death among women in the UK. Cigarette smoking among women also needs to be a focus for prevention, with national policy and local interventions, particularly in low income groups.

Lastly, more research including women as well as men is urgently needed. Traditionally, most of the research studies on CHD have been carried out only among men. Although the situation may now be changing, it remains unclear how effective most procedures are among women, because few women have been included in the research on preventive and therapeutic interventions. Health authorities also need to carry out audits of sex differences in referral rates for CHD, at each stage of the diagnostic and therapeutic pathway, to gain a better understanding of the most appropriate clinical practice, for both women and men.

Note

Many of these issues and more are covered in the National Heart Forum report, *Coronary Heart Disease: Are Women Special?*, which reviews the scientific and policy research evidence, and sets out recommendations for action. Copies are available from: Women and Heart Disease, PO Box 7, London W52GQ. Price £9.95 including postage and packing. Please make cheques payable to BSS.

References

Activity and Health Research (1992) *Allied Dunbar National Fitness Survey: A Report on Activity Patterns and Fitness Levels.* London: Sports Council and Health Education Authority.

Amos, A. (1993) In her own best interests? Women and health education: a review of the last fifty years. *Health Education Journal*, 52: 140–50.

Ayanian, J.Z. and Epstein, A.M. (1991) Differences in the use of procedures between women and men hospitalised for coronary heart disease. *New England Journal of Medicine*, 325 (4): 221–5.

British Heart Foundation (1995) *Women and Heart Disease Publicity Campaign.* London: British Heart Foundation.

Calnan, M. and Williams, S. (1992) *Coronary Heart Disease Prevention: The Role of the General Practitioner.* Final report of a national study commissioned by the Department of Health with the Health Education Authority. Canterbury: University of Kent.

Clarke, K.V.V., Gray, D., Keating, N.A. and Hampton, J.R. (1994) Do women with acute myocardial infarction receive the same treatment as men? *British Medical Journal*, 309: 563–6.

Dowler, E. (1994) Diet: What are the policy implications for women? In I. Sharp (ed.) *Coronary Heart Disease: Are Women Special?* London: National Heart Forum.

Friedman, M. and Rosenman, R.H. (1959) Association of specific overt behaviour pattern with blood and cardiovascular findings: blood cholesterol level, blood clotting time, incidence of arcus senilis and clinical coronary artery disease. *Journal of the American Medical Association*, 169: 1286–96.

Guiry, E., Conroy, R.M., Hickey, N. and Mulcahy, R. (1987) Psychological response to an acute coronary event and its effects on subsequent rehabilitation and lifestyle change. *Clinical Cardiology*, 10: 256–60.

Health Education Authority (1990) *Heartbeat: An Evaluation of 'Look After Your Heart' Publicity Campaign. Trend volume: November 1990.* Research carried out by the British Market Research Bureau on behalf of the Health Education Authority.

Healy, B. (1991) The Yentl syndrome. *New England Journal of Medicine*, 325: 274–6.

Hjerman, J., Byre, K.V., Holme, I. and Leren, P. (1981) Effect of diet and smoking intervention on the incidence of coronary heart disease: report from the Oslo Study Group of a randomised trial in healthy men. *Lancet*, 2: 1303–31.

Hsia, J. (1993) Gender differences in diagnosis and management of coronary disease. *Journal of Women's Health*, 2 (4): 349–52.

Information and Statistics Division, National Health Service in Scotland (1994) *Scottish Health Statistics 1993.* Edinburgh: Common Services Agency.

Julian, D. and Marley, C. (1991) *Coronary Heart Disease: The Facts.* Oxford: Oxford University Press.

Kaduskar, S., Bradshaw, H. and Rayner, M. (1997) *Coronary heart disease statistics, 1997 edition.* London: British Heart Foundation.

Kee, F., Gaffney, B., Currie, S. and O'Reilly, D. (1993) Access to coronary catheterisation: fair shares for all? *British Medical Journal*, 307: 1305–7.

Kennedy, J.W., Killip, T., Fisher, L.D., Alderman, E.L., Gillespie, M.J. and Monk, M.B. (1982) The clinical spectrum of coronary artery disease and its surgical and medical management, 1974–9. The coronary artery surgery study. *Circulation*, 66 (Supplement 3): 16–23.

Khan, S.S., Nessim, S., Gray, R., Czer, L.S., Chaux, A. and Matloff, J. (1990) Increased mortality of women in coronary artery bypass surgery: evidence for referral bias. *Annals of Internal Medicine*, 112: 561–7.

Kornfield, J. (1991) Coronary disease in women. *Cardio*, August: 5.

Lipid Research Clinics Program (1984) The Lipid Research Clinics Coronary Primary Prevention Trial, results I. Reduction in incidence of coronary heart disease. *Journal of the American Medical Association*, 251: 351–64.

Marmot, M.J., Rose, G., Shipley, M. and Hamilton, P.J.S. (1978) Employment grade and coronary heart disease in British civil servants. *Journal of Epidemiology and Community Health*, 32: 244–9.

McGee, H.M. and Horgan, J.H. (1992) Cardiac rehabilitation programmes: are women less likely to attend? *British Medical Journal*, 305: 283–4.

MRFIT Research Group (1982) Multiple Risk Factor Intervention Trial: risk factor changes and mortality results. *Journal of the American Medical Association*, 248: 1465–77.

Nursing Times (1994) *Women's Health: A Nursing Times Special Publication*. London: Macmillan Magazines.

Office of National Statistics (1996) *Smoking among Secondary School Children*. London: HMSO.

Oldridge, M.B., Lasalle, D. and Jones, N.L. (1980) Exercise rehabilitation of female patients with coronary heart disease. *American Heart Journal*, 338: 1366–7.

Osler, W. (1892) *Lectures on Angina and Allied States*. New York: Appleton.

Pettigrew, M., McKee, M. and Jones, J. (1993) Coronary artery surgery: are women discriminated against? *British Medical Journal*, 306: 1164–6.

Rahimtoola, S.H., Bennett, A.J., Grunkemeier, G.L., Block, P. and Starr, A. (1993) Survival at 15 to 18 years after coronary bypass surgery for angina in women. *Circulation*, 88 (2): 71–8.

Shaper, A.G., Pocock, S.J., Walker, M., Cohen, N.M., Wale, C.J. and Thomson, A.G. (1982) British Regional Heart Study: cardiovascular risk factors in middle-aged men in 24 towns. *British Medical Journal*, 283: 179–86.

Sharp, I. (ed.) (1994) *Coronary Heart Disease: Are Women Special?* London: National Heart Forum.

Sharpe, P.A., Clark, N.M. and Janz, N.K. (1991) Differences in the impact and management of heart disease between older women and men. *Women and Health*, 17: 25–43.

Shaw, D.G. (1990) Gender and heart disease – is there a difference? A study of the possible relationship between gender and the psychological impact of heart attack, Unpublished MSc research project. City University.

Sketch, M.N., Mohiuddin, S.M., Lynch, J.D., Zencka, A.E. and Runco, V. (1975) Significant sex differences in the correlation of electrocardiographic exercise testing and coronary arteriograms. *American Journal of Cardiology*, 36: 169–73.

Steingart, R.M., Packer, M., Hamm, P. *et al.* (1991) Sex differences in the management of coronary artery disease. *New England Journal of Medicine*, 325 (4): 226–30.

Stern, M.J., Pascale, L. and Ackerman, A. (1977) Life adjustment post myocardial infarction. *Archives of Internal Medicine*, 137: 1680–5.

Sullivan, K.S., Holdright, D.R., Wright, C.A., Sparrow, J.L., Cunningham, D. and Fox, K.M. (1994) Chest pain in women: clinical, investigative and prognostic features. *British Medical Journal*, 308: 883–6.

Tobin, J.N., Wassertheil-Smoller, S., Wexler, J.P., Steingart, R.M., Budner, N., Lense, L. *et al.* (1987) Sex bias in considering coronary bypass surgery. *Annals of Internal Medicine*, 107: 19–25.

Tunstall-Pedoe, H. (1994) Cholesterol levels in women: what are the policy implications? In I. Sharp (ed.) *Coronary Heart Disease: Are Women Special?* London: National Heart Forum.

Vetter, N.J., Cay, E.L., Philip, A.E. and Stranger, R.E. (1977) Anxiety on admission to the coronary care unit. *Journal of Psychosomatic Research*, 21: 73–8.

Weintraub, W.S., Wenger, N.K., Jones, E.L., Craver, J.M. and Guyton, R.A. (1993) Changing clinical characteristics of coronary surgery patients: differences between men and women. *Circulation*, 88 (2): 79–86.

Wenger, N.K. (1990) Gender, coronary artery disease, and coronary bypass surgery. *Annals of Internal Medicine*, 112: 557–8.

WHO European Collaborative Group (1980) Multifactorial trial in the prevention of coronary heart disease. Recruitment and initial findings. *European Heart Journal*, 1: 73–80.

Wiklund, I., Herlitz, J., Johansson, S., Bengston, A., Karlson, B.W. and Persson, N.G. (1993) Subjective symptoms and well-being differ in women and men after myocardial infarction. *European Heart Journal*, 14: 1315–19.

Wilkinson, P., Laji, L., Ranjadayalan, K., Parsons, L. and Timmins, A.D. (1994) Acute myocardial infarction in women: survival analysis in first six months. *British Medical Journal*, 309: 566–9.

7

•

Cause for concern: women and smoking

•

Kate Woodhouse

Introduction

Smoking is the leading behavioural cause of illness and death among women in the UK. Although smoking prevalence is falling, there has been little change among the most disadvantaged women, and an upward trend among girls. Globally, prevalence is increasing, particularly in newly industrialized countries.

There is some evidence that women are more at risk of tobacco-related damage than men, and reproductive effects have been of additional concern. Smoking behaviour is influenced by class and ethnic group, and gender differences in conditions at home and work. Women also lead diverse lives, in which cigarettes may play a complex role. Smoking should therefore be understood and addressed on many levels, from the biological to the social. A range of tobacco control strategies have been developed – but who should benefit, and bear the costs, and over what timescale? Such decisions are ultimately political.

This chapter examines the background to policy decisions: patterns of smoking behaviour, the health impact of tobacco use, influences on smoking, and gender issues in cessation and tobacco control strategy. British data are used, unless otherwise stated.

Smoking behaviour among girls and women

A recent model has identified four stages in the development of tobacco use within a country. For example, during stage 1 prevalence is very low but

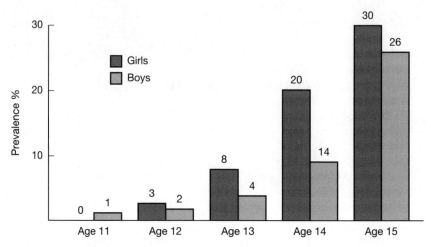

Figure 7.1   Regular (weekly) smoking prevalence, among young people in England aged 11–15.
Source: Diamond and Goddard 1995

increasing markedly, as in many African nations, whereas during stage 4 rates are still high but falling, as in the 'mature markets' of the USA and UK (Amos 1996).

In 'developed' countries, smoking is usually established during adolescence. Across the countries of the UK roughly one in eight girls under 16 smoke regularly, at least weekly (Figure 7.1). By around age 16 a quarter or more smoke at least weekly, but among young women aged 16–19 a quarter smoke every day. Classification changes thus perhaps obscure the increase in habitual smoking around this age. Smoking among girls under 16 increased across the UK during 1988–94, and a class gradient is becoming apparent (HEA 1996). As with most Westernized countries, more girls smoke than boys, and in England, for example, this gender gap has appeared at increasingly younger ages (Diamond and Goddard 1995; HPA for Northern Ireland 1995).

A quarter of adult women smoke daily, compared with nearly a half 30 years ago (HEA 1996; OPCS 1996). Tobacco use, and more recently cigarette use, has fallen just as rapidly as among men (Jarvis 1994). However, there has been a slight upward trend at age 20–24, where prevalence peaks at around two-fifths – compared with a fifth at age 60+ (OPCS 1996).

Since the 1960s a steep class gradient has emerged, and smoking is now strongly linked to disadvantage, for example as marked by occupation (Figure 7.2). Poorer women are also less likely to be able to stop than those with more access to resources. During the two decades to 1994 smoking prevalence halved among 'professional' women, but fell by only a fifth among women classified as 'unskilled manual' (OPCS 1996). Smoking among lone mothers, who have borne the brunt of increased poverty, remained

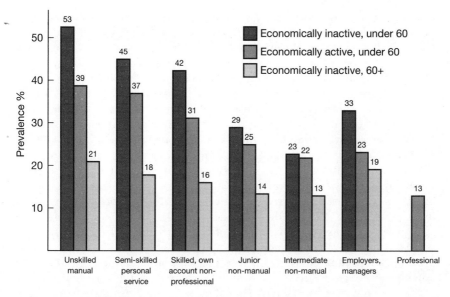

Figure 7.2 Regular (daily) smoking prevalence among women by own employment status
Source: OPCS 1996

unchanged at around six in ten over the period 1976–90 (Marsh and McKay 1994; see also Graham, this volume). In developing countries, however, it is the affluent, educated woman who is most likely to smoke (Amos 1996).

Smoking during pregnancy is also closely linked with poor circumstances (HEA 1994b; Owen and Bolling 1996). One in three pregnant women in England smoke, and there is evidence of an upward trend (HEA 1997). Around one in five women do stop before ten weeks' gestation, but at least half relapse within a month of the birth (McBride and Pirie 1990; HEA 1997). Despite greater disadvantage, women from black and ethnic minority groups are generally less likely than white women to use tobacco. About one in five African–Caribbean women in England smoke, but recorded rates among Asian women are very low (HEA 1994a). Prevalence may be higher among other groups, for example Turkish women.

Smoking: a women's health issue

Women who smoke suffer more ill-health, disability and increased risk of premature death, and may be at greater risk than men (Amos 1996). In 1995 an estimated 49,000 female deaths were caused by smoking, that is one in six of those among women over 35, or around half of all deaths among women smokers (Peto *et al.* 1994). Smoking-related mortality continues to rise among older women (Peto *et al.* 1994). There is a lag of several decades between peak prevalence and peak mortality, but globally over half a million female deaths a year are already linked to smoking (Amos 1996). Yet relatively few studies have looked at the long-term effects of smoking on women (Amos 1993). In the discussion that follows the estimates of relative risk (RR) for women smokers are taken from a major American study (Peto *et al.* 1994).

In the UK, coronary heart disease is the main cause of death for both sexes. About one in four female deaths are ascribed to CHD, and mortality is falling more slowly among women than among men (Khaw and Sharp 1994). Smoking roughly doubles women's risk of dying from the disease (RR 1.8, or 3.0 under age 65). Long term smokers of 30 'peak years' run three times the risk of comparable male smokers (Prescott *et al.* 1998). Smoking-related atherosclerosis also increases the risk of cerebrovascular disease, or stroke (RR 1.8, or 4.8 under age 65). An additional hazard for some women is use of oral contraception, which further increases risk of arterial disease (WHO Collaborative Study 1996).

Lung cancer ranks third as a cause of death among women, but second among older women in Scotland and northern England, exceeding breast cancer. Lung cancer mortality is almost entirely smoking-related (RR 11.9), and is expected to increase into the next century in all parts of the UK (Faculty of Public Health Medicine 1995). Smoking at a young age, before the mid-twenties, particularly increases risk in later life, possibly more so than among men (Hegmann 1993). Other parts of the respiratory and digestive tracts are vulnerable, particularly the larynx (RR 17.8) and oesophagus (RR 10.3). Cancers of the stomach, pancreas, kidney and bladder are also established as smoking-related. Among cancers specific to women, smoking at least doubles risk of cervical cancer, and may promote breast cancer, but reduces the risk of endometrial cancer (Chollat-Traquet 1992; Bennicke *et al.* 1995; Baron 1996).

Smoking is the main cause of chronic obstructive pulmonary disease (COPD) (RR 10.5), and again mortality is increasing among older women. Women smokers show a more rapid decline in lung function than men (Xu *et al.* 1994). Smoking is also implicated in deaths from other respiratory diseases, such as pneumonia. There are steep social class gradients in mortality from smoking-related illness. For example, the incidence of COPD among women classified as 'unskilled manual' is five times that among 'professional' women (Townsend 1995). Smoking behaviour provides only a partial explanation for these differences.

Besides premature death, women smokers of all social classes suffer more sickness absence, long-standing illness or disability, and poorer subjective health (Chollat-Traquet 1992; Graham 1993). Other conditions which contribute to poor health include respiratory infections, exacerbation of asthma, stomach and duodenal ulcers, and delayed healing (Chollat-Traquet 1992). Smoking has also been linked to pelvic infections, urinary incontinence, some bowel disorders, and adult-onset diabetes, though precise causal mechanisms are not always fully established. Girls who smoke show increased respiratory symptoms and increased coronary risk factors (ASH Working Group 1990). Older women smokers have increased risk of sensory impairment, Alzheimer's disease and osteoporosis, all major causes of disability (ASH Working Group 1995).

Tobacco use may also damage the health of both mother and child, throughout pregnancy and after the birth (RCP 1992). Smokers have higher incidence of infertility, ectopic pregnancy and spontaneous abortion, and are more prone to vomiting, urinary infections and bleeding in later pregnancy (Golding 1994; HEA 1994b). Smokers' babies weigh some 200gm less on average at birth, and are at greater risk of perinatal or neonatal mortality, and sudden infant death (HEA 1994b). Passive smoking also contributes to risk of childhood respiratory problems including asthma, bronchitis and pneumonia, and chronic middle ear effusion, which impairs hearing (ICRF-CRC 1991; RCP 1992).

The effects of stopping smoking

A major report on the effects of smoking cessation concluded that 'there are major and immediate benefits for men and women of all ages . . . with and without smoking-related disease' (USDHHS 1990).

Within six months levels of blood DNA-carcinogen complex halve, indicating reduced cancer risk, and pre-cancerous cervical lesions shrink markedly (Mooney *et al.* 1995; Szarewski *et al.* 1996). Cancer mortality falls significantly; for example excess risk of bladder cancer halves within a few years. Lung cancer risk falls 30–50 per cent within ten years, but some excess may persist for many decades, and there is evidence of irreversible changes (USDHHS 1990).

Gender-specific studies have shown that women's cardiovascular health improves rapidly, with excess risk of heart attack falling by a third within two years, and minimal excess risk of stroke within four years (Kawachi *et al.* 1993; Prescott *et al.* 1998). Respiratory symptoms decrease, and decline in lung function may be reduced. Other physiological systems also benefit: fertility recovers, risk of low birthweight falls, and early menopause and osteoporosis become less likely. Ulcers and post-operative wounds heal more rapidly, and stress levels eventually fall below those while smoking (Parrott 1995). Smoking cessation may also improve finances, with benefit to family health.

However, ex-smokers commonly experience acute craving, physical symptoms, sleep disturbance, and poor mood and concentration (Hughes *et al.* 1994). Daily routine and social relations are often disrupted. Thus worry about smoking-related illness may conflict with the need to feel and function well. Most ex-smokers also gain weight initially, women generally gaining more, and for longer (Gritz *et al.* 1995). Weight gain does not contribute to 'central obesity' and is not thought to be a health risk (Lissner *et al.*

1992), but women's size and shape is a matter of intense social concern, and any increase in weight may severely damage confidence and self-esteem.

Early influences on smoking behaviour

Many disciplines, from neurobiology to social learning theory, have contributed to our understanding of smoking behaviour. As with eating, going without may cause physical discomfort. However, research suggests that biology alone does not fully explain smoking behaviour. Smoking, like eating, is woven into daily life – to give a break or 'breathing space', control mood, create closeness or distance, or symbolize social identity (see Graham, this volume). This applies both to young girls struggling with adolescence, and to adult women.

Girls have more positive expectations of smoking than boys, more often believing that cigarettes can control weight or improve mood, and they may more easily become nicotine dependent (Charlton and Blair 1989; Goddard 1990). Although findings are inconsistent, some research links smoking with poor self-image, girls suffering a greater loss of self-esteem than boys in their early teens (Minagawa *et al.* 1993). Girl smokers also tend to be rebellious and reject school. Some studies suggest that girls are more susceptible than boys to parental, sibling and then peer influence (Stead *et al.* 1996). Girls mature earlier, and make a greater transition to peer influence in their early teens (Goddard 1990). All these factors would tend to promote tobacco use.

Young women may also discover painful conflicts within the female role. These conflicts may include sexual double standards, tensions between 'feminine' and 'adult' behaviour, and academic pressure combined with low expectations of achievement (Greaves 1996). Cigarettes may then seem the ideal accessory to manage conflicting emotions, self-images, and social expectations, being 'both forbidden and normal, alternative and accessible' (Stead *et al.* 1996).

Despite extensive research, the continuing high level of teenage smoking, especially among girls, is poorly understood (Waldron *et al.* 1991). Additional factors may include 'non-conformist' smoking, and membership of an 'education resistant' group (Reid *et al.* 1995). A generally drug-positive youth culture increases acceptability, while relatively low prices may have eased access (Townsend 1995). The role of increased family poverty is largely unexplored. However, although the great majority of children try cigarettes, it is the poorest who become adult smokers.

Influences on women's smoking

Nicotine has complex effects on mental function, and women are more likely than men to report mood control as a reason for smoking, and stress as a relapse trigger (Gritz *et al.* 1995). Depression and anxiety are more common, particularly among disadvantaged women, and are strongly linked with both smoking and relapse (Anda *et al.* 1990). Poor mood may in turn be linked to lack of social power and high levels of responsibility, both at home and possibly at work. Traumatic experiences of powerlessness, such as childhood abuse or partner violence, are also linked with smoking (Greaves 1996). In these circumstances, to buy and consume cigarettes may be to claim power otherwise denied – over time, personal space, resources and identity.

For women on low incomes, smoking is independently linked to social housing, to dependence on means-tested benefit, to lone parenthood, to manual work, and to lack of educational qualifications. Seven out of ten lone mothers with two or more of these characteristics smoke, yet smoking prevalence among poor households with none of these disadvantages is no more than average (Marsh and McKay 1994). This again suggests that lack of social power may be a key factor.

Very few women want to continue smoking, and around two-thirds in all social groups 'would like to stop', with perhaps two-fifths making a serious attempt in any one year (Reid *et al.* 1992; OPCS 1996). Although immediate withdrawal symptoms are similar for both sexes, women are less confident about stopping, more concerned about weight and mood changes, and possibly more likely to respond to symptoms with relapse (Gilbert 1995; OPCS 1996). Weight gain is seen as a major barrier to stopping, although seldom cited as reason for relapse (West 1995). Withdrawal symptoms and relapse are more likely during the second half of the menstrual cycle, which may be of practical value in planning cessation (Craig *et al.* 1992).

Mass interventions

Research suggests that key strategies to reach short-term adult targets are brief health service interventions, and use of mass media (Reid *et al.* 1992; Buck and Godfrey 1994). Although relatively limited in their effectiveness, such interventions reach the majority of women who do not seek formal support. However, research can only provide illumination for policy decisions. Strategies to address disadvantage may in future be given higher priority, and new developments will change our perspective. Such developments may include novel pharmacological techniques, and psychological interventions tailored to cognitive changes during cessation (Prochaska *et al.* 1993).

Brief opportunistic advice from a GP promotes cessation among both adult women and girls. Women make greater use of primary healthcare, and other workers, including pharmacists or family planning staff, may also have a role to play (Sanders 1992). However, nurse-led CHD checks may be ineffective in promoting cessation, and poorer women less often use specialized services such as health promotion clinics (Sharp 1995). Health workers are more likely to take action if they are trained in cessation support, and patient notes are marked as a reminder (Sanders 1992). Effectiveness appears to be increased by use of a protocol, and by additional interventions such as demonstrations of smoking-related damage, or self-help booklets (Sanders 1992). However, easily readable material is seldom available. Offer of follow-up is important, and some women may benefit from nicotine replacement therapy, particularly those who tend to anxiety or depression (Silagy *et al.* 1994; Stapleton *et al.* 1995).

An HEA review of interventions during pregnancy concluded that both self-help material and counselling may be effective, with the most promising approach combining initial advice with mailed self-help booklets (HEA 1994b). Yet there are major obstacles to good practice, particularly lack of time and counselling skills, social barriers, and poor staff coordination (Jones and McCleod Clark 1993). Local targets, and appointment of local coordinators, may promote development of an integrated strategy (HEA 1994b). Enhanced cessation rates among younger women have been ascribed to pregnancy (Jarvis 1994). However, many women stop before conception, and most relapse after the birth, so some commentators argue for a broader approach to promoting cessation (Greaves 1996).

Paid advertising can play an important part in promoting smoking cessation (Buck and Godfrey 1994). Unpaid news items, particularly linked to No Smoking Day, are also of established value (Reid *et al.* 1992). Effectiveness is enhanced by linked community programmes, and HEA evaluation of a recent UK-based trial seems promising (HEA 1997). However, publicity may have less impact on poorer women (Townsend *et al.* 1994). Some women, and some health workers, have seen media campaigns in the UK as blaming, or simply irrelevant, but in other countries the theme of empowering women has been given more emphasis (Greaves 1996). Youth media often glamorize smoking, but may also be a useful health promotion resource. HEA publicity in girls' magazines has changed attitudes, and a Finnish programme using various mass media had an immediate effect on smoking among the girls targeted, apparently by promoting discussion (Ryan 1991; Hafstad *et al.* 1996).

Many teenage girls wish to stop smoking and attempt to do so, but relapse rates are very high. Efforts have focused on prevention, yet even the best projects may only delay regular smoking. Reviews suggest that broad-based community campaigns may be most effective, together with legislation and reduced adult smoking (Reid *et al.* 1995; Stead *et al.* 1996). Specific smoking education may have less impact on girls, and broader health education programmes are easier to implement (Reid *et al.* 1995; Stead *et al.* 1996). School and college smoking policies sometimes reduce smoking prevalence (Stead *et al.* 1996). Girls may also derive at least short-term benefit from activity-based projects focusing on self-image, assertiveness, physical activity or arts (Doward *et al.* 1996). Multi-agency alliances are perhaps best placed to take health promotion into the 'real world', especially for young school leavers, who currently receive little attention. In developing countries community-based or media campaigns are more likely to reach girls, who often get little schooling.

Additional support

Women may gain particular benefit from coping strategies such as relaxation, or skills to deal with depression and weight gain, but opportunities to learn and to practise are limited (Gritz *et al.* 1995). Women smokers are also more likely than men to seek out and benefit from support, whether from health workers, friends or colleagues (Gritz *et al.* 1995); however, the value of partner support is uncertain. Stop-smoking groups are seldom cost-effective, and often impractical, especially during pregnancy, but group support may boost the effect of nicotine replacement therapy (Hajek 1994). Women also appear to value group exploration of the role of smoking, or the effects of passive smoking, without the explicit aim of cessation (Greaves 1996).

Community-based support projects have focused on areas of deprivation. The 'Women, Low Income and Smoking' initiative has established a database of relevant work, and QUIT is also piloting interventions (Crossan and Amos 1994). Careful design of these initiatives can help all participants benefit. For example, a Coventry project employed local women in peer-support, while protecting benefits income, and Birmingham's 'Towering Inferno' trained tower-block residents in research techniques (see Amos *et al.*, this volume).

Political responses

The development of a strategic and collaborative response to poverty is perhaps one of the greatest challenges facing the NHS (Benzeval *et al.* 1995; Laughlin and Black 1995). Effective strategies to reduce smoking among women might include improved training and job opportunities, better childcare, and initiatives to reduce isolation, with particular attention to lone mothers (ASH Working Group 1993). Much can also be done within routine practice through provision of more accessible or home-based services, particularly for antenatal and child health, and the offer of information and support in relation to housing, benefits and debt (Blackburn and Graham 1993). Community development approaches may also improve social organization and local facilities. Although smoking is often a low priority for participants, particularly in the early stages, cessation may follow once needs such as childcare are addressed (Ewles *et al.* 1996).

Legislation has been a key influence on smoking behaviour. NHS workers have promoted legislative change through publicity, support for pressure groups, and multi-agency alliances such as Parents Against Tobacco. Advocacy of this kind is not always seen as appropriate 'health work', but it has played a significant role in creating a climate conducive to smoking cessation.

Price is thought to have been the main determinant of adult smoking levels since 1980 (Reid *et al.* 1992). Girls and women are more price sensitive than males, and poorer social groups are generally more responsive, with the possible exception of the most disadvantaged (Townsend *et al.* 1994). Fiscal control has been a mainstay of government policy, and 1997 brought very substantial price increases. However, it has been argued that, to avoid 'taxing poverty', revenue should be redirected to subsidized nicotine replacement or community-based health education (ASH Working Group 1993; Marsh and McKay 1994).

It is now widely accepted that tobacco promotions reinforce and possibly initiate teenage smoking, and increase adult tobacco consumption (Aitken and Eadie 1990; ASH 1992). A ban may reduce consumption by around 7.5 per cent, and more among the young, particularly girls (Townsend 1995). A phased abolition of promotions was announced in May 1997, but industry pressure soon led to modifications. Globally, enticing promotions are thought to have been crucial in expanding female markets, and again restrictions are more effective among girls (Amos 1996). Legislation also affects the availability and acceptability of cigarettes. For example, American research suggests that vigorous implementation of sales laws can substantially reduce teenage smoking (Altman *et al.* 1992). Under-age girls can buy cigarettes more easily than boys, and the great majority have never been refused (Diamond and Goddard 1995). American data also suggest that the extent of smoke-free provision affects population smoking rates, although the effect on individual smokers is inconsistent (Reid *et al.* 1992). The UK target of 80 per cent policy coverage has not been met, even for health centres, and legislation is a possibility. As the UK's largest employer of women, and a key service provider, the NHS has an important role in promoting smoke-free facilities.

Towards an integrated strategy

Smoking should be addressed on many levels, to recognizing the complexity of smoking behaviour, and exploiting the cumulative effect of different interventions. Globally, there is a need to increase awareness of the issue through research and campaigning – those countries which have developed appropriate policy have seen marked changes in smoking behaviour. In the UK further development of multi-agency alliances may promote combined approaches, to both include gender awareness in programme planning and prioritize the needs of disadvantaged women.

An integrated strategy should include:

- relevant legislation, both on tobacco control and social welfare;
- full use of unpaid media opportunities, and community back-up to paid media campaigns;
- improved training for health workers, to increase understanding of disadvantage and coping strategies, and improve counselling skills;
- access to support within community-based programmes;
- broad-based community programmes to address teenage smoking;
- further investigation of gender-specific approaches, and relapse prevention techniques.

Such a strategy would aim to be sensitive to both social context and the needs of individual women, and to move towards current targets, while planning for a sustained reduction in smoking among women into the next century.

Acknowledgements

With thanks to Norma Daykin, Anne Upton and Patti White for comments on an earlier draft of this chapter.

Note

For projects on women and smoking outside the UK please contact INWAT Europe International Network of Women Against Tobacco), c/o ASH Scotland, 8 Frederick St, Edinburgh EH2 2HB.

References

Aitken, P.P. and Eadie, D.R. (1990) Reinforcing effects of cigarette advertising on under-age smoking. *Journal of Addiction*, 88: 399–412.

Altman, D., Carol, J. and Chalkley, C. *et al.* (1992) Report of the Tobacco Policy Research Study Group on access to tobacco products in the United States. *Tobacco Control*, 1(Supplement): 45–51.

Amos, A. (1993) In her own best interests? Women and health education: a review of the last fifty years. *Health Education Journal*, 52: 140–50.

Amos, A. (1996) 'Women and Smoking', *British Medical Bulletin*, 52 (1): 74–89.

Anda, R.F., Williamson, D.F., Escobedo, G. *et al.* (1990) Depression and the dynamics of smoking. *Journal of the American Medical Association*, 264: 1541–5.

ASH (1992) *Tobacco Advertising Bans Work – Official*. London: Action on Smoking and Health.

ASH Working Group on Women and Smoking (1990) *Teenage Girls and Smoking*. London: Action on Smoking and Health.

ASH Working Group on Women and Smoking (1993) *Her Share of Misfortune: Women, Smoking and Low Income*. London: Action on Smoking and Health.

ASH Working Group on Women and Smoking (1995) *As Time Goes By: Smoking and the Older Woman*. London: Action on Smoking and Health.

Baron, J.A. (1996) Beneficial effects of nicotine and cigarette smoking: the real, the possible and the spurious. *British Medical Bulletin*, 52 (1): 58–73.

Bennicke, K., Conrad, C., Sabroe, S. and Sorensen, H.T. (1995) Cigarette smoking and breast cancer. *British Medical Journal*, 310: 1431–3.

Benzeval, M., Judge, K. and Whitehead, M. (ed.) (1995) *Tackling Inequalities in Health: An Agenda for Action*. London: King's Fund.

Blackburn, C. and Graham, H. (1993) *Smoking among Working Class Mothers: Information Pack*. Coventry: Department of Applied Social Studies, University of Warwick.

Buck, D. and Godfrey, C. (1994) *Helping Smokers Give Up: Guidance for Purchasers on Cost-Effectiveness*. London: Health Education Authority.

Charlton, A. and Blair, V. (1989) Predicting the onset of smoking in boys and girls. *Social Science and Medicine*, 7: 813–18.

Chollat-Traquet, C. (1992) *Women and Tobacco*. Geneva: World Health Organisation.

Craig, D., Parrott, A. and Coomber, J. (1992) Smoking cessation in women: effects of the menstrual cycle. *International Journal of the Addictions*, 27 (6): 697–706.

Crossan, E. and Amos, A. (1994) *Under a Cloud: Women, Low Income and Smoking*. Edinburgh: Health Education Board for Scotland.

Diamond, A. and Goddard, E. (1995) *Smoking among Secondary School Children in 1994*. London: HMSO.

Doward, F.C., McKenna, S.D. and Ryan, H. (1996) *Teenage Smoking Programme – Innovative Pilot Project Scheme: Summary Report*. London: Health Education Authority.

Ewles, L., Miles, U. and Velleman, G. (1996) Lessons learnt from a coronary heart disease prevention project. *Journal of the Institute of Health Education*, 34 (1): 15–19.

Faculty of Public Health Medicine (1995) *UK Levels of Health: Third Report of a Working Party*. London: FPHM.

Gilbert, D.G. (1995) *Smoking: Individual Differences, Psychopathology and Emotion*. London: Taylor and Francis.

Goddard, E. (1990) *Why Children Start Smoking*. London: HMSO.

Golding, J. (1994) 'The Consequences of Smoking in Pregnancy'. Paper presented at HEA conference on smoking in pregnancy, Health Education Authority, London.

Graham H. (1993) *When Life's a Drag: Women, Smoking and Disadvantage*. London: HMSO.

Greaves, L. (1996) *Women's Smoking and Social Control*. London: Scarlet Press.

Gritz, E.R., Brooks, L. and Nielsen, I. (1995) Gender differences in smoking cessation. In K. Slama (ed.) *Tobacco and Health*. New York: Plenum Press.

Hafstad, A., Aaro, L.E. and Langmark, F. (1996) Evaluation of an antismoking mass-media campaign targeting adolescents: the role of affective responses and interpersonal communication. *Health Education Research*, 11 (1): 29–38.

Hajek, P. (1994) Treatments for smokers (Review). *Addiction*, 89 (11): 1543–9.

HEA (1994a) *Black and Minority Ethnic Groups in England: Health and Lifestyles Survey*. London: Health Education Authority.

HEA (1994b) *Helping Pregnant Smokers Quit*. London: Health Education Authority.

HEA (1996) *Health Update: Smoking*. London: Health Education Authority.

HEA (1997) Health Education Authority, unpublished data.

Hegmann, K.T. (1993) The effect of age at smoking initiation on lung cancer risk. *Epidemiology*, 4: 444–8.

HPA for Northern Ireland (1995) *Health Behaviour of Schoolchildren in Northern Ireland: A Report on the 1994 Survey. A WHO Collaborative Study*. Belfast: Health Promotion Agency for Northern Ireland.

Hughes, J.R., Higgins, S.T. and Bickel, W.K. (1994) Nicotine withdrawal versus other drug withdrawal syndromes: similarities and dissimilarities (Review). *Addiction*, 89 (11): 1461–70.

ICRF-CRC (1991) *Passive Smoking: A Health Hazard.* London: Imperial Cancer Research Fund/Cancer Research Campaign.

Jarvis, M.J. (1994) Gender differences in smoking cessation: real or myth? *Tobacco Control*, 3: 324–8.

Jones, K. and McLeod Clark, J. (1993) *A Review of Effective Interventions in Smoking and Pregnancy.* London: Health Education Authority.

Kawachi, I., Graham, A. and Colditz, A. (1993) Smoking cessation and decreased risk of stroke in women. *Journal of the American Medical Association*, 269 (2): 232–6.

Khaw, K. and Sharp, I. (1994) The scale of the problem: should we be concerned? In I. Sharp (ed.) *Coronary Heart Disease: Are Women Special?* London: National Forum for Coronary Heart Disease Prevention.

Laughlin, S. and Black, D. (ed.) (1995) *Poverty and Health: Tools for Change.* Birmingham: Public Health Trust.

Lissner, L., Bengtsson, C., Lapidus, L. and Bjorkelund, C. (1992) Smoking initiation and cessation in relation to body fat distribution. *American Journal of Public Health*, 82: 273–5.

McBride, C.M. and Pirie, P.L. (1990) Post partum relapse. *Addictive Behaviour*, 15: 165–8.

Marsh, A. and McKay, S. (1994) *Poor Smokers.* London: Policy Studies Institute.

Minagawa, K., While, D. and Charlton, A. (1993) Smoking and self-perception among secondary school children. *Tobacco Control*, 2: 215–21.

Mooney, L.A., Santella, R.M., Covey, L. *et al.* (1995) Decline of DNA damage and other biomarkers in peripheral blood following smoking cessation. *Cancer Epidemiology Biomarkers and Prevention*, 4 (6): 627–34.

OPCS (1996) *Living in Britain 1994.* London: HMSO.

Owen, L. and Bolling, K. (1996) *Smoking and Pregnancy: Developing a Communications Strategy for Cessation.* London: Health Education Authority.

Parrott, A.C. (1995) Stress modulation over the day in cigarette smokers. *Addiction*, 90: 233–44.

Peto, R., Lopez, A.D., Boreham, J. *et al.* (1994) *Mortality from Smoking in Developed Countries 1950–2000.* Oxford: Oxford University Press.

Prescott, E., Hippe, M., Schnohr, P., Hein, H. and Vestbo, J. (1998) Smoking and risk of myocardial infection in women and men: longitudinal population study. *British Medical Journal*, 316: 1043–7.

Prochaska, J.O., DiClemente, C.C., Velicer, W.F. and Rossi, J.S. (1993) Standardized, individualized, interactive, and personalized self-help programs for smoking cessation. *Health Psychology*, 12 (5): 399–405.

RCP (1992) *Smoking and the Young.* London: Royal College of Physicians.

Reid, D.J., McNeill, A.D. and Glynn, T.J. (1995) Reducing the prevalence of smoking in youth in Western countries: an international review. *Tobacco Control*, 4: 266–77.

Reid, D.J., Killoran, A.J., McNeill, A.D. and Chambers, J.S. (1992) Choosing the most effective health promotion strategies for reducing a nation's smoking prevalence. *Tobacco Control*, 1: 185–97.

Ryan, H. (1991) Tackling teenage smoking: the research strategy. *Health Education Journal*, 50 (1): 53–5.

Sanders, D. (1992) *Smoking Cessation Interventions: Is Patient Education Effective? A Review of the Literature.* London: London School of Hygiene and Tropical Medicine.

Sharp, I. (1994) Attitudes to women and coronary heart disease. In I. Sharp (ed.) *Coronary Heart Disease: Are Women Special?* London: National Forum for Coronary Heart Disease Prevention.

Sharp, I. (1995) *Preventing Coronary Heart Disease in Primary Care – The Way Forward.* London: HMSO.

Silagy, C., Mant, D., Fowler, G. and Lodge, M. (1994) Meta-analysis on efficacy of nicotine replacement therapies in smoking cessation. *Lancet*, 343 (8890): 139–42.

Stapleton, J.A., Russell, M.A., Feyerabend, C. *et al.* (1995) Dose effects and predictors of outcome in a randomized trial of transdermal nicotine patches in general practice. *Addiction*, 90 (1): 31–42.

Stead, M., Hastings, G. and Tudor-Smith, C. (1996) Preventing adolescent smoking: a review of options. *Health Education Journal*, 55: 31–54.

Szarewski, A., Jarvis, M.J., Sasieni, P. *et al.* (1996) Effect of smoking cessation on cervical lesion size. *Lancet*, 347 (9006): 941–3.

Townsend, J. (1995) The burden of smoking. In M. Benzeval, K. Judge and M. Whitehead (eds) *Tackling Inequalities in Health.* London: King's Fund.

Townsend, J., Roderick, P. and Cooper, J. (1994) The economic influences on smoking by socioeconomic group, age and gender. *British Medical Journal*, 309: 923–7.

USDHHS (1990) *The Health Benefits of Smoking Cessation. A Report of the Surgeon General.* Rockville, MD: US Department of Health and Human Services.

Waldron, I., Lye, D. and Brandon, A. (1991) Gender differences in teenage smoking. *Women and Health*, 17 (2): 65–90.

West, R. (1995) *Escaping the Nicotine Trap: A Report on Smoking Cessation in the UK.* London: No Smoking Day.

WHO Collaborative Study of Cardiovascular Disease and Steroid Hormone Contraception (1996) Ischaemic stroke and combined oral contraception: results of an international, multicentre, case-control study. *Lancet*, 348 (9026): 493–7.

WHO Collaborative Study of Cardiovascular Disease and Steroid Hormone Contraception (1996) Haemorrhagic stroke and combined oral contraception: results of an international, multicentre, case-control study, *Lancet*, 348 (9026): 505–10.

Xu, X., Weiss, S.T., Rijcken, B. and Schouten, J.P. (1994) Smoking, changes in smoking habits, and rate of decline in FEV1: new insight into gender differences. *European Respiratory Journal*, 7 (6): 1056–61.

Part 2

•

Principles into practice

8

•

Maternity and health links: an advocacy service for Asian women and their families

•

Fenella Starkey

Historical context

In the early 1980s, poor perinatal health amongst South Asian populations in Britain in comparison to the general population was becoming an increasing area of concern amongst policy makers. The work of the Select Parliamentary Committee on perinatal and neonatal mortality led to the publication in 1980 of the 'Short Report' (House of Commons Social Services Committee 1980), which focused upon high perinatal and neonatal mortality rates amongst South Asian women and called for action to improve these rates.

This action took the form of the Asian Mother and Baby Campaign (AMBC), launched in 1984 in 16 district health authorities by the Department of Health and Social Security and the Save the Children Fund. The three-year campaign aimed to improve the antenatal and post-natal care available to South Asian women via two initiatives.

The first was a community-based health education campaign which provided South Asian families with information on health services and the value of antenatal care (Parsons *et al.* 1993). The second, a two-year linkworker scheme, was also launched in 1985. Linkworkers were South Asian women, recruited by the health districts from the same communities as those of the patients, fluent in English in addition to at least one Asian language, and who had also received maternity services. These linkworkers were intended to act as a 'bridge' (Hicks and Hayes 1991) between Asian women and health professionals, facilitating communication by interpreting, explaining cultural differences and providing women with information on services in order to encourage their uptake (Smaje 1995). Linkworker services were available to women from the time of their first booking visit until six weeks after the birth of their baby (Parsons *et al.* 1993).

The AMBC has been criticized on a structural level for its focus on a 'cultural' model of communication facilitation, ignoring factors such as class, deprivation and racism which might contribute to higher perinatal mortality rates (Rocheron 1988; Smaje 1995). The Campaign's emphasis on 'ethnic group' as an explanation for 'ill-health' independent of the above factors has been interpreted as reinforcing the concept of a 'Black pathology' (Rocheron 1988), thereby stigmatizing all South Asian women. The implicit assumption that removing 'cultural barriers' such as knowledge of diet and customs will remove 'racist barriers' has also been challenged (Rocheron 1988). It is perhaps worth noting that none of the districts that participated in the AMBC formulated a strategic anti-racist policy as a framework within which linkworkers would operate (Smaje 1995).

Despite these criticisms, the evaluation of the campaign showed it to be a practical success, facilitating communication, personalizing care and improving knowledge of services amongst South Asian communities (Smaje 1995; Warrier 1996). One health authority attributed a 50 per cent increase in antenatal services uptake to the AMBC (Smaje 1995).

Models of language and social support

The concept of the linkworker has lasted into the 1990s, with several health authorities still employing (mainly South Asian) linkworkers in maternity services and other clinical settings. In addition to linkworker schemes, other services have been established in order to address the maternity needs of women from minority ethnic communities. Such services are scattered across Britain, and vary in aims and philosophies.

Warrier (1996) has identified three models of language and social support which categorize current services. The 'linguistic' model refers to 'pure' interpreting services, used by many service providers, particularly hospitals, to address the language barrier between patients and health professionals. Warrier defines an interpreter as a 'language transmitter' between the two parties. Interpreters have to explain and elucidate but they are not expected to intervene in the interaction unless there has been a misunderstanding, nor are they expected to take responsibility for the outcome of the consultation or interview (Warrier 1996: 10). Varying forms of interpreting services are used by health providers, including the use of bilingual members of staff and private telephone interpreting services.

The 'professional team' model is used by Warrier to describe linkworker services such as those developed by the AMBC, where linkworkers are NHS employees who work alongside professionals in order to facilitate communication with patients and disseminate appropriate health information. Evaluations of linkworker services based on this model have generally shown positive outcomes for Asian women. Warrier reports on a randomized controlled trial of 50 Asian women at risk of giving birth to a 'low birthweight' infant, which found that linkworker interventions 'contributed to happier pregnancies, reduction in maternal morbidity, increased health awareness and a lower use of analgesia during labour' (Warrier 1996: 11). The study also found that the mean birthweight of babies born to the women who received linkworker support was greater than that of the control group.

However, despite practical improvements in care, the extent to which linkworkers directly employed by the NHS are able to challenge discriminatory practices and racist attitudes experienced by patients is questionable. Similar criticisms to those levelled at the Asian Mother and Baby Campaign regarding its exclusive focus on 'cultural' issues of communication can be applied to present-day linkworker services operating this model.

The 'client-centred' model refers to bilingual advocacy schemes which attempt to address the power issues involved in accessing health services. Warrier describes the role of the bilingual advocate thus:

> Based on their understanding of their client's needs, expectations and preferences and a knowledge of the agency involved, the provider of language support could, where necessary, offer advice and additional information to enable the client to make informed decisions, challenge discrimination and insensitive or inappropriate care, increase clients' awareness of the full range of services and their entitlements, and advocate on their behalf to ensure that clients' rights are protected.
>
> (Warrier 1996: 12)

The focus of health advocacy schemes is firmly on the needs of the patient, rather than on those of the health professionals. Smaje argues that the health advocacy model 'therefore provides a less internal and less consensual model of organisational change than that implicit in the linkworker scheme' (Smaje 1995: 128). However, the extent to which schemes following this model can remain truly 'client-centred' as voluntary organizations move towards contracting with NHS bodies to provide services is an issue which requires careful consideration, particularly where the composition of those services is defined by the contracting agency rather than the advocacy organization.

For the 'client-centred' approach to be effective, it is generally believed that an advocacy service should be provided by an organization whose management structure allows workers to be closely associated with NHS management yet independent of it (Larbie *et al.* 1987). The Hackney Multi-ethnic Women's Health Project is a well-known example of such an organization, receiving funding directly from the local health authority while being managed by the City and Hackney Community Health Council. Based upon the American concept of 'patient advocacy', the Hackney project was the first of its kind in the country, and aimed to establish an advocacy ethos as an essential part of the health services' interactions with non-English speaking patients. Such an ethos appears to have been established in the hospital in which the project operates, and workers have also succeeded in bringing about policy changes in the way in which health services are provided for minority ethnic patients (Larbie *et al.* 1987; City and Hackney Community Health Council 1991).

Current policy context

The NHS reforms of the 1990s have focused upon the importance of contracting for the needs of local populations, and include an emphasis on tailoring services to meet the varying needs of individuals. To this end, standards regarding the quality of care which patients can expect to receive have been laid down and include some recognition of the needs of people from minority ethnic groups.

The Patient's Charter

The *Patient's Charter* is intended to put the *Citizen's Charter* into practice in the NHS, and lays down standards of care which individuals have the right to expect in their interactions with health services. With regard to access to services, it includes a right to 'receive healthcare on the basis of your clinical need, not on your ability to pay, your lifestyle or any other factor...' (Department of Health 1995: 5), in addition to an expectation that the NHS will 'make it easy for everyone to use its services...' (Department of Health 1995: 6). Of particular relevance to people from minority ethnic communities is the expectation that the NHS will 'respect your privacy, dignity and religious and cultural beliefs at all times and in all places' (Department of Health 1995: 6).

These standards place responsibility upon service providers to ensure that their services are fully accessible to all, including minority ethnic groups. This implies easy access to language and cultural support, the provision of written and verbal information accessible to all minority ethnic groups, and an awareness on the part of health staff of cultural and religious needs. It might also require anti-racist training for health staff to enable them to recognize the ways in which institutions and individuals might act to discriminate against minority ethnic people within healthcare settings.

The Charter also lays out standards relating to the provision of information, giving patients the right to 'have any proposed treatment, including any risks involved in that treatment and any alternatives, clearly explained to you before you decide whether to agree to it' (Department of Health 1995:

6) and to 'receive detailed information on local health services' (Department of Health 1995: 7). This clearly implies the provision of appropriate translated information and of interpreting and advocacy services to ensure that treatment options are fully understood so that informed consent can be given.

In addition to the rights and expectations laid out in the *Patient's Charter* for all patients, the *Patient's Charter and Maternity Services* (Department of Health 1994) for pregnant women and new mothers provides expectations regarding information and advice on antenatal and post-natal care, such as appropriate diet and methods of feeding. Again, for these expectations to be fulfilled for women from minority ethnic communities, the provision of language and cultural support may be necessary so that information and advice given is both sensitive and effective.

While the need for interpreting and advocacy services is therefore implied in the above Charters, they do not mention language as a specific factor which may affect the quality of care received by people from minority ethnic communities. An example of a government document which does so is the Department of Health's *Changing Childbirth* report (1993).

Changing Childbirth

The *Changing Childbirth* report (1993) was produced by the Expert Maternity Group headed by Baroness Cumberlege. It lays out guidelines for maternity care which focus upon the importance of each individual woman being at the centre of decisions made regarding her care, able to make decisions in the light of full discussions with the professionals concerned. This degree of control clearly implies the provision of information in a language which the woman fully comprehends. This point is made explicit within the document:

> At her first visit to the midwife or GP the woman should be able to discuss her views and wishes and feel confident that she will receive unbiased information about the options open to her. Where her first language is not English, interpretation facilities must be organised as early as possible and the woman given the name of a contact person who speaks her language.
>
> (Department of Health 1993: 11)

Changing Childbirth acknowledges that language support alone may not be adequate in ensuring that the needs of minority ethnic women are met by focusing upon linkworker and advocacy schemes:

> When a maternity unit is providing services to significant numbers of women who are unable to communicate in English, it is essential that providers should develop link worker and advocacy schemes. Women who do not speak English must be given the means of expressing their wishes and exercising choice. They should be kept fully informed of all matters relevant to their care. Link workers and advocates should not

be seen as optional extras to the service. They should be fully integrated into the maternity care team, with clearly defined roles, appropriate training and education opportunities.

(1993: 55)

This recognition by the Department of Health that non-English speaking women should have access to fully trained, professional linkworkers or advocates, working as part of their healthcare team, is a very important one. It acknowledges the central role that linkworkers and advocates must play if a woman whose first language is not English is going to be able to make real decisions about her own care and to feel in control of what is happening to her. It also suggests a preference for language and social support services to follow the 'professional team' or 'client-centred' models, rather than the 'linguistic' model of pure interpreting. However, the number of such schemes is limited, particularly in areas outside London. One exception to this is a long-standing programme, Maternity and Health Links, based in Bristol.

Maternity and Health Links

Origins

Maternity Links was established in April 1984, in the light of the concern over perinatal mortality rates mentioned earlier and acknowledgement that many Asian women in Bristol were not benefiting fully from the maternity services available. The organization's work focused initially on helping Asian women to learn English during their pregnancies. However, it was acknowledged that such tuition would not in itself be sufficient to enable Asian women to cope with maternity services. It was therefore decided that Maternity Links should also provide support to pregnant Asian women in their mother tongue via linkworkers who would advocate and interpret for them in their contacts with health professionals.

In 1987, this advocacy and interpreting service was extended via the 'Health Links' project, a pilot scheme funded by the Bristol Inner City Health Project and based at a local health centre. Linkworkers were employed to attend to the wider health needs of people whose first language was not English. The two groups amalgamated in 1993 to form Maternity and Health Links (MHL), comprising a structure which the present-day organization has retained.

Aims

Recognizing that the needs of people from different cultures using different languages are not currently met by mainstream healthcare provision, Maternity and Health Links works towards the following aims:

- to provide interpreting and advocacy for Asian and other minority ethnic group families in their use of health services;
- to provide information, advice and educational support on an individual and group basis to minority ethnic families with health-related problems;
- to bring to the attention of health professionals and other statutory and voluntary bodies the needs of Asian and other minority ethnic communities;
- to provide an individual home-based English tuition and health education service for pregnant women from minority ethnic communities.

The work of Maternity and Health Links is based upon a 'user-led' approach to health service provision similar to Warrier's 'client-centred' model, emphasizing the needs and wishes of the patients and working to empower service users by attempting to ensure that they are able to make informed choices regarding their care.

Services

Maternity and Health Links provides a wide and expanding range of services to minority ethnic communities in Bristol. It currently employs seven South Asian linkworkers, who advocate for patients at an inner city health centre, GP surgery and at a maternity hospital. Between them, these linkworkers are able to provide interpreting and advocacy services in Urdu, Punjabi, Bengali, Sylheti and Hindi. In recognition of the dispersed nature of the Chinese population in the area, a 'mobile' Chinese linkworker is also employed. The organization is currently investigating the extension of its linkworker services to Bristol's Somali communities. In 1994/5, the service was used by 1299 people via Maternity Links and 3093 people via Health Links.

The provision of English home tuition for pregnant women from minority ethnic communities is also an important part of Maternity and Health Links' activities. Thirty-two volunteer tutors offer to women one hour a week of one-to-one tuition, centred around maternity care, until six months after the birth of their baby. Such tuition may be vital for women who encounter difficulties in attending mainstream education classes, and the experience of learning English in this 'safe' way can raise their confidence when using maternity services.

Maternity and Health Links has also produced a video called *Healthy Pregnancy, Safe Birth* which explains antenatal, labour and post-natal procedures at the local health centre and maternity hospital, and is available in English, Urdu, Punjabi, Bengali, Hindi, Gujarati, Cantonese and Vietnamese. This video is currently being updated, and will also be available in Somali, Serbo-Croat, Farsi and Amharic. The new video will contain more general information and will therefore be available as a national resource. Other health education activities include the organization of keep-fit and parentcraft classes for women from minority ethnic communities, as well as an Asian mother peer-counselling scheme.

Maternity and Health Links has recently been awarded a grant by the local health authority to undertake research and development work in relation to the health needs of homeless Asian families in Bristol. Training in cultural awareness, focusing on health and welfare issues, is also provided to a wide range of statutory and voluntary organizations in Bristol and neighbouring areas.

MHL: strengths and weaknesses

Many of the strengths of Maternity and Health Links derive from its status as a community-based voluntary organization which has responded to the expressed needs of local minority ethnic communities. But as we shall see, many of these strengths can also be potential weaknesses. This has become especially evident with the growth of the 'contract culture' and the 'professionalization' of independent organizations associated with this process. The future of MHL will depend to a considerable extent on the ways in which this growing tension can be managed.

Maternity and Health Links' work involves advocacy on both an individual and a community level. In addition to advocating for individual patients in their interactions with health services it also has a broader community orientation, working with statutory agencies and other voluntary organizations to highlight the health and support needs of minority ethnic communities. The location of MHL outside the NHS itself is therefore an important element in its success.

Although MHL receives funding both from the health authority and a local NHS Trust, it is an independent voluntary organization, run by a management committee consisting of local women and health service co-optees. Its office is based within the inner city area of Bristol, close to many of the communities with which it works. This accessibility is increased by the location of linkworkers in community health settings used most frequently by patients from minority ethnic communities, including an inner city health centre and a general practice surgery.

The majority of MHL's linkworkers have been with the organization since its inception 11 years ago, and demonstrate considerable commitment to their work and to the communities to whom they provide a service. They frequently use their own time to accompany patients to appointments in health settings at which they are not contracted to work or to be with patients at times of emergency outside their working hours (Starkey 1995). The linkworkers see themselves as more than just interpreters and advocates, providing vital emotional support and befriending services to patients (Harding 1988).

The presence of both maternity linkworkers and generic health linkworkers within one organization (with some of the linkworkers assuming both functions) facilitates continuity of care for women and their families, enabling relationships of trust to be developed. At the same time, the linkworkers are viewed as colleagues by the majority of the health professionals with whom they work, and many see their presence as invaluable (Starkey 1995). Linkworkers attend regular meetings with health visitors at the health centre in which they are based in order to facilitate effective teamwork and clarify any issues or problems which may arise during their work.

The positive benefits of an independent organization like MHL are therefore evident. However, considerable disadvantages can also be identified both in Bristol and in similar services in other parts of the country (Hicks and Hayes 1991; Hayes 1995; Warrier 1996).

The demand for Maternity and Health Links' services continues to exceed the levels of provision funded within existing resources. Current service level agreements barely cover the cost of providing the contracted level of service, and linkworkers' goodwill results in many extra unpaid hours being worked. Thus the commitment of linkworkers mentioned above as a strength may also be regarded as a weakness for MHL, rendering staff vulnerable to exploitation due to their relatively weak position in the workforce.

The need for linkworker services which operate outside office hours, 24 hours a day and at weekends, has been highlighted by research around the country (Hicks and Hayes 1991; Warrier 1996). Such a need is particularly acute in maternity services, where women often go into labour at weekends or during the night and may be in need of support to help them through the experience. However, MHL is currently limited by funding levels to providing a Monday to Friday daytime service.

Maternity and Health Links currently holds service-level agreements with two directorates of one local NHS Trust. Two neighbouring Trusts do not provide funding for MHL's services. The impact of such funding arrangements on continuity of care for patients from minority ethnic communities is considerable, with linkworkers frequently unable to accompany a patient from GP consultations to appointments at hospitals within the same Trust or to respond to requests for their services from community and acute settings in the neighbouring Trusts (Starkey 1995). This arrangement can clearly lead to inefficient use of a well-established service, as well as causing the linkworkers and their clients considerable distress. The local health authority has recently provided MHL with money to develop their services further, but this is unlikely to match the demand for linkworker services across three NHS Trusts, a variety of clinical specialties and a range of minority ethnic communities.

During the 1990s, there has been a shift away from traditional grant-funding arrangements between statutory agencies and voluntary organizations towards the use of contracts or service-level agreements as a means of purchasing specified services. This use of contracting mechanisms can be seen as a way of improving services by defining explicit standards, monitoring achievement and enhancing accountability (NCVO 1989). However, for an organization like MHL, this 'contract culture' is problematic on a number

of levels. A primary concern is funders' expectations regarding desired outputs and performance indicators. The emphasis by some funders on the quan-
tification of MHL's service in terms of number of people seen by linkworkers
ignores the quality of the service provided by linkworkers and goes against
MHL's philosophy of working according to the needs and wishes of the
patient. There is clearly a tension between desired outputs as specified by
funders and desired outcomes, which are by their nature more difficult to
measure and require extensive consultation with patients (Phillips *et al.* 1994).
Such requirements from funders call into question the extent to which
MHL can remain 'independent', both in organizational and service delivery
terms.

Maternity and Health Links is also experiencing requests to show 'value
for money' by measuring the number of people seen as a percentage of all
people from minority ethnic groups in the area. However, the absence of a
systematic assessment of the general healthcare needs of the area's black
and minority ethnic communities, and their need for language support in
particular, makes such requests problematic.

Finally, the increasing focus in service-level agreements on the provision
of linkworker hours in specified settings limits MHL's ability to maintain its
broader community focus as described above – organizing health education
events, for example. This community orientation has been identified by
recent research as a highly desirable aspect of linkworker and advocacy
schemes (Warrier 1996). However, its continuation relies on MHL's success
in raising funds from elsewhere, a time-consuming task in relation to the
relatively small amounts of money needed to organize such activities.
Maternity and Health Links' ability to respond flexibly to the needs of local
minority ethnic communities is therefore being threatened by the increasingly narrow focus of the contracting process.

Maternity and Health Links' linkworkers often receive requests from patients for help and support in other aspects of their lives, such as housing
and welfare benefits (Harding 1988). Such requests are clearly outside the
linkworkers' remit, as MHL only holds contracts with health agencies. However, with the development of community care and the continued blurring
of boundaries between health and social care, this issue highlights potential
benefits in joint funding and interdisciplinary training for linkworkers to
enable them to fulfil a broader role within care in the community.

Conclusions: ways forward

Government guidelines such as the *Patient's Charter* and *Changing Childbirth*
have now formulated an explicit expectation of equality of opportunity in
the provision of health services and set standards against which service providers can be measured. For patients whose first language is not English
equality must be facilitated by the provision of language and social support.

Maternity and Health Links attempts not only to overcome language barriers, but also to improve access to health services for women from minority ethnic groups and their families via its advocacy service. Evaluation of health advocacy projects has shown that their users are 'better equipped to access NHS provision, receive more information about services, have better access to health education, and are more able to interact with NHS services' (Parsons and Rudat 1994).

As a provider of health advocacy services, MHL – like similar services elsewhere – has an important role to play in any local strategies aimed at addressing inequalities in healthcare for minority ethnic groups. The need for strategic planning in the purchasing and providing of services geared towards the health needs of minority ethnic communities is well recognized in relevant literature (Hicks and Hayes 1991; Audit Commission 1993; Warrier 1996). However, this same literature reports that such planning in the area of interpreting, linkworker and advocacy services is currently limited, with 'a worrying mismatch between client need and service planning' (Hicks and Hayes 1991: 89). A lack of needs assessment, inadequate funding and patchy service provision appear to be common characteristics of such services in England.

If organizations such as MHL are to succeed in providing effective services which appropriately meet the language and social support needs of local minority ethnic communities, they need to operate within a strategic framework which acknowledges and attempts to address these needs. Such a framework should start from the basis of comprehensive needs assessments carried out in full consultation with members of minority ethnic communities, which feed into the formulation of an appropriate purchasing plan. The purchaser/ provider split is in this sense a valuable mechanism for change, as the contracting and monitoring process allows for the setting of quality standards and 'equal opportunities' practices. Formal evaluation of services such as MHL should also feed into this process. By these means linkworker and advocacy services will be able to ensure that their services are meeting the needs of minority ethnic communities in the most effective manner.

Acknowledgements

Many thanks to the Management Committee and staff of Maternity and Health Links for their support and inspiration for this chapter. Particular thanks to Liz Lloyd for her helpful comments on initial drafts of this piece.

References

Audit Commission (1993) *What Seems To Be the Matter?: Communication between Hospitals and Patients*. London: HMSO.

City and Hackney Community Health Council (1991) *Multi-ethnic Health Project: Experiments in Health Advocacy.* London: City and Hackney CHC.

Department of Health (1993) *Changing Childbirth Part 1: Report of the Expert Maternity Group.* London: HMSO.

Department of Health (1994) *The Patient's Charter and Maternity Services.* London: Department of Health.

Department of Health (1995) *The Patient's Charter and You.* London: Department of Health.

Harding, T. (1988) *Health Links Scheme Evaluation Report.* Bristol: Bristol Inner City Health Project.

Hayes, L. (1995) Unequal access to midwifery care: a continuing problem? *Journal of Advanced Nursing,* 21: 702–7.

Hicks, C. and Hayes, L. (1991) Linkworkers in antenatal care: facilitators of equal opportunities in health provision or salves for the management conscience? *Health Services Management Research,* 4 (2): 89–93.

House of Commons Social Services Committee (1980) *Perinatal and Neonatal Mortality: Second Report from the Social Services Committee.* House of Commons Paper 663–1 (Session 1979–80) vol. 2. London: HMSO.

Larbie, J., Mares, P. and Baxter, C. (1987) *Trainer's Handbook for Multi-racial Healthcare.* Cambridge: National Extension College.

National Council for Voluntary Organisations (1989) *Contracting – In or Out? The Contract Culture: The Challenge for Voluntary Organisations.* London: National Council for Voluntary Organisations.

Parsons, L., Macfarlane, A. and Golding, J. (1993) Pregnancy, birth and maternity care. In W. Ahmad (ed.) *'Race' and Health in Contemporary Britain.* Buckingham: Open University Press.

Parsons, L. and Rudat, K. (1994) The power of advocacy. *Health Service Journal,* 104 (5429): 31.

Phillips, C., Palfrey, C. and Thomas, P. (1994) *Evaluating Health and Social Care.* Basingstoke: Macmillan.

Richards, D. (1994) *A Study of the Training Needs for Health Staff at Charlotte Keel Health Centre in Working with Linkworkers of Maternity and Health Links.* Bristol: Bristol Area Specialist Health Promotion Services.

Rocheron, Y. (1988) The Asian Mother and Baby Campaign: the construction of ethnic minorities' health needs. *Critical Social Policy,* 22 (Summer). 4–23.

Sharif-Dashty, M. (1994) 'A study to examine the health visitors' perception of the effectiveness of Linkworkers with respect to their communication and advocacy roles', unpublished BSc (Hons) Nursing Studies dissertation. University of the West of England, Bristol.

Smaje, C. (1995) *Health, 'Race' and Ethnicity: Making Sense of the Evidence.* London: King's Fund Institute.

Starkey, F. (1995) *Linking Communities: The Need for Advocacy and Language Support in Bristol's Health Services.* Bristol: University of the West of England.

Warrier, S. (1996) *Consumer Empowerment: A Qualitative Study of Linkworker and Advocacy Services for Non-English Speaking Users of Maternity Services.* London: The Maternity Alliance.

9

•

The establishment of a women-centred gynaecology assessment unit

•

Katharine Bell

The idea of a gynaecology assessment unit at Watford General Hospital was first conceived in January 1995. The hospital is part of the merged Watford and Mount Vernon Hospital NHS Trust which serves a combined population of 600,000. The gynaecology services are provided within the Women's Services Department which also incorporates midwifery and obstetrics. In the autumn of 1994, managers and staff realized that there was an escalating problem with both the volume and the appropriateness of admissions to the gynaecology ward.

The ward had 24 beds and catered for all elective and emergency gynaecology surgery for the Trust. Emergency admissions were referred by GPs directly to the ward, bypassing the Accident and Emergency department, unless the patient had collapsed and required emergency resuscitation. In the previous 12 months ward staff had dealt with 2,180 attendances averaging 181 a month. These women had been referred as emergencies but only about 30 per cent required hospital admission. Of the total attendances, 70 per cent were women in the early stages of pregnancy who had developed slight bleeding with or without abdominal pain.

In recent years it had also been observed that GPs were immediately referring to the hospital any women who presented with signs of bleeding. Previously, they would have advised such patients to rest in bed and await events. However, things have now changed. Women themselves are more likely to expect active reassurance about the viability of the pregnancy. At the same time the workload of GPs has greatly increased and the time needed to reassure an anxious woman is not always available. Hence the reasons for referral to the hospital were often psycho-social rather than medical in the narrow sense. This unplanned and unanticipated increase in referrals for early pregnancy bleeding was creating problems for both the service providers and for the women themselves.

The ward was usually busy when women arrived and they often had to wait between two and four hours to be assessed by a doctor. They then had a further wait for an ultrasound scan, depending on whether the department was open or not. The doctor for both day and night would be the senior house officer who would have had limited training and experience in managing early pregnancy bleeding. If the woman was admitted at night, most facilities were unavailable and she would spend the night waiting for a diagnostic scan at 9 o'clock in the morning. It seemed evident, therefore, that most women would gain little from emergency admission during unsocial hours and this was reflected in an increase in complaints. The service was haphazard, disorganized and of extremely poor quality.

At the same time, the Trust's response to the national commitment to reducing junior doctors' hours meant that medical staff were finding it very difficult to accommodate all the tasks that had to be done in the care of the growing number of ward attendees (Dowling *et al*. 1995; NHSME 1994). The nursing team, acutely aware of the poor service, queried whether it was necessary for a doctor to see every potential admission, particularly if the presenting condition was non-urgent. It was clear that GPs were unlikely to change their habits, whatever the impact on patients. The majority were fundholders who were very vocal and it would be difficult to influence their clinical practice. Thus women with bleeding in early pregnancy were not going to be managed in primary care. But did the hospital setting necessarily have to involve treatment by a doctor? Discussion among ward staff was focused around the following issues:

- Do women who are clearly not emergency cases have to see a doctor?
- How could we develop a high quality, efficient service meeting both the clinical and psychological needs of these women?
- What clinical work does the doctor undertake that could be undertaken by a nurse/midwife?
- Could we relocate the service away from the gynaecological ward?
- How much would such a service cost and where would the funding come from?

Analysis of the situation revealed that the harassed junior doctor is not always able to undertake an ultrasound scan due to inexperience and a lack of training but can take blood samples to confirm pregnancy, identify whether a fetal heart is present and exclude tubal pregnancy. There was agreement that a nurse or midwife could be trained to take on the responsibilities previously undertaken by the junior doctor and ultrasound department. It was also recognized that if s/he was trained in counselling, the nurse or midwife could provide substantial psychological support to the women using the service. The activity could also be relocated to another area within the maternity block, thus removing some of the outpatient ward workload.

Having recognized the potential of this new way of organizing care, a bid was submitted to the (then) North Thames Regional Health Authority Task Force New Deal Initiative. Under the general umbrella of reducing junior doctors' hours, funding was agreed to establish the project, to cover administrative costs and to pay the salary of a nurse or midwife practitioner. The new gynaecology assessment unit was to be consultant-led but managed by a nurse or midwife practitioner who would undertake clinical duties previously undertaken by a senior house officer or registrar. The clinic would be open from Monday to Friday between 8 a.m. and 4 p.m.

It was agreed that the new service would also provide Hormone Replacement Therapy (HRT) by implant. The provision of HRT was another area in which the quality of care was recognized to be poor. An internal HRT clinic was held in a lunch-time slot in the main out-patient department. In the short time of one hour, up to 15 women would be seen by a senior house officer. There was barely time for inserting the implant let alone providing the appropriate screening and counselling. There was also a lack of continuity of care, since whichever senior house officer was available would attend. It was therefore decided that the midwife/nurse practitioner would be ideally placed to provide a higher quality and more effective service.

The purchase of an ultrasound machine was funded from capital funds within the Trust, and a midwife practitioner was appointed in July 1995. She was selected because she had a strong gynaecological background, had recently qualified as a midwife and was felt to be highly motivated and able to take the initiative. The main training needs identified were in ultrasound scanning and the management of HRT. Both internal and external training was provided for the ultrasonography and the consultant gynaecologist taking the lead for the service provided all other clinical training. He also assisted in the development of the protocols and procedures that would be required.

An action plan was agreed and processes were developed and implemented for the following aspects of the service:

- Administration processes for GP referral and the Patients Administration System (PAS). This was in anticipation of charging fundholding GPs for the provision of a non-emergency service.
- Protocols and operational policies incorporating medical referral and clearly identifying the roles and responsibilities of both the midwife practitioner and the doctor.
- Incorporation of training experience for junior doctors in order to enable them to be more skilled in the management of early bleeding in pregnancy as well as HRT.
- Development of a patient waiting and treatment area to provide privacy and comfort. This was felt to be particularly important as those women

attending with early pregnancy bleeding were likely to be anxious and would require a relaxed, pleasant environment.

- Development of a strategy promoting the service to GPs within and outside the Trust's immediate catchment area.
- Publicizing the service to women themselves via the local press.
- Ensuring that all internal staff – medical, nursing, midwifery and administration – understood the clinic and its functions.
- Establishment of a system of statistical collection and monitoring processes in order to assist with clinical audit and user evaluation of the service.
- Development of a training programme to enable other midwives or nurses to provide cover in cases of absence of the nurse practitioner.

In early October 1995 the practitioner commenced the HRT service at the unit. This proved to be an instant success with the women attending, most of whom felt that they were talking to someone who was sympathetic, understanding and able to take time to answer their questions. Both verbal and written communications described how much the users felt the service had improved:

> I attend the clinic for HRT implants. The first couple of times I saw a doctor in the outpatients department in his lunch hour, he inserted the implant but I could see that he really didn't have time to answer my questions. This time it was different. The midwife was gentle and kind. She also answered all my questions.

> I used to dread attending the HRT clinic. I never saw the same doctor twice. This clinic is now so different. I really feel as if I know the nurse. It makes such a difference being able to ask all your questions without feeling silly.

> When I used to attend the HRT clinic in the outpatients department, I used to feel embarrassed and felt I was in a cattle market or on a conveyor belt. There was always at least ten of us sitting in a little room waiting to be called. This new system is more than 100 per cent better.

On average, 50 women attend the gynaecology assessment unit and are assessed by the midwife each month. The unit officially opened for early pregnancy referral in November 1995 when the practitioner had completed her training. GPs were requested to refer all women with non-emergency early pregnancy problems directly to the unit. The gestation for referral should be 12 weeks or less. At the time of writing, a total of 600 women with problems in early pregnancy have attended the unit and 75 per cent of these have returned for a follow-up scan.

There has been substantial support for the unit both within the hospital and outside it. Internally, the team effort to enable the clinic to be successful has been admirable. The only weak area within the team proved to be the ultrasound department who despite being very unhappy at their increased workloads, stubbornly continued to accept referrals from GPs rather than attempting to redirect the workload in the direction of the midwife practitioner. It was apparent that professional pride was being ruffled despite apparent enthusiastic agreement during discussions and meetings. This problem slowly resolved itself following constant monitoring and active management by the senior management team.

Externally, the clinic has proved popular with GPs. A number have taken the trouble to write in and praise the service. Unfortunately, however, a significant minority continue to refer haphazardly despite the on-call senior house officer trying to redirect them to the clinic. The scheme has been marketed continuously to GPs but some did not read these communications. Those who persisted in bypassing the service for whatever reason were contacted personally, but as yet even this has failed to change practice in some cases.

In response to requests from a number of GPs it is now planned to extend the clinic hours in order to provide a service during evening surgery hours. The idea is that the gynaecology assessment unit would run in tandem with evening surgery enabling GPs to refer directly to the unit rather than the ward. This would also enable the women to be scanned quickly and go home rather than spend a worrying night in hospital awaiting a diagnosis.

In April 1996 a small charge was made to the GPs in order to cover the costs of the service and maintain its financial viability. Charging for the service will also enable funds to be potentially available for service expansion, particularly with the plans to start an evening clinic.

The midwife practitioner appointed to provide the clinical expertise has ensured that the service is provided to a high standard. She has bravely adapted to her new role and has set an example of the opportunities for both professional and clinical development now available to both nurses and midwives (Read and Graves 1995). As the service develops, she has extended her skills and is now able to undertake vaginal as well as abdominal ultrasonography.

The women who have used the clinic have been very supportive. A formal evaluation has been undertaken which demonstrated the value most attach to the new service. Quotes from the evaluation forms returned have included the following:

> I have miscarried before and had to wait for hours in the ward before I was seen by the doctor. It was also upsetting not knowing whether I was pregnant or not. This time I started bleeding slightly. My GP rang the unit and I was quickly seen and scanned by the midwife. Everything was all right and I was out in no time.

> I read about the clinic in the local paper. When I started bleeding I asked my GP to refer me as I had a friend who had already been there and said it was good. I think I embarrassed my GP because he went a bit

pink and said he had received something in the post about it but hadn't read it. Anyway he did refer me and I felt really cared for. Caroline [midwife] was really kind and understanding. I had to attend for two scans before the bleeding settled and everything was OK.

I wanted to write and thank you for the marvellous care I received when I attended the gynaecology assessment unit. I felt like I was receiving private care. It was so smooth and efficient. I really felt my needs were met. Sadly, I lost my baby but it really helps to feel that the care I received was so good. Thank you.

Formal evaluation of the gynaecology assessment unit is now being carried out and includes both quantitative analysis and more qualitative observations from users. A questionnaire will be sent to GPs and also to the women who have attended and results will be anonymized. The findings of the evaluation will be circulated to the GPs and it is hoped that positive views from the women will assist in further developing the GPs' support for the unit.

The process of implementing the gynaecology assessment unit has not been easy. The idea of a nurse or midwife taking on some of the responsibilities of a doctor continues to be a problem to some in the medical profession and for some nurses too. However, there is no doubt that it is now well established. Future plans include the possibility of expansion into a general menopause service and also the redirection of other gynaecological ward attendees to the outpatient service.

We feel that the future of the gynaecology assessment unit is secure. We are also confident that in working towards the reduction of junior doctors' hours, we have created an opportunity to improve the service provided to our female clientele. We have seen no evidence that quality of care has been devalued. Indeed, the opposite seems to be the case as a number of evaluations of similar initiatives in other settings have indicated (Doyal *et al.* 1998; Read and Graves 1995). The service now provided is a great improvement on the past, is women-centred and sets a high standard for the future.

References

Dowling, S., Barrett, S. and West, R. (1995) With nurse practitioners who needs house officers? *British Medical Journal*, 312: 1211–14.

Doyal, L., Dowling, S. and Cameron, A. (1998) *Challenging Roles: An Evaluation of Four Innovatory Nursing Posts in the South West*. Bristol: Policy Press.

NHS Management Executive (1994) *The New Deal: Plan for Action*. London: Department of Health.

Read, S. and Graves, L. (1995) *Catching the Tide: New Voyages in Nursing?* Sheffield: Sheffield Centre for Health and Related Research.

10

•

Gender, sexuality and healthcare: improving services

•

Tamsin Wilton

Policy makers and health professionals alike are paying increasing attention to the links between gender, health and healthcare. This concern is amply demonstrated by mushrooming well woman clinics, an established literature on women's health and a newly emergent focus on men's health. However, it has not yet been matched by comparable interest in issues of sex and sexuality. This gap in our knowledge poses considerable difficulties, since some of the most basic issues in 'women's health' (or 'men's health') are intimately bound up with sexual behaviours and identities. So, in a book whose subject matter is women's relationship with the health services, it is essential that we examine the place of sexuality within medical practice.

In the arena of sexual health, the links between the biological and social components of health may be highly visible, and their complexity easy to perceive. The World Health Organisation (WHO), for example, recognizes that sexual health is 'much more than sexual functioning; [it is] concerned with lifestyles, sexual roles and relationships'. WHO identifies possible barriers to sexual health as including:

> myths, taboos and attitudes, over-concentration on the physical aspects of male sexuality, stereotypical images of female sexuality, discrimination against lesbians and gay men, and denial of sexuality in disabled, mentally handicapped and elderly people.
>
> (Langfeldt and Porter 1986: 5)

However, the potential impact of sexuality on health and healthcare goes even further beyond the specifics of what is usually defined as sexual health.

It is deeply interwoven with our sense of ourselves, with our self-esteem and with our closest relationships. As such, it is potentially an important element in the care experience of all NHS users (Savage 1987; Wilton 1997a). Despite this, sexuality is all too often treated in a cursory or inadequate way in the training of healthcare professionals, with the result that its significance may be overlooked in diagnosis, treatment or care (Jessop and Thorogood 1988).

In order to provide appropriate and high quality care to women (and, indeed, to men) health professionals need to have a thorough grounding in questions of sexuality and sexual identity. Healthcare services need to incorporate a high level of awareness of these issues into their practice at every level. Yet the question of sexuality has only recently begun to receive attention within the National Health Service. This chapter will highlight the importance of sexuality for healthcare provision within the NHS and identify examples of good practice in this area. This can then be used by providers, purchasers and managers as a resource in developing more efficient and effective services for women in general and for lesbian users in particular.

Sex and medicine: a troubled history

In order to understand current debates around sexuality within the culture of the NHS it is important to have some insight into the recent history of medicine. One key issue here has been the *medicalization* of sexuality.

Healthcare as provided within the NHS is no longer rigidly tied to a biomedical model of health. The value of holistic care is increasingly recognized, and it is becoming more commonplace for treatments such as aromatherapy, homoeopathy or chiropractic to be recommended (or even practised) by NHS professionals (Baggott 1994). However, such changes are relatively recent.[1] Historically, the NHS has been dominated by a reductionist biomedical approach, with its by now well-recognized shortcomings. This dominance has had particular consequences for the way in which the healthcare professions have engaged with sexuality.

Biomedicine's exclusive focus on the biological body has been demonstrably effective in the development of appropriate techniques for curing certain physical ailments. However, it may impede our ability to understand and respond effectively to pain and distress which cannot be reduced to the level of physiology. Yet, historically, European biomedicine has laid claim to more and more of such areas of the human experience in a process generally referred to as *medicalization* (Hart 1985). Sexuality is one such area. From the mid-nineteenth century onward, all aspects of human sexual expression were brought under the aegis of medical science (Foucault 1976; Weeks 1986).

With this medicalization of sexuality came the pathologization of those sexual desires, experiences and behaviours which deviated from what medical science – dominated by middle-class European males – perceived to be 'normal'. Since medical science was exclusively the domain of men from privileged socio-economic groups, the sexual norms of the time were inextricably entwined both with men's fantasies about how women *should* behave and with the middle-class etiquette of ladylike conduct (Jeffreys 1990). The sexual behaviour of other groups, especially that of the working class and of the native populations of colonized nations, was labelled abnormal and dangerous (McClintock 1995; Wilton 1997b). At the same time same-sex relations were pathologized, and the homosexual as a pathological 'type' was created (Foucault 1976).

The troublesome legacy of this nineteenth-century process of medicalization is with us today. In the absence of informed and thoughtful consideration of sexuality in the training of medical and healthcare professionals, it continues to influence the attitudes, beliefs and practices of doctors, nurses and others (Stern 1993; Das 1996).

An alternative view

Within the social sciences, increasingly sophisticated theories of sexuality have developed over the last 40 years (Plummer 1981; Altman *et al.* 1989; Stein 1992). These theories have explored the complex interrelationships between individuals, their behaviour, the cultural context in which they move, and the various meanings which they give to certain acts and feelings. Out of this intricate web sexual identities are spun. Sexuality is, therefore, a complicated issue that resists containment within a biomedical model. It encompasses ideas of 'normality' which are culturally bound, and it has tenuous (and hotly contested) links with biology and with gender (see essays in Rosario 1997). Yet the sophistication and increasing subtlety of these ideas are not reflected in training, clinical practice or service provision within the NHS.

Moving towards good practice: identifying the problems

It has been argued that the current failure of the NHS properly to incorporate the question of sexuality into practice has wide-ranging consequences for all service users (Savage 1987; Tiefer 1995). Of immediate concern here, however, are the effects on women in general, and on lesbians in particular.

Problems for service users who are women

Research into the healthcare which women in Britain receive indicates that medical and nursing staff alike are ill-prepared to provide even basic information and support concerning sex and sexual activity (Webb 1985, 1986), and that staff all too often hold and express judgemental attitudes about the sexuality of their patients/clients (Macintyre 1977; Dockery 1996). This is hardly surprising, since the question of sexuality continues to receive little or no attention in either basic or post-basic training in any of the professions (Savage 1987; Das 1996; Jones 1996).

The failure of health carers to address the issue of sexuality is especially problematic in the arena of sexual rehabilitation – for example, following treatment for certain cancers, stroke, heart attack or gynaecological complaints – and for disabled people in particular (see essays in Browne *et al.* 1985). The inadequacy of the support available lies not simply in basic ignorance about varieties of sexual technique or in embarrassment and unwillingness to discuss sexual activity directly, but in a profound failure to recognize the interaction of sexuality and gender.

'Sex' is by and large perceived in very narrow terms as heterosexual penis-in-vagina intercourse defined by and culminating in male ejaculation. There is a continuing silence and ignorance about female sexuality, whether heterosexual or lesbian in expression: 'Most books [on rehabilitation] assume that sexual readjustment is easier for a woman, and stress how to be attractive to men rather than how to get sexual satisfaction' (Rakusen 1989: 111). As Rakusen suggests, the medical model of sexuality is more than simply secretive and repressive; it is associated with a very specific understanding of what constitutes proper and 'normal' gender behaviour.

Feminist researchers have argued that the biomedical model of 'normal' sexuality – a model with all the social and cultural status of medical 'knowledge' – has been an important element in disempowering women and maintaining their secondary social status relative to men (Martin 1987; Waldby 1996). The dominant cultural belief about heterosexuality is that to be masculine is to be sexually active, initiatory and possessed of a potent 'sex drive', which must be controlled and directed. To be feminine, on the other hand, is to be sexually passive, responsive and driven by a desire for emotional contact and for pregnancy rather than for sexual pleasure *per se* (Savage 1987; D'Emilio and Freedman 1988; Wilton 1996a).

This set of beliefs is simply the product of a particular society at a particular moment in its history. However, it has been promoted by medical science as 'normal', with the attendant assertion that behaviours which do not fit this narrow set of culturally determined parameters are abnormal and hence unhealthy, sick or pathological. Apart from its obvious implications for women's experience of sexuality, this medicalization of sexual behaviours has been an effective agent in the social control of women, by labelling as sick or maladjusted behaviour which is socially unacceptable.

It is no coincidence that the key campaigns of the women's health movement have been around reproduction – questions of abortion, contraception, new reproductive technologies and childbirth – for it is in these arenas that the medical control of women has been most clearly visible (Richardson 1993; Doyal 1995). Medical discourse has tended to define women in relation to their reproductive function, to the extent that women are deemed capable of achieving full emotional and physical health only through childbearing – and childbearing within marriage is regarded as healthier than childbearing without (Richardson 1993). Indeed, the simplistic biomedical model of female-ness is founded on the assumption that the social relations of matrimony are inextricable from that vaguely biologized notion the 'maternal instinct'. 'At its crudest this leads to the position that the maternal instinct only operates in married women and not in unmarried women' (Macintyre cited in Richardson 1993: 76). Within the terms of this model childbearing on the part of unmarried women, and especially lesbians, is pathologized.

Problems for service users who are lesbians

The medicalization of sexuality, which has had such destructive consequences for lesbians and gay men, has been successfully challenged within some areas of the NHS. It is in the context of psychiatry that the separation of sexuality from a purely medical framework has been at least partially achieved. After decades of 'treating' lesbian and gay desire as either a psychopathology *per se* or as symptomatic of underlying pathology, the medical profession in Brit-ain and the United States now no longer officially supports this position.[2] This move away from an understanding of homosexuality as pathological was motivated by concerted activism on the part of lesbian and gay commu-nities, and by members of the medical profession who were themselves lesbian or gay. In Britain the shift was encouraged by the efforts of the Counter-Psychiatry Group, founded in London in 1971 in order to challenge current attitudes towards lesbians and gay men within the medical profes-sion (Stewart 1995).

This shift within psychiatry, however partial, at least makes it more likely that lesbian and gay clients will receive respectful and appropriate psychiat-ric treatment. This has not been reflected in healthcare practice more gener-ally, although major transformations have been set in motion in the wake of the HIV pandemic. One of the positive consequences of the appalling tragedy that is AIDS has been a truly startling improvement in the quality of care available to gay men in some quarters within the NHS.

It is important to recognize the very real achievements of the NHS in this area, but it is equally important to recognize that there remains a very long way to go. Gay men continue to report encounters with homophobic NHS staff, especially outside major urban areas, and there is evidence that the improvements in healthcare provision to gay male service users have not been matched by similar improvements for lesbian users (Dockery 1996; Muir-Mackenzie and Orme 1996). This situation is unsurprising, given the historical positioning of sexuality within biomedicine.

If the dominant biomedical model of sexual health depends on the no-tion of socially sanctioned reproductive heterosexuality, then lesbian and gay sexuality is *by definition* labelled unhealthy. Indeed, biomedical science has devoted much time and energy (not to mention precious resources) in attempting to track down the causes of (and, by implication, a cure for) the love and desire which a significant proportion of individuals feel for members of their own sex. Such 'explanations' shift as the focus of medical interest alters, but are flawed by a continuing tendency to confuse sexual object choice with gender identity.

Indeed, homosexuality has been conceptualized within post-enlightenment European cultures primarily as a disorder of gender (Wilton 1995). The very act of desiring a man is regarded as inherently female or feminizing, and the act of desiring a women similarly seen as inherently male or masculinizing. Thus early attempts to establish an aetiology of lesbianism led researchers to suggest that the signs (indeed, symptoms) and causes of women's desire for each other lay in the masculinization or imperfect feminization of their bodies.

Lesbians, it was proposed, had enlarged (penis-like) clitorises, excess body hair, thick wrists and were 'more solid' than heterosexual women (Ruse 1988). Some researchers claimed to have identified characteristic 'sex-variant' labia, pelvis structure, hymen formation and even nipple shape (Henry 1950). As the technology of medical investigation developed so the proposed 'symptomatology' of same-sex desire shifted, from the grossly anatomical to the biochemical (hormones) to the neurological (brain shape or function) to the neurogenetic (the so-called 'gay gene'). Significantly, lesbians were generally ignored in such studies in favour of gay men, but the baseline assumption continued to be that same-sex desire was a marker or result of a *gender* disorder.

This very basic failure to understand gender identity and sexual orientation as distinct issues left researchers simply unable to comprehend the 'masculine' gay man or 'feminine' lesbian (see essays in Stein 1992), let alone the 'feminine' heterosexual man or 'masculine' heterosexual woman. This has been an issue in nursing, for example, where it is assumed that, since the caring and nurturing aspects of nursing (not to mention its low status and poor pay) are regarded as properties of the female role, therefore all male nurses must be gay (Savage 1987).

This history has important consequences for the relationship of lesbians to the medical profession. In the nineteenth century, the biologically determinist model of homosexuality was generally welcomed by lesbians and gay men, who felt (as did sexologists such as Havelock Ellis) that the scientifically sanctioned 'third sex' theory offered a strong base from which to argue for social tolerance and an end to persecution. Indeed, Radclyffe Hall's famous novel *The Well of Loneliness* was written precisely in order to popularize the idea of the lesbian as a member of the third sex and make a plea for acceptance. As the social movement for lesbian and gay liberation grew in confidence and as sophisticated models of sexual identity developed within the social sciences, lesbians were no longer so inclined to believe the medical experts who told them they were biological freaks or that their desire was the product of physiological malfunction.

Although a minority within the lesbian and gay community continues to insist that a biological model of same-sex desire offers the most coherent foundation for a liberation campaign (see Stein 1992; Simon 1996), very few would now subscribe to an illness model. Indeed, there is a lively and informed community debate around the nature/nurture question of whether lesbians and gay men are born or made. Yet, as we have seen, the failure to address sexuality in basic training means that few in the healthcare professions have the opportunity to develop more than a crude understanding of these complex issues.

It is difficult to have faith or trust in anyone whose treatment of you is informed by her/his continued belief that your closest intimate relationships are sick, dysfunctional or abnormal. In addition, there is ample evidence to suggest that homophobia or simple ignorance on the part of doctors, nurses and other healthcare workers can lead to neglect or malpractice in treating known lesbians (Hemmings 1986; Savage 1987; Trippet and Bain 1992; McClure and Vespry 1994).[3]

Nor is ignorance the only problem for lesbians who seek medical care. The pathologization of same-sex desire resulted, relatively recently, in attempts to 'treat' or 'cure' lesbians and gay men, many of which were humiliating, harmful or downright sadistic (Wilton 1995). In addition, there is now an extensive body of research from Britain and the United States which indicates that lesbians who disclose their sexuality when seeking healthcare often meet with hostility, judgemental attitudes and poor treatment (Stevens 1993; James *et al.* 1994; Wilton 1996a). Lesbians and gay men in Britain are likely to be well informed about such matters, and their willingness to be open about their sexuality with healthcare providers may be influenced as a result.

Implications for healthcare provision

The biomedical model of sexuality, founded as it is in a naively asocial understanding of the 'naturalness' of gender, has profound implications for the healthcare available to women in the NHS. One consequence, for example, is that enormous sums are spent on making new reproductive technologies available to childless married heterosexual couples, whereas such services are hard to access or simply unavailable to unmarried women, whether heterosexual or lesbian (Saffron 1994).

Another troubling effect is that the collection of clinical and/or epidemiological data may be significantly flawed by the assumption that reproductive, penetrative heterosex is the norm. In the context of diagnosis the question, 'When did you last have sex?' is of little value when the word 'sex' has different meanings for patient and professional. On the wider epidemiological level, an example from a Bristol hospital demonstrates the extent to which the resulting data may be flawed.

A specialist breast care clinic in the hospital asks patients to fill in a questionnaire which asks what contraception they use/have used, how long they used it for, and how long after they ceased using it they became pregnant. This assumes that all women are heterosexually active, that all heterosexually active women have penetrative sex and depend on contraceptives to avoid pregnancy, and that the only reason for ceasing to use contraception is to conceive. Women whose only sexual activity has been with female partners, or who made a transition from heterosexuality to lesbianism and stopped using contraceptives in consequence, or who prefer non-penetrative heterosex, or who ceased using contraception for reasons other than to get pregnant (perhaps the end of a heterosexual relationship, or dissatisfaction with available contraceptives), do not 'fit' the questions asked.

Any research into the prevalence of breast cancer among specific groups or into its cause relative to sexual activity that makes use of data gathered through this research instrument will lack methodological rigour. This is especially worrying in the light of research findings which seem to suggest that lesbians are at disproportionate risk of breast cancer (Wilton 1996a).[4]

Healthcare services available to women, then, are seriously flawed by homophobia (fear and dislike of lesbians and gay men) and by heterosexism (the unquestioning assumption that heterosexuality is natural, normal and right). As Sue Rosser (1993: 183) concludes, 'Not only does homophobia discourage lesbians from seeking necessary health care, but it also prevents health care workers from tying appropriate diagnoses and treatments to risk behaviours.' Clearly this situation is unacceptable, since it militates against all women, and lesbians in particular, receiving appropriate healthcare, and hampers effective research into many health issues which affect women.

Moving forward: examples of good practice

Cultural beliefs about gender and sexuality are deeply held, and among the most resistant to change. Moreover, the social marginalization of lesbian and gay citizens in Britain is given powerful political and ideological sanction by legislation such as Section 28 of the 1988 Local Government Act.[5] Yet the HIV pandemic with its Red Ribbon Campaign, the increasing confidence of the lesbian and gay communities, closer political and social links with other European nations (many of whom are more tolerant of their lesbian and gay citizens than Britain) and other social shifts less easy to quantify – such as the inclusion of sympathetic lesbian and gay characters on mainstream network television – seem to be leading to a liberalization of attitudes. This has in turn facilitated the growth of lesbian healthcare initiatives both at a grass-roots community level and, more recently, within the statutory sector. Cross-sectoral collaboration has proved especially beneficial in this sensitive area, with statutory bodies funding community initiatives and community activists providing fundraising and publicity for statutory sector ventures.

Community organizing

Lesbian and gay communities in most Euro-American countries, including Britain, have developed complex networks of service provision, both private and voluntary, in an attempt to compensate for the widespread failure of statutory services to meet their needs. This network, which incorporates legal, social, cultural and political elements, is increasingly likely to offer some healthcare services, and the women's health movement has sometimes (though by no means always) also supported lesbian healthcare initiatives.

As long ago as 1973, lesbian paramedics established a lesbian night at St Mark's Clinic, a drop-in clinic in the East Village area of New York (Waitkevicz 1978), while healthcare information for lesbians is almost exclusively published and distributed through feminist or lesbian and gay networks and publishing houses (see for example Hepburn and Gutierrez 1988; McClure and Vespry 1994; Lynch and Woods 1996). In the UK a group of lesbian volunteers in Birmingham have set up a lesbian health group, 'Lesbewell' to coordinate activism, provide a resource archive, raise awareness about lesbian health and consolidate networking among researchers and practitioners in this field.[6] Their newsletter, *Dykenosis*, offers regular health updates for lesbian subscribers, and is an invaluable resource for service providers within the NHS wishing to keep informed about the needs of lesbian service users.

Good practice within the NHS

Encouraged by a slow liberalization of social attitudes to sexual minorities, and building on a tradition of community organizing, lesbians working within the NHS have taken the lead in establishing services for lesbians and in challenging homophobic attitudes within the broader culture of the NHS.

The Royal College of Nursing Working Party on Lesbian and Gay Nursing Needs has carried out extensive research into the healthcare experiences of lesbians and gay men using the NHS, and into nurse training in sexuality. As well as writing regular articles in professional journals, members of the Working Party have published an RCN statement, *The Nursing Care of Lesbians and Gay Men* (Royal College of Nursing 1994), which acts as a guide to good professional practice with this client group.

Such initiatives are extremely significant, since they send a clear signal to the profession that homophobia and the prejudicial treatment of lesbian and gay patients is unprofessional and will not be condoned by the Royal College. This is an important baseline in establishing the right of lesbian and gay service users to fair and appropriate treatment, and in supporting those within the profession who are themselves lesbian or gay or who are concerned to challenge homophobia in the NHS.

The most substantial developments to date in terms of the service/user interface within the NHS have been the setting up of lesbian-specific genito-urinary medicine (GUM)/sexual health clinics attached to NHS hospitals. The first of these, North West Thames Regional Health Authority's Bernhard

Clinic, was based at the GUM department of Charing Cross Hospital in London, and opened in April 1992. Its success was such that the doctor responsible was invited by the North East Thames Regional Health Authority to set up a second, the Audre Lorde Clinic, at the Royal London Hospital in October 1993.

Demand for this service was so great that both clinics were fully booked months in advance, and women travelled from all over the country in order to attend for sexual health screening, advice and treatment (Farquhar and Kavanagh, personal communication). As well as providing a much-needed service, the clinics were well-placed to collect important empirical data on lesbian sexual health and sexual behaviour, information which has been notoriously difficult to collect in other circumstances (Wellings 1988). Their success in London has led to the establishment of a similar facility in Oxford, the Vita Clinic, and has provoked interest in other parts of the country.

The high levels of demand experienced by these lesbian-specific GUM clinics indicate that they are tapping into a very real need. By advertising in the lesbian press, by recruiting lesbian or lesbian-friendly staff and by making use of their insider knowledge of lesbian culture (the clinics are all named after famous lesbian/bisexual women), they have succeeded in their aim of widening access to preventative sexual health services for lesbians.

However, the fact that the clinics concentrate on sexual health is in itself problematic, since it tends to reinforce the stereotype that lesbians are primarily interested in sex, and that lesbian sex is harmful to health, when in fact studies suggest that it is less harmful for women than heterosex (Doyal 1995; Wilton 1997a). More worryingly, it also appears to suggest that what lesbians primarily need from the NHS is a service which takes account of their sexual *behaviour*. In fact, copious research indicates that it is sexual *identity*, or more accurately heterosexual prejudice and discrimination against women whose sexual identity is lesbian, which causes most problems for lesbians seeking healthcare (Stern 1993; Dockery 1996; Wilton 1997a).

This is not to deny the importance of these pioneering clinics. They demonstrably meet a very real need, and their ability to encourage the uptake of preventative care and screening amongst a group of women who all too often do not attend for routine smears or blood pressure measurement offers enormous benefits for users and providers alike. Nevertheless, clinics like the Bernhard, the Audre Lorde and the Vita should be seen as examples of what needs to be done more generally within the NHS. This includes not just a wider geographical spread of services but also a diffusion of lesbian awareness into different specialties, beyond genito-urinary medicine.

Such diffusion has been foreshadowed in the setting up of a Lesbian Health Service as part of the Centre for Women's Health in Glasgow. The Centre is funded on a three-year pilot basis by Greater Glasgow Health Board, Strathclyde Regional and Glasgow District Councils, with support from the Community and Mental Health Services NHS Trust (see Laughlin, this volume). Centrally located in the main shopping street, it takes a non-medical approach to women's health, and operates on a drop-in basis from Tuesday to Thursday from 10.00 a.m. to 9.00 p.m. (there is an appointment system for Mondays and Fridays). The lesbian health service has relatively restricted access, running on alternate Thursdays from 5.30 p.m. to 8.30 p.m., but has proved extremely popular.

Moving away from a narrow focus on sexual health, the service offers PMT and menopause counselling, cervical smears, breast examination, contraception advice and pregnancy testing as well as a confidential counselling service using trained lesbian counsellors. Lesbians are also welcome to use the Centre's many other facilities, including a reference library, health advice service, crèche and various support groups. Building on the tried and tested model of the community-based well woman centre, the innovative aspect of this particular initiative lies in the provision of a specific, well-publicized service for lesbians.

The real world? In the broader NHS context

It would clearly represent a major step forward if such services were more widely available to lesbians in Britain. But even this would not address the wider issue of endemic heterosexism within the NHS. To tackle this continuing problem requires political will and a substantive (albeit not costly) investment in training and self-education on the part of service purchasers, providers and managers.

Most substantial resources on lesbian and gay health are published in the United States or Canada and do not 'translate' directly to an NHS context, although they contain much which is useful. However, there is a steadily growing list of British publications in this area (see References). There is, in addition, a lesbian and gay press in Britain with a few specifically lesbian magazines such as *Diva*, and most carry articles about lesbian health issues.

One beneficial consequence of the HIV pandemic is that most health authorities now have access to high-quality training around homophobia, lesbian and gay equality and sexual health issues, run by voluntary sector organizations (Wilton 1996b). This availability of resources is particularly important in the light of a recent World Health Organisation finding that sexuality training in healthcare contexts is most effective when delivered by facilitators outside the healthcare system itself (Savage 1987). Hence, purchasers and providers no longer have an excuse for failing to address these issues.

Strategies for change need to be broad based, and research strongly suggests that effective education of health and social care professionals must be the first priority (James *et al.* 1994; Das 1996; Dockery 1996; Muir-Mackenzie and Orme 1996). All healthcare professionals from consultants to porters, nurse managers to radiographers, should receive basic training in non-discriminatory practice and in the needs of lesbian (and gay) service users. In order to avoid flawed data collection, information-gathering instruments, for both audit and research purposes, should not be designed on the assumption that reproductive heterosexuality is the unquestioned norm. Most importantly of all, building on the good practice which has been developed to counteract racism in the NHS, local lesbian and gay communities should be consulted as a matter of course by healthcare providers, both to identify local need and to establish links in the attempt to address the issues of homophobia.

It is often relatively straightforward to improve aspects of the service available to lesbian clients. For example, reading material addressed to lesbians (back issues of lesbian magazines and community newspapers) should be available in all hospital/clinic/GP-centre areas used by women. This may seem unimportant, but even such a tiny gesture sends out strong signals to lesbian service users that their existence is recognized and that some trouble is being taken to make services accessible and safe for them. In the wider context of a homophobic society, where lesbian issues are relegated to late-night minority interest slots on television, such gestures mean a lot. Such publications can be obtained in the same way as other women's magazines, by putting up notices asking users to donate their unwanted back issues. Contrary to homophobic expectation, such magazines are not pornographic, and many contain a far smaller proportion of sexually explicit material than magazines such as *Cosmopolitan* or *Company*.

None of this is particularly difficult, and none of it is expensive. It is difficult to quantify the economic consequences of homophobia in the NHS. However, we know that many lesbians either delay seeking treatment or refuse all contact with allopathic medicine; that the stress of facing abuse, hostility or mistreatment from healthcare professionals delays healing; that inappropriate or even punitive treatment is sometimes given to lesbian patients; and that failure to account for sexual orientation may throw into question the effectiveness of clinical and epidemiological research. As a result, resources may be wasted in prescribing inappropriate diagnostic or therapeutic interventions (Rosser 1993; Stevens 1993). All of these carry fiscal as well as humanitarian costs.

Given the relative simplicity and low cost of potential solutions to these problems, it would make sense for NHS policy makers, managers, purchasers and providers to confront the problem of homophobia. The existence of gay men as a distinct client/patient group has been at least partially recognized in the wake of HIV/AIDS. The time is now right for recognizing the existence of lesbians, and the consequences of homophobia for the healthcare of all women. Significant steps forward have already been made; all that is now required is the will to continue.

Acknowledgements

Lesbian health is an expanding field of research, but remains underfunded and marginalized. It is only possible to write a piece such as this with the cooperation of those dedicated and courageous enough to carry out the research and/or to disseminate the findings. I am indebted to many such individuals, especially Pat Stevens of the University of Wisconsin–Milwaukee, Gisela Dütting of the Woman's Global Network for Reproductive Rights, Grindl Dockery of the Specialist Health Promotion Service for South and East Cheshire, Nancy Worcester of the University of Wisconsin–Madison, Hazel Platzer of the Royal College of Nursing's Lesbian and Gay Nursing Issues Working Party, Rosie Ilett of the Centre for Women's Health in Glasgow and Clare Farquhar of South Bank University. Thanks also to Lesley Doyal for her customarily rigorous and sympathetic editing, and to Professor Steve West for that all-important institutional support.

Notes

1 Indeed, the growing interest in 'complementary' healthcare among some NHS practitioners does not in itself indicate that biomedical reductionism is on the wane. The demand that complementary therapies must be evaluated according to biomedical standards of effectiveness, or that the 'active ingredient' of herbal medicines be extracted and delivered to patients in the more 'scientific' form of tablets, injections etc. are clear indicators that biomedicine is striving to assert its dominance over non-reductionist healing traditions.

2 Although the official position of the profession has shifted towards depathologizing same sex desire and sexual activity, there are still prominent individuals who publicly adhere to the position that sexual desire between women or between men is pathological. Moreover, following the American Psychiatric Association's decision to remove homosexuality from the list of recognized psychiatric disorders, a group of the Association's members lobbied (unsuccessfully) to have it reinstated. Nevertheless, the general trend within the medical profession since the mid-1970s has been away from a medical model of homosexuality.

3 While writing this chapter I was invited to give a presentation on lesbian users of the maternity services for an ENB study day at John Radcliffe Hospital in Oxford. Afterwards a practising midwife came up to ask me, in complete seriousness, what was done with any boy babies born to lesbian mothers. She went on to explain that, since all lesbians loathed anything male, they would obviously want to get rid of any male infants they gave birth to. Although such horrifying depths of ignorant superstition are not in any way typical of NHS staff, in my experience they are not uncommon. Perhaps incidents such as this go some way to explaining why lesbian service users seldom feel secure enough to disclose their sexual identity in healthcare settings (and, in turn, why one participant commented on her evaluation form that she had no need of information about lesbians because 'there are no lesbians in our practice').

4 In fact a critical examination of the data strongly suggests that it is childless women, rather than lesbians, who form a 'risk group'. Nevertheless, it is probably the case that lesbians are less likely than non-lesbian women to have children, and there is considerable concern among lesbian communities (especially in the US) about this issue.

5 Section 28 of the 1988 Local Government Act prohibits local authorities from funding the 'promotion' of homosexuality. For more detail about the law and its effects see Colvin and Hawksley (1989).
6 Anyone wishing to be kept informed of lesbian health issues in Britain should be on the Lesbewell mailing list. An annual subscription to their newletter, *Dykenosis*, costs only £6, and their address is: LesBeWell, PO Box 4048, Moseley, Birmingham B13 8DP. Other contact numbers are as follows: The Audre Lorde Clinic 0171 377 7312, The Bernhard Clinic 0181 846 7606/1576, Glasgow's Centre for Women's Health 0141 211 6700 and the Vita Clinic in Oxford 01865 246 036.

References

Altman, D., Vance, C., Vicinus, M. and Weeks, J. (1989) *Which Homosexuality? Essays from the International Scientific Conference on Lesbian and Gay Studies*. London: Gay Men's Press.

Baggott, R. (1994) *Health and Health Care in Britain*. London: Macmillan.

Brandt, A. (1987) *No Magic Bullet: A Social History of Venereal Disease in the United States since 1880* (revised ed.). New York: Oxford University Press.

Bremmer, J. (ed.) (1989) *From Sappho to de Sade: Moments in the History of Sexuality*. London: Routledge.

Browne, S., Connors, D. and Stern, N. (eds) (1985) *With the Power of Each Breath: A Disabled Women's Anthology*. San Francisco: Cleis Press.

Caplan, P. (ed.) (1987) *The Cultural Construction of Sexuality*. London: Routledge.

Colvin, M. and Hawksley, J. (1989) *Section 28: A Guide to the Law*. London: Liberty.

Das, R. (1996) 'The power of medical knowledge: systematic misinformation and the perpetuation of lesbophobia in medical education'. Paper presented at the Medical Sociology Group of the British Sociological Association annual conference, University of Edinburgh, September.

D'Emilio, J. and Freedman, E. (1988) *Intimate Matters: A History of Sexuality in America*. New York: Harper and Row.

Dockery, G. (1996) *Final Report of the Research on the Sexual Health Needs of Lesbians, Bisexual Women and Women who have Sex with Women in Merseyside/Cheshire*. Liverpool: SHADY.

Doyal, L. (1995) *What Makes Women Sick: Gender and the Political Economy of Health*. London: Macmillan.

Ehrenreich, B. and English, D. (1979) *For Her Own Good: 150 Years of the Experts' Advice to Women*. London: Pluto Press.

Fee, E. and Fox, D. (eds) (1988) *AIDS: The Burdens of History*. Berkeley, University of California Press.

Foucault, M. (1976, trans. 1979) *The History of Sexuality Vol. 1: An Introduction*. Harmondsworth: Penguin.

Grau, G. (1995) *Hidden Holocaust? Gay and Lesbian Persecution in Germany 1933–45*. London: Cassell.

Hart, N. (1985) *The Sociology of Health and Medicine*. Ormskirk: Causeway.

Hemmings, S. (1986) An overdose of doctors. *Spare Rib*, 162 (January):11–14.

Henry, G. (1950) *Sex Variants: A Study of Homosexual Patterns*. London: Cassell.

Hepburn, C. and Gutierrez, B. (1988) *Alive and Well: A Lesbian Health Guide*. Freedom: Crossing Press.

James, T., Harding, I. and Corbett, K. (1994) Biased care? Lesbians and gay men. *Nursing Times*, 90 (51): 28–31.

Jeffreys, S. (1990) *Anticlimax: A Feminist Perspective on the Sexual Revolution*. London: Women's Press.

Jessop, L. and Thorogood, N. (1988) Sexuality and health. *Radical Community Medicine*, Winter: 3–8.

Jones, L. (1996) *The Social Context of Health and Health Work*. London: Macmillan.

Langfeldt, T. and Porter, M. (1986) *Sexuality and Family Planning: Report of a Consultation and Research Findings*. Geneva: World Health Organisation.

Llewellyn-Jones, D. (1985) *Herpes, AIDS and other Sexually Transmitted Diseases*. London: Faber and Faber.

Lynch, L. and Woods, A. (eds) (1996) *Off the Rag: Lesbians Writing on Menopause*. Norwich, VT: New Victoria Publishers.

McClintock, A. (1995) *Imperial Leather: Race, Gender and Sexuality in the Colonial Contest*. London: Routledge.

McClure, R. and Vespry, A. (eds) (1994) *Lesbian Health Guide*. Toronto: Queer Press.

Macintyre, S. (1977) *Single and Pregnant*. London: Croom Helm.

Martin, E. (1987) *The Woman in the Body*. Buckingham: Open University Press.

Muir-Mackenzie, A. and Orme, J. (eds) (1996) *Health of the Lesbian, Gay and Bisexual Nation: 1996 Conference Official Report*. Plymouth: The Harbour Group.

Panos Institute (1990) *The Third Epidemic: Repercussions of the Fear of AIDS*. London: Panos/Norwegian Red Cross.

Plummer, K. (ed.) (1981) *The Making of the Modern Homosexual*. London: Hutchinson.

Rakusen, J. (1989) Sexuality. In A. Phillips and J. Rakusen (eds) *The New Our Bodies Ourselves: A Health Book by and for Women*. Harmondsworth: Penguin.

Richardson, D. (1990) *Safer Sex: The Guide for Women Today*. London: Pandora.

Richardson, D. (1993) *Women, Motherhood and Childrearing*. London: Macmillan.

Rosario, V. (ed.) (1997) *Science and Homosexualities*. London: Routledge.

Rosser, S. (1993) Ignored, overlooked or subsumed: research on lesbian health and health care. *National Women's Studies Association Journal*, 5 (2): 183–203.

Royal College of Nursing (1994) *The Nursing Care of Lesbians and Gay Men: An RCN Statement*. London: RCN.

Ruse, M. (1988) *Homosexuality: A Philosophical Inquiry*. Oxford: Basil Blackwell.

Saffron, L. (1994) *Challenging Conceptions: Planning a Family by Self-Insemination*. London: Cassell.

Savage, J. (1987) *Nurses, Gender and Sexuality*. London: Heinemann.

Simon, W. (1996) *Postmodern Sexualities*. London: Routledge.

Stein, E. (ed.) (1992) *Forms of Desire: Sexual Orientation and the Social Constructionist Controversy*. London: Routledge.

Stern, P.N. (ed.) (1993) *Lesbian Health: What are the Issues?* London: Taylor and Francis.

Stevens, P. (1993) Lesbian health care research: a review of the literature from 1970 to 1990. In P. Noerager Stern (ed.) *Lesbian Health: What Are the Issues?* London: Taylor and Francis.

Stewart, W. (1995) *Cassell's Queer Companion: A Dictionary of Lesbian and Gay Life and Culture*. London: Cassell.

Terry, J. and Urla, J. (eds) (1995) *Deviant Bodies: Critical Perspectives on Difference in Science and Popular Culture*. Bloomington, IN: Indianapolis University Press.

Tiefer, L. (1995) *Sex is Not a Natural Act and Other Essays*. Oxford: Westview Press.

Trippet, S. and Bain, J. (1992) Reasons American lesbians fail to seek traditional health care. In P. Noerager Stern (ed.) *Lesbian Health: What are the Issues?* London: Taylor and Francis.

Turner, B. (1987) *Medical Power and Social Knowledge.* London: Sage.

Waitkevicz (1978) Lesbian health issues. In G. Vida (ed.) *Our Right to Love: A Lesbian Resource Book.* New Jersey: Prentice-Hall.

Waldby, C. (1996) *AIDS and the Body Politic: Biomedicine and Sexual Difference.* London: Routledge.

Webb, C. (1985) *Sexuality, Nursing and Health.* Chichester: Wiley.

Webb, C. (1986) Women as gynaecology patients and nurses. In C. Webb (ed.) *Feminist Practice in Women's Health Care.* London: Wiley.

Weeks, J. (1985) *Sexuality and its Discontents.* London: Routledge and Kegan Paul.

Weeks, J. (1986) *Sexuality.* London: Routledge.

Wellings, K. (1988) Sexual behaviour research: prospects and problems. *Radical Community Medicine,* Winter: 9–13.

Wilton, T. (1992) *Antibody Politic: AIDS and Society.* Cheltenham: New Clarion Press.

Wilton, T. (1995) *Lesbian Studies: Setting an Agenda.* London: Routledge.

Wilton, T. (1996a) Genital identities: an idiosyncatic foray into the gendering of sexualities. In L. Adkins and V. Merchant (eds) *Sexualising the Social: Power and the Organization of Sexuality.* London: Macmillan.

Wilton, T. (1996b) Caring for the lesbian client: homophobia and midwifery. *British Journal of Midwifery,* 4 (3): 126–32.

Wilton, T. (1997a) *Good For You: A Handbook on Lesbian Health and Wellbeing.* London: Cassell.

Wilton, T. (1997b) *En/Gendering AIDS: Deconstructing Sex, Text, Epidemic.* London: Sage.

11

•

The care of women with breast cancer: research, policy and practice

•

Nichola Rumsey and Diana Harcourt

Introduction

This chapter explores the links between research, policy and practice in the care of women with abnormalities of the breast. The psychosocial needs of women diagnosed with breast cancer are considered, with particular reference to the period around diagnosis and the applicability of counselling interventions at this time. Recent advances in diagnostic procedures have made it possible to provide women with the results of diagnostic tests within a single clinic visit. An investigation into the psychosocial implications of speeding up the diagnostic process is described and the findings of this research are summarized. The need for evidence to underpin policy and practice in current care provision is highlighted throughout the chapter.

Breast cancer: incidence, treatment and prognosis

Breast cancer is the most common malignancy found in women, accounting for one in five of all female cancers (Cancer Research Campaign 1991). In the UK, approximately 230,000 women with breast abnormalities are referred to consultants each year. Of these, nearly 25,000 women are newly diagnosed with breast cancer. In the region of 15,000 women die from the disease per annum (Cancer Relief Macmillan Fund 1995). The mortality rates are worse in the UK than in other European countries and the US. It is currently estimated that one in twelve British women will develop breast cancer at some time in their lives (Cancer Research Campaign 1991).

Despite the high incidence of breast cancer, the pathogenesis of the disease is poorly understood, though some risk factors have been identified. The incidence increases with age and is greatest amongst populations with high economic status. The differences in incidence rates between socio-economic groups is thought to be related to reproductive patterns (women with no children and those aged more than 30 at the birth of their first child are thought to be at twice the risk of developing breast cancer as those who gave birth at under 20 years of age). Other known risk factors include age at menopause (the later the onset, the greater the risk of developing a malignant breast lump), the age of onset of menstruation (the earlier, the greater the risk) hormone levels (including the taking of oral contraceptives and hormone replacement therapy) and family history of the disease (Bristol Cancer Epidemiology Unit 1995).

Four main types of treatment are currently used: surgical removal of the tumour through mastectomy or wide local excision (removal of the lump and a surrounding margin of healthy tissue), radiotherapy, chemotherapy and hormonal (anti-oestrogen) therapy. These treatments are often used in combination.

Prognosis will depend on the histological type of tumour and the stage of development reached by the time of diagnosis. Breast tumours are known to be more amenable to successful treatment in the early stages of development. As the pathogenesis is so poorly understood, the possibilities for effective primary prevention are clearly limited. Consequently both *Health of the Nation* and *Our Healthier Nation* targets have focused on reducing mortality through effective awareness, screening campaigns and efforts to treat the disease at an early stage.

The provision of care for women with breast cancer

The methods by which the NHS is currently managing the high prevalence of breast cancer have recently come under close scrutiny. Along with examples of good practice have come complaints of poor quality care, the failure to apply research findings in clinical practice and a lack of consistency of approach between different hospitals and services.

A 'wide gulf' has been described between the best and worst practice in the diagnosis and management of breast disease (BASO 1995), and it is clear that nationally there are considerable variations in treatment patterns. Some women are treated in specialist breast cancer units, while others may be referred to a general surgeon.

The impact on prognosis of differences in the provision of care is not entirely clear. Some studies offer support for the specialist units. An audit of breast cancer care carried out prospectively in the UK showed that those surgeons identified as having specialist skills had significantly improved survival rates in their patient populations with an 8.9 per cent better outcome in survival at five years and 7.6 per cent at ten years after treatment (Gillis *et al.*, cited in the Expert Advisory Group on Cancer to the Chief Medical

Officers of England and Wales 1995). Despite the fact that not all studies have confirmed the impact of specialized care in breast cancer, the Expert Advisory Group on Cancer to the Chief Medical Officers of England and Wales (1995) Policy Framework for Commissioning Cancer Services (referred to as the Calman Report 1995) highlights the fact that no study has shown a disadvantage. This report emphasizes that patients are interested in the quality as well as the quantity of their survival and proposes specialist centres for all cancer services with the aim of making the best treatment available to all.

The lack of agreement in outcome studies emphasizes the continuing need to base policy and practice on evidence-based research. Whilst the NHS Executive's manual (1996a) and The Research Evidence (1996b) for the provision of care for breast cancer patients made recommendations based on research, it remains to be seen to what extent this will be reflected in future service provision.

The provision of psychosocial support and the impact on women of developments in diagnostic procedures both highlight the tenuous relationship that currently exists between research, policy and practice in the provision of patient care. These issues are examined in more detail in the remainder of this chapter.

The psychosocial needs of women with breast cancer

The psychosocial needs of people with cancer have been increasingly recogn ized over the past 20 years (Holland 1992) and it is now widely accepted that quality of life is as important as survival. Recently, when outlining principles for treating patients with cancer, the Calman Report (1995: 6) stressed that '. . . psychosocial aspects of cancer care should be considered at all stages'.

Many studies have emphasized the psychological impact of breast cancer and its treatment. These include anxiety provoked by screening (Lerman *et al.* 1991); the psychological impact of recurrence (Weisman and Worden 1986; Northouse *et al.* 1995); threats to self-esteem and femininity (Polivy 1977); body image problems following treatment (Lasry *et al.* 1987; Mock 1993); and adjuvant therapy such as chemotherapy or radiotherapy. Reports of the incidence of psychological morbidity amongst cancer patients vary depending upon the sample studied and the timing and method of assessment. It is generally accepted that around half to one-third of cancer patients experience some kind of psychological problem at any one time.

The impact of diagnosis

There is no uniform or typical psychological response following a diagnosis of cancer. Psychological morbidity may include depression, anxiety, body image problems, sexual difficulties, cognitive disorders, sadness, anger, guilt, loss of interest, lowering of mood, and physical symptoms including weakness, tiredness and loss of weight. Although specific stages such as diagnosis, treatment and recurrence may be common to all cancers, individual reactions and psychosocial needs vary at each stage of the disease and its treatment.

More specifically, Goldberg *et al.* (1992) reported that 51 per cent of a sample of 166 women diagnosed with breast cancer experienced severe anxiety pre-operatively, reducing to 29 per cent six months and 27 per cent one year post-operatively. This compared with rates for patients with a benign diagnosis of 37 per cent, 16 per cent and 18 per cent at each of these assessment points. Levels of depression, sexual problems, physical symptoms and body image problems were also higher amongst patients who had received a cancer diagnosis. These followed a similar slowly declining trend over the first six months. Within the cancer group, Goldberg *et al.* found no relationship between extent of surgery and psychological distress, supporting the notion that psychological problems are more heavily influenced by the type of diagnosis than by the type of treatment received.

There are a number of limitations with much of the research examining the psychological ramifications of a diagnosis of breast cancer, yet it is these studies on which policy and practice have been based. Firstly, the majority of studies consider psychological morbidity in terms of standardized measures of anxiety and depression. Whilst important, the limited focus on only these two aspects may represent an incomplete or distorted understanding of women's reactions to diagnosis. Tjemsland *et al.* (1996) tried to overcome this by applying a model of post-traumatic stress disorder, employing both interviews and self-report measures of psychological well-being and distress. Almost half of the women in their study reported high levels of thoughts relating to the illness in the days following diagnosis and one-third experienced acute symptoms of distress. Although a high proportion of patients suffered emotional pain at this time, the majority of cases did not justify a diagnosis of post-traumatic stress disorder. However, this study illustrated the need for a more comprehensive assessment of the psychological impact of cancer in order to account for individual differences.

Most studies have focused on distress *following* diagnosis. However, a woman is likely to experience considerable emotional disturbance *pre-diagnosis* from the time she first notices a symptom that prompts her to seek medical attention (Fallowfield 1991). In a review of literature concerning the diagnostic phase, Poole (1997) introduced the concept of 'the waiting game' and emphasized the need for more studies to investigate this stage. A retrospective study by Benedict *et al.* (1994) reported anxiety levels to be extremely high in the period from discovery of a breast problem to receiving a definite diagnosis. Macfarlane and Sony (1992) found that the emotions most commonly reported during this period are fear, worry, anxiety, nervousness and concern over the possible diagnosis. Unusually, both these studies were concerned with women whose biopsy results proved to be negative.

The findings throw into sharp relief the need to learn more about the 200,000 women each year who are referred to a consultant for examination of a breast problem which is non-malignant. The Breast Surgeons Group of the British Association of Surgical Oncology Guidelines (BASO 1995: 9) recognize that 'even women with benign conditions may sometimes have questions and need information'. This statement, however, gives the impression that this is an exceptional rather than natural request.

The needs of women with a benign diagnosis

Two studies have retrospectively examined the psychological status of women prior to discovery and diagnosis of a breast abnormality. Hughes *et al.* (1986) found that, when compared with women receiving a diagnosis of cancer, those receiving a benign diagnosis reported a higher incidence of 'severe' depression, mood disturbance and psychosocial stress in the year preceding their initial breast clinic consultation. Hughson *et al.* (1988) compared the psychosocial morbidity of women awaiting breast biopsy with those awaiting general surgery. Patients whose breast biopsy was later diagnosed as benign were found to experience higher levels of anxiety, depression and irritability than either general surgery patients or those whose breast biopsy was subsequently found to be malignant.

Both Hughes *et al.* (1986) and Hughson *et al.* (1988) concluded that in comparison with women diagnosed with breast cancer, women who develop benign lumps may be more prone to psychosocial problems and dysfunction in addition to concerns about their symptoms and possible diagnosis. However, Morris and Greer (1982) reported that women attending a breast clinic experienced legitimate concern rather than exceptional personality characteristics or neurotic anxiety.

A recent study of a counselling intervention (Rumsey *et al.* 1995) found that patients with a benign diagnosis still reported concerns about their diagnosis and treatment six months after surgery. However, levels of anxiety amongst these women were lower than those found in the studies outlined above, which may reflect the benefits derived from the provision of counselling and psychosocial support for all women within this study.

Recent research indicates that women with benign breast problems are a neglected group. To date, their needs have not been adequately addressed by policy makers, researchers or care providers. In the current climate of shrinking resources and increasing incidence of malignancies, priority in policy decisions and the provision of care is given to women with a diagnosis of cancer.

Psychosocial support and counselling interventions

In breast cancer, specialist units generally include a skill-mix appropriate to the ongoing treatment and support of patients, including a dedicated surgeon and breast care nurse. In many teams, the role of the breast care nurse has expanded to include counselling. This has led to a debate concerning the most appropriate way to identify and meet the psychosocial needs of patients. Several studies have explored the effectiveness of psychological interventions, the majority of which have been provided by specialist breast care nurses.

An early study of a counselling intervention for women who had undergone mastectomy (Maguire *et al.* 1980) found that although counselling by a specialist nurse did not prevent psychological morbidity, levels of anxiety and depression 12 months after surgery were lower in the counselled group than in a control group receiving only routine care. The authors concluded that this reflected the specialist nurse's ability, through regular monitoring of patients, to identify problems and to refer on to psychological or psychiatric services any patients warranting further specialist support.

In a similarly designed study, Watson *et al.* (1988) evaluated the impact of a counselling intervention available from the time of diagnosis. Three months after a mastectomy, women who received counselling were significantly less depressed than those who received only routine care. However, twelve months after diagnosis there were no significant differences between the two groups.

Burton *et al.* (1995) found a pre-operative intervention to be beneficial. Although intervention by a trained counsellor was preferable, significant benefits, in terms of reduced levels of body image distress, anxiety and depression, were also reported amongst women whose only intervention was a pre-operative chat with their surgeon! More recently, McArdle *et al.* (1996) reported that in a randomized controlled trial, counselling from a breast care nurse resulted in significantly greater benefits than support provided by a voluntary counselling group, routine ward care or a combination of counselling by the breast care nurse and the voluntary organization.

Links between research, policy and practice

It is clear that the inclusion of the breast care nurse in the specialist team has gone some way to addressing the needs of women with abnormalities of the breast. Policy documents now include recommendations relating to the inclusion of a specialist nurse in breast care teams. In their guidelines for women concerned about breast cancer, the Cancer Relief Macmillan Fund (1994) stated that the availability of a breast care nurse should be considered as a minimum acceptable standard of care. Similarly, the BASO (1995) guidelines stressed the need for access to specialist nurses. However, despite evidence supporting the benefits of psychosocial support and intervention, there is still a lack of clarity concerning the most appropriate structure, content and method of delivery of this support.

Watson *et al.* (1988) proposed a general framework which should be employed in a counselling process. This includes emotional support and facilitation of adjustment, information about physical state and practical advice on breast prostheses. However, it appears that breast care nurses generally receive little guidance on how to carry out their role effectively. This problem was highlighted by Fallowfield and Roberts (1992) in a survey of people whose work involved counselling people with cancer. Only 25 per cent of respondents had any formally recognized counselling qualification, only 43 per cent used a particular framework or approach to the counselling they offered and more than one-third did not receive any supervision. Whilst not suggesting that the counselling offered by these people was inadequate, this survey highlights the scope for facilitating the work of breast care nurses, and exploring further how counselling and support might best be delivered.

In recent years, researchers have explored more rigorously the individual and situational factors which might buffer or reduce the distress experienced by women with abnormalities of the breast. A nurse counsellor intervention is typically first available *after* the patient has received her diagnosis of malignant disease, yet the consultation in which the diagnosis is given is likely to be crucial in the patient's adjustment. The impact of the actual diagnosis may be such that women find it difficult to take in additional information given to them (for example, concerning treatment and prognosis). This in itself may be anxiety-provoking and can impinge upon the ability of women to make informed choices about their treatment (Scott 1983).

Attempts have therefore been made to 'soften the blow' of receiving the diagnosis, with the aim of increasing patients' feelings of control and involvement in treatment. Hogbin and Fallowfield (1989) found it beneficial to tape record the 'bad news' consultation, enabling women, their families and friends to listen to the recording of the consultation after the initial shock of the diagnosis. However, this procedure has not been widely adopted. The reluctance to adopt this approach might be due to a number of factors. Some surgeons lack confidence in their handling of such situations, others may fear complaint or litigation if the treatment or prognosis later deviates from original expectations. The tape recording is only as clear and informative as the consultation itself and may be of little benefit if surgeons communicate badly or fail to provide all the necessary information.

Policy makers, care providers and researchers in breast cancer have in many instances failed to capitalize on findings in potentially relevant areas. Studies of individual differences suggest that psychological adjustment is likely to be enhanced by improvements in staff–patient communication, patient involvement in decision making, the provision of clear and relevant information, sufficient opportunity for questions and expression of concerns (Sarafino 1994). The implications of an extensive psychological literature on coping are that women vary in their need for information and involvement in decision making. However, policy documents offer contradictory recommendations.

BACUP (1995: 6) suggests that 'information should be tailored to meet the individual need of the person with cancer'. In a rather different vein, the Calman Report (1995: 6) recommends that 'patients, families and carers should be given clear information and assistance in a form they can understand about treatment options and outcomes available to them at all stages of treatment from diagnosis onwards'. Healthcare providers should be aware that not all the people want all of the information all of the time.

In an attempt to bridge the gap between research and practice, a framework for counselling that aims to ensure each patient's needs are met at the time of diagnosis has been developed and implemented at the Breast Care Centre at Frenchay Hospital, Bristol (Rumsey *et al.* 1995). In contrast to the conventional approach to counselling, this intervention begins *prior* to the diagnosis being given. At this stage, the breast care nurse meets with the patient and tries to elicit her main concerns. Together they prepare a list of questions the patient would like answered in the subsequent consultation. The breast care nurse then accompanies the patient into the consultation where, if necessary, she acts as the patient's advocate and ensures all her questions are answered by the consultant. Counselling continues after the diagnosis on an 'as needed' basis, in line with the more conventional approach.

A controlled study (Rumsey *et al.* 1995) compared this advocacy intervention with the more conventional, post-diagnosis counselling approach. All women, regardless of diagnosis, were allocated to one of the two groups. Levels of psychological morbidity in both groups were lower than those generally reported in the literature. No significant differences in measures of anxiety, depression, self-esteem, body image and physical symptoms were found between the two groups. The low incidence of 'severe' anxiety and depression in both groups suggests that counselling support is beneficial for all women, regardless of diagnosis. The study further reinforced the importance of considering the needs of women with a benign diagnosis as, in comparison with cancer patients, they reported less understanding of their diagnosis, of the reasons why surgery was offered and what it would entail.

Despite the lack of significant differences in the quantitative data, qualitative responses to open-ended questions were highly supportive of the advocacy approach. The breast care nurse and the surgeon also expressed a clear preference for this approach. The methodology has subsequently been adopted in the standard provision of care for breast cancer patients, providing an example of how research can affect practice even in the absence of what standard experimental procedures would regard as confirming evidence!

The counselling provided by breast care nurses in the majority of specialist units is widely acknowledged to be useful, though further progress needs to be made in developing a more systematic and patient-led approach to the provision of this aspect of care. However, pressures from advances in technology and the need to reduce costs are leading to changes in clinic provision which in many respects mitigate against the provision of comprehensive psychosocial support.

Developments in diagnostic procedures and the provision of care

Until the 1970s diagnosis was typically made by frozen section, with the biopsy and, if necessary, mastectomy carried out under the same general anaesthetic. With increased recognition of the anxiety engendered by this procedure and the need for patient involvement in decision making, this procedure is now rarely performed. The BASO guidelines (1995) state that 90 per cent of breast cancer patients should be diagnosed pre-operatively, with less than 10 per cent of breast cancer operations being frozen section procedures.

In the early 1980s most clinics used breast biopsy to ascertain diagnosis. This involves surgical removal of the suspicious area of the breast. The results of analysis are available at a subsequent clinic visit. More recently, fine needle aspiration biopsy (FNAB) has become the preferred method of investigation, in conjunction with clinical examination, mammography and, occasionally, ultrasound scanning. FNAB involves the removal and analysis of cells to confirm diagnosis. This procedure avoids the need for anaesthetic and surgery prior to diagnosis, thus facilitating the earlier involvement of women in decisions regarding their treatment.

The advent of 'one-stop' clinics

Until recently, clinical examination, FNAB and ultrasound scanning were carried out at the first clinic visit, with mammography, if necessary, being conducted at a second appointment. Women returned a minimum of one week later for their diagnosis. It appears that in some instances the gap between clinic visits has been considerable, as guidelines issued by the Cancer Relief Macmillan Fund (1994) suggested that the waiting time should be kept down to a maximum of four weeks.

In the last few years technological advances have resulted in more immediate access to radiological and pathological services for the rapid evaluation of breast lumps. 'One-stop' clinics have been established in which the patient is seen by the consultant at the beginning of a clinic and necessary investigations are performed immediately. The results are available 2–3 hours later, when the patient sees the consultant once more to receive the diagnosis and to discuss treatment options before returning home.

Recent policy documents support the desirability of the one-stop clinic. For example, the BASO guidelines (1995) promote the ideal that breast clinics should be structured to produce a rapid and multi-disciplinary assessment of women with breast disease and that diagnostic tests should involve the minimum number of hospital visits. The NHS Executive (1996a) recommended that results should be made available with as little delay as possible and the Labour Party's (1997) pre-election pledge on breast cancer supported the extension of same-day diagnostic clinics throughout the country.

Patient attendance rates are likely to be better if results are available the same day. Patients' travelling costs will be reduced by a single clinic visit. The throughput of patients may be higher if only one clinic visit is required, thus optimizing the use of specialist staff time. General practitioners are likely to favour a system which reduces the distressing wait between the discovery of a breast lump and the results of investigations. Fundholding practices may prefer a system which will cut costs by reducing the numbers of hospital visits.

Therefore, the one-stop approach clearly offers potential advantages from the point of view of healthcare providers and purchasers. This model is now being implemented in many district general hospitals. *The Macmillan Directory of Breast Cancer Services in the UK* published by the Kings Fund in February 1995 suggested that 40 per cent of those hospitals listed were offering a same-day service. By 1996 this figure had increased to 48 per cent and it seems likely that numbers will have continued to increase (Cancer Relief Macmillan Fund 1995, 1996). However, the consequences for the women attending these clinics have yet to be researched in a systematic way. Those who assume it will be beneficial are the policy makers, budget holders and medical personnel. Information and data from patients themselves are notable by their absence.

Despite the case for one-stop clinics, many issues need to be addressed before definitive recommendations can be made. Although intuitively it seems desirable to try to reduce the anxiety associated with the wait for diagnosis, research is needed to clarify the short- and long-term impact of more immediate versus delayed communication of results on the psychological well-being of women with breast abnormalities. The relative impact of benign compared with malignant results is not yet fully understood. The relationship of the timing of diagnosis to individual coping styles and strategies is unknown. Whilst accepting the stress associated with waiting for diagnosis, speedier results may heighten anxiety levels for women who have used denial as a coping mechanism. A degree of anxiety or worry may be necessary to facilitate the use of effective coping strategies: 'unhappiness and worry during certain periods of the illness cannot be avoided altogether, indeed for many patients a limited period of emotional distress is probably a prerequisite for realistic long-term adjustment' (Hughes 1987: 456).

The Calman Report has stated that patients, families and carers should be given clear information and assistance in a form they can understand about treatment options and outcomes at all stages of treatment, from diagnosis onwards. In recognition of the impact of diagnosis and treatment on patients and their families, this report noted that good communication between professionals and patients is especially important and that psychosocial aspects of cancer care should be considered at all stages. The time pressures experienced in one-stop clinics may make it difficult to address these issues fully.

Research by the authors and others has demonstrated the benefits derived by women with breast lumps from the support offered to them by the specialist nurse. However, in a one-stop clinic, the results of investigations are not usually available until the end of the session. After waiting in the hospital environment for a minimum of two hours (during which time the patient may feel largely unsupported), she may be given her diagnosis at a time when the clinic is coming to an end. She may feel guilty for detaining staff and consequently may not fully address her concerns. Childcare arrangements or work commitments compounded by a lengthy clinic stay may further increase the pressure upon her to leave quickly. The provision of sufficient time to address patient concerns in the context of a one-stop clinic needs careful consideration.

Evaluating the impact of a one-stop clinic

Research evidence relating to the implementation of one-stop clinics is so far notable by its absence. A detailed literature search has revealed two studies. From the experience of only four clinics, Gui *et al.* (1995) suggested that the one-stop clinic allows 'optimum patient management' by maximizing utilization of hospital outpatient resources. Without supporting data, the authors claim it minimizes anxiety associated with symptomatic breast disease.

Ubhi *et al.* (1996) found high anxiety levels in a sample of 53 women attending a one-stop clinic and in 69 patients receiving the diagnosis at the second visit. When the lump was found to be benign, earlier communication of the results led to more significant decreases in anxiety in the one-stop sample than in the delayed results group. However, there was no significant difference in the anxiety displayed in the 17 women with a malignant diagnosis between the two groups. The results of Ubhi *et al.* indicate that the benefits of one-stop clinics for women with a malignant diagnosis are far from clear-cut.

In order to address the lack of research evidence, a prospective randomized controlled trial (Harcourt *et al.* 1997) comparing a one-stop clinic with the more conventional two-stop arrangement was conducted at Frenchay Hospital, Bristol. A one-stop clinic was established here in 1994 in response to GP fundholder demand for such a service. In line with the recommendations of the Calman Report (1995) all breast care services, including outpatient clinics for diagnosis, follow-up, reconstructive surgery and planning of adjuvant (chemotherapy or radiotherapy) treatment are conducted in the specialist Breast Care Centre. This centre also provides a base for counselling and support available from the specialist breast care nurse. Women attending the clinic undergo clinical examination, ultrasound scanning of the breast and, if necessary, FNAB and mammography in a single outpatient appointment. Results of these tests are generally available two to three hours later.

Assessments in this study comprised quantitative and qualitative data collected during the patient's first attendance, with follow-up six days later. At this point women attending the one-stop clinic had received their diagnosis and those attending the two-stop clinic were still awaiting their results. A final assessment eight weeks later evaluated the longer term adjustment of the two groups. The assessments were designed to evaluate levels of psychological distress, adjustment, quality of life and current coping strategies. Women were also asked to indicate their satisfaction with the care they received. Comparisons of measures obtained from benign and cancer patients were made at each assessment point.

The advocacy style of intervention outlined above was available in both styles of clinic. The clinic evaluation monitored whether demands placed upon the specialist nurse and the timing of each clinic enabled sufficient attention to be devoted to this aspect of patient care.

More than 580 women completed all 3 assessments, of whom 65 were diagnosed with cancer. High levels of psychological distress were evident amongst both clinic groups at their first attendance, with 28 per cent of all women reporting clinically high levels of anxiety, i.e. 'caseness', at this stage. Whilst the speedier provision of diagnosis reduced this to 11 per cent amongst women given the 'all clear', a more rapid diagnosis of breast cancer increased this rate to 57 per cent. In the delayed results group, 44 per cent of women who would be told they had breast cancer showed high levels of anxiety the day prior to diagnosis.

In the period between initial consultation and receiving results, women attending the two-stop clinic experienced significantly greater levels of anxiety, worry, distress, disturbed sleep, lack of concentration and disrupted daily routine. Following diagnosis, women receiving benign results at the one-stop clinic reported a significant reduction in levels of anxiety. However, anxiety reported by women diagnosed with cancer in this clinic *increased* significantly following diagnosis and were higher than those reported by women still awaiting results. Eight weeks later, anxiety was significantly higher amongst women with cancer, regardless of the style of clinic attended. Disturbingly, at this stage, levels of depression reported by women diagnosed with breast cancer in a one-stop clinic were higher than those women diagnosed with a malignancy in the delayed, two-stop system. This difference was significant (p = 0.05).

Although women receiving news of a malignancy were satisfied with the time available to discuss their diagnosis and treatment, women given the 'all clear' were less satisfied and would have preferred more time to discuss their individual concerns, regardless of the style of clinic they had attended. If implemented, this could prove particularly difficult within the time pressures of a busy clinic offering a same-day service.

These results suggest that for women receiving a benign diagnosis, immediate availability of results may reduce psychological distress in the short term. However, a more rapid diagnosis may be to the detriment of women receiving a diagnosis of cancer. The study illustrates the need for policy makers and care providers to consider both the psychological implications of speeding up the diagnostic process and also the logistics of running a same-day service capable of providing the emotional and psychological support women need at the time of diagnosis.

Conclusions

In this examination of the provision of care for women with breast abnormalities, we have attempted to describe how treatment has developed over the recent past and how a body of knowledge is accumulating in relation to the psychological consequences of diagnosis and treatment. In particular, we have explored the links between research, policy and practice in this area. There are examples in which policy has been formulated on sound research evidence, yet in other instances the interpretation of research has been dubious. In some cases, particularly in relation to the implementation of one-stop clinics, research on psychological sequelae has been notable by its absence. In the ongoing development of guidelines for best practice in the care of women with abnormalities of the breast, there is clearly great potential in close working relationships between policy makers, care providers and researchers.

Acknowledgements

The authors wish to acknowledge the extensive role played by Nicholas Ambler, Simon Cawthorn and Jane Barker in the research outlined in this chapter.

References

BACUP (1995) *The Right to Know: A BACUP Guide to Information and Support for People Living with Cancer*. London: BACUP.

BASO (Breast Surgeons' Group of the British Association of Surgical Oncology) (1995) Guidelines for surgeons in the management of symptomatic breast disease in the United Kingdom. *European Journal of Surgical Oncology*, 21 (Supplement A): 1–13.

Benedict, S., Williams, R.D. and Baron, P. (1994) Recalled anxiety: from discovery to diagnosis of a benign breast mass. *Oncology Nurses Forum*, 21 (10): 1723–7.

Bristol Cancer Epidemiology Unit (1995) *Cancer of the Female Breast in the South and West*. Bristol: Department of Social Medicine, University of Bristol.

Burton, M.V., Parker, R.W. with Farrell, A., Bailey, D., Conneely, J., Booth, S. and Elcombe, S. (1995) A randomised controlled trial of preoperative psychological preparation for mastectomy. *Psycho-Oncology*, 4 (1): 1–19.

Cancer Relief Macmillan Fund (1994) *Breast Cancer: How to Help Yourself*.

Cancer Relief Macmillan Fund (1995) *The Macmillan Directory of Breast Cancer Services in the UK*. London: Kings Fund.

Cancer Relief Macmillan Fund (1996) *The Macmillan Directory of Breast Cancer Services in the UK*. London: Kings Fund.

Cancer Research Campaign (1991) *Breast Cancer: Factsheet 6*. London: CRC.

Expert Advisory Group on Cancer to the Chief Medical Officers of England and Wales (1995) *A Policy Framework for Commissioning Cancer Services*. (The Calman Report) London: DoH and Welsh Office.

Fallowfield, L. (1991) *Breast Cancer*. London: Routledge.

Fallowfield, L. and Roberts, R. (1992) Cancer counselling in the United Kingdom. *Psychology and Health*, 6: 107–17.

Fallowfield, L., Baum, M. and Maguire, G.P. (1986) Effects of breast conservation on psychological morbidity associated with diagnosis and treatment of early breast cancer. *British Medical Journal*, 293: 1331–4.

Goldberg, J.A., Scott, R.N., Davidson, P.M., Murray, G.D., Stallard, S., George, W.D. *et al.* (1992). Psychological morbidity in the first year after breast surgery. *European Journal of Surgical Oncology*, 18: 327–31.

Gui, G.P.H., Allum, W.H., Perry, N.M., Wells, C.A., Curling, O.M., McLean, A. *et al.* (1995) One-stop diagnosis for symptomatic breast disease. *Annals of the Royal College of Surgeons of England*, 77: 24–7.

Harcourt, D.M., Cawthorn, S.J., Ambler, N. and Rumsey, N. (1997) A randomised controlled trial investigating the psychological impact of some-day diagnosis at a 'one stop' breast clinic versus conventional clinic arrangement. Abstracts of the 5th Nottingham International Breast Cancer Conference. *The Breast*, 6 (4): 253.

Hogbin, B. and Fallowfield, L. (1989) Getting it taped: the 'bad news' consultation with cancer patients. *British Journal of Hospital Medicine*, 41: 330–3.

Holland, J.C. (1992) Psycho-oncology: overview, obstacles and opportunities. *Psycho-oncology*, 1: 1–13.

Hughes, J. (1982) Emotional reactions to the diagnosis and treatment of early breast cancer. *Journal of Psychosomatic Research*, 26 (2): 277–83.

Hughes, J.E. (1987) Psychological and social consequences of cancer. *Cancer Survey*, 6 (3): 455–75.

Hughes, J.E., Royle, G.T., Buchanan, R. and Taylor, I. (1986) Depression and social stress among patients with benign breast disease. *British Journal of Surgery*, 73: 997–9.

Hughson, A., Cooper, A., McArdle, C.S. and Smith, D.C. (1988) Psychosocial morbidity in patients awaiting breast biopsy. *Journal of Psychosomatic Research*, 32 (2): 173–80.

Labour Party (1997) *Labour's Pledge on Breast Cancer*. London: Department of Health.

Lasry, J.-C.M., Margolese, R.G., Poisson, R., Shibata, H., Fleischer, D., Lafleur, D. *et al.* (1987) Depression and body image following mastectomy and lumpectomy. *Journal of Chronic Disease*, 40 (6): 529–34.

Lerman, C., Trock, B., Rimer, B.K., Jepson, C., Brody, D. and Boyce, A. (1991) Psychological side effects of breast cancer screening. *Health Psychology*, 10 (4): 259–67.

McArdle, J.M., George, W.D., McArdle, C.S., Smith, D.C., Moodie, A.R., Hughson, A.V.M. *et al.* (1996) Psychological support for patients undergoing breast cancer surgery: a randomised study. *British Medical Journal*, 312: 813–16.

Macfarlane, M.E. and Sony, S.D. (1992) Women, breast lump discovery and associated stress. *Health Care for Women International*, 13: 23–32.

Maguire, P., Tait, A., Brooke, M., Thomas, C. and Sellwood, R. (1980) Effect of counselling on the psychiatric morbidity associated with mastectomy. *British Medical Journal*, 281: 1454–6.

Mock, V. (1993) Body image in women treated for breast cancer. *Nursing Research*. 42 (3): 153–7.

Morris, T. and Greer, S. (1982) Psychological characteristics of women electing to attend a breast screening clinic. *Clinical Oncology*, 8: 113–19.

Morris, J. and Royle, G.T. (1988) Offering patients a choice of surgery for early breast cancer: a reduction in anxiety and depression in patients and their husbands. *Social Science and Medicine*, 26 (6): 583–5.

NHS Executive (1996a) Improving Outcomes in Breast Cancer: The Manual. London: Department of Health.

NHS Executive (1996b) Improving Outcomes in Breast Cancer: The Research Evidence. London: Department of Health.

Northouse, L.L., Laten, D. and Reddy, P. (1995) Adjustment of women and their husbands to recurrent breast cancer. *Research in Nursing and Health*, 18: 515–24.

Polivy, J. (1977) Psychological effects of mastectomy on a woman's feminine self-concept. *Journal of Nervous and Mental Disease*, 164 (2): 77–87.

Poole, K. (1997) The emergence of the waiting game: a critical examination of the psychosocial issues in diagnosing breast cancer. *Journal of Advanced Nursing*, 25: 273–81.

Rowland, J.H. and Holland, J.C. (1990) Breast cancer. In J.C. Holland and J.H. Rowland (eds) *Handbook of Psycho-oncology*. Oxford: Oxford University Press.

Rumsey, N., Ambler, N., Harcourt, D., Khan, F. and Cawthorn, S. (1995) Counselling breast cancer patients: evaluation of an advocacy style of intervention. *Proceedings of the British Psychological Society*, 4 (1): 37.

Sarafino, E.P. (1994) *Health Psychology. Biopsychosocial Interactions*, 2nd ed. Chichester: Wiley.

Scott, D. (1983) Anxiety, critical thinking and information processing during and after breast biopsy. *Nursing Research*, 32: 24–8.

Tjemsland, L., Soreide, J.A. and Malt, U.F. (1996) Traumatic distress symptoms in early breast cancer 1: acute response to diagnosis. *Psycho-oncology*, 5: 1–8.

Ubhi, S.S., Wright, S., Clarke, L., Black, S., Shaw, P., Stotter, A. *et al.* (1996) Anxiety in patients with symptomatic breast disease: the effects of immediate versus delayed communication of results. *Annals of the Royal College of Surgeons of England*, 78: 466–9.

Watson, M., Denton, S., Baum, M. and Greer, S. (1988) Counselling breast cancer patients: a specialist nurse service. *Counselling Psychology Quarterly*, 1 (1): 25–34.

Weisman, A.D. and Worden, J.W. (1986) The emotional impact of recurrent cancer. *Journal of Psychosocial Oncology*, 3 (4): 5–16.

12

•

Women, low income and smoking: developing a 'bottom-up' approach

•

Amanda Amos, Elizabeth Crossan and Paula Gaunt-Richardson

Introduction

This chapter describes the work of 'Under a Cloud' – a Scottish project which developed community-based approaches to tackling the issues around smoking among women on low income (Crossan and Amos 1994). The first part of the chapter gives the findings of a survey of the views of a wide range of people and agencies in Scotland who work with women on low income. The second part focuses on a conference which drew together over 100 participants from differing backgrounds to consider how best to empower and enable women who want to stop smoking, and to identify ways in which smoking among women on low income could be addressed in the future. The final part describes the action that has been taken as a result of the participants' recommendations, and gives some examples from around the UK of projects which are trying to address this issue in innovative ways.

Background to the project

Smoking is a major health issue and a challenge to all who are concerned about the well-being of women. It is increasingly associated with those living on low income and in materially disadvantaged circumstances and women are over-represented in this group (see Graham and Woodhouse, this volume). Because smoking plays a complex role in the daily lives of women struggling to survive with little money (Graham 1993, 1994; Nicotinell 1993; Greaves 1996) those working with such women may be tempted to avoid the issue – to think that smoking is the least of their problems. But smoking is a major cause of inequalities in health among women in Scotland, as in the rest of the UK. It is the single most important preventable cause of ill health and death among women in Scotland and rates of smoking-related diseases are highest among women trying to survive life on a low income. While smoking has declined among women over the past ten years, this decline has been much slower among working-class women and those living on low incomes (Graham 1994; Marsh and MacKay 1994; Bennett *et al.* 1996).

Reducing smoking has been identified as a priority for improving the health and well-being of the people of Scotland (Scottish Office 1992). A review of tobacco use in Scotland (Amos *et al.* 1992) concluded that while there had been general progress in reducing smoking, there were few initiatives designed to meet the needs of women living on low income. In addition there seemed to be some reluctance among those working with such women to discuss the issue of smoking. It was concluded that new approaches which would support smoking reduction among this group were needed which involved both health and community workers, and which would establish a dialogue between the tobacco control/health promotion agencies and those working with women living on low income in Scotland. It was to address these concerns that the 'Under a Cloud – Smoking Among Women on Low Income' project was initiated.

'Under a Cloud'

The aims of the project were to:

- engage in a wide-ranging consultation with individuals and organizations throughout Scotland who were playing, or who potentially could play, a role in reducing smoking among women living on low income;
- identify ways in which current and future initiatives could be developed including consideration of possible obstacles and how they might be overcome;
- organize a national conference on the theme of 'Smoking Among Women on Low Income – The Way Forward', to address the needs expressed in the consultation phase, and consider how to develop future action on this issue.

The project was divided into two main phases. Phase 1 involved in-depth telephone interviews with a sample of individuals and organizations through-out Scotland who were playing, or who could play, a role in this area of work. Phase 2 involved a one-day national conference and the production and dissemination of the project report.

Phase 1: Consultation

Interviews were carried out with 37 community projects from all over Scotland, and 12 of the 15 Scottish health promotion departments. The aim was to find out the current range of activities which addressed, either directly or indirectly, smoking reduction among women living on low income. The experiences of those involved in these initiatives were drawn on to identify factors which influenced the effectiveness of their work, and to see how such initiatives could be further developed. Views were also collected from those not currently involved in such activities about perceived barriers to work concerning women and smoking, and how these difficulties might be overcome. Smoking in relation to work in community projects was a difficult area to research as there were initiatives which, while not ostensibly addressing 'smoking', could potentially support smoking reduction in more indirect ways. For this reason the interviews were kept as flexible as possible.

Just under half (17) of the community projects reported that they were, or had recently been, involved in initiatives directly concerned with smoking, i.e. where smoking was identified as the single, main or part focus. These included smoking cessation groups and groups providing support for smokers to cut down or give up. A further twelve community groups were involved in initiatives which they felt could indirectly support smoking reduction. That is, activities where smoking had not been the identified focus, but smoking reduction had been a by-product. These included aromatherapy sessions, stress management groups, exercise and 'away weekends'. The remaining eight of those interviewed were not currently involved in initiatives which they felt addressed the issue of smoking either directly or indirectly.

Five of the twelve health promotion departments had officers with a smoking remit, three had officers with women's health as their remit, and a further two had community development officers who worked specifically with women. Although few departments had initiatives on women and smoking, several were involved in broader smoking initiatives such as 'Glasgow 2000' and 'Port Smoke Alert'. Many departments stated that they were not involved in as much work on this issue as they would like due to lack of staff and heavy workloads.

Overall, the interviews highlighted a range of community and locally based initiatives, which were at different stages of development, which could support smoking reduction among women living on low income. These findings challenged somewhat the notion that those who work with women living on low income tend to avoid the issue of smoking. Many people were currently working in this area, and others were keen to develop work and to become involved.

The interviews also highlighted the need for further discussion around a number of key issues which the workers themselves identified. These included questions about the most appropriate people to work on initiatives with women – whether it was community workers or health professionals for example, where funding could be found, and where women could get support after an initiative had ended. Several interviewees felt that the materials and resources currently available, as well as national initiatives such as 'No Smoking Day' and 'Smokeline', did not meet the needs of women on low income. There was also felt to be a need to focus on specific groups such as the young, older women, women from ethnic groups and women with mental health problems or learning difficulties. A major concern voiced by many was that potential funders and health promotion agencies often had inappropriate and unrealistic expectations of what could be achieved through community work. For example, funders often seemed to be only interested in how many women had quit whereas community projects tended to focus more on the process involved in helping smokers to start thinking about the issues and ways in which they might address their smoking.

Phase 2: Dissemination

The dissemination phase began with a one-day conference which brought together people interviewed in Phase 1 and others who work with women on low income. It generated a huge interest and was over-subscribed. One of the main strengths of the day was that it attracted participants from a wide variety of backgrounds including health promotion specialists, community workers, researchers, midwives, health visitors, welfare and advice workers, social workers and community educators.

The issues

Irrespective of their current level of involvement on this issue participants welcomed the opportunity to share views and experiences, and hear about research and initiatives. Several spoke of their need to 'recharge' and find new enthusiasm, as well as collecting ideas for action for themselves and their colleagues. Many recognized the links between gender, material disadvantage and smoking and argued that work with women must acknowledge these key issues, though some had not appreciated how marked this association was. Others raised issues such as women's caring role, poverty, stressful lives, poor housing, and powerlessness.

Several participants from cessation-based projects raised concerns that their current approach might inadvertently be doing more harm than good. In contrast, others seemed relieved that their experiences were confirmed, that smoking could not be tackled in isolation. In particular, those who had been involved in indirect initiatives felt that their experiences had been legitimated. They felt that initiatives which addressed assertiveness training,

raising self-esteem, trying to reduce isolation and giving women new opportunities and experiences should be recognized as having an important role
to play in supporting smoking reduction. A point stressed by many was the
need to avoid victim blaming by working in a non-judgemental way, understanding the meaning and significance of smoking for women.

Although many worked with women who smoked, the point was made
that not all women living in disadvantaged circumstances smoke. Thus there
should be further research into the ways in which non-smokers cope. Several participants from community projects felt that a major challenge facing
them was that smoking was not a priority issue for many women because of
the other problems that they had to deal with. However, while some women
could not and did not want to address their own smoking, many were
concerned about the effects of passive smoking on their children.

Health professionals spoke about their feelings of isolation, demoraliza-
tion, and lack of training about how to raise the issue of smoking in ways
that were not victim blaming. Some participants reported that offering
alternative therapies such as aromatherapy was successful as it enabled
women to feel good about themselves. Others stressed the need to recognize
the addictiveness of nicotine, and the sometimes counter-productive impact
of blanket smoking bans in community venues. A variety of strategies were
identified for moving forward at community, regional and national levels.

At community level, participants felt that women themselves should be
enabled to take more control over developments; to decide the focus, the
language and who should facilitate. Peer education projects were thought
by many to have considerable potential – training local women about how
to run initiatives themselves, and how to train other women. Funding was
needed to pay local women to undertake this work and to experiment with
new approaches.

Many thought that training should emphasize a holistic approach, with
smoking cessation seen as a process which involves assessing whether or not
people want to change and then increasing their motivation. This can be
a long process and while not all approaches will result in increased rates of
quitting in the short term, they may have an impact in the long term.
Evaluation, therefore, needs to focus on both process and outcome. Another
training issue discussed was when and how to raise the issue of smoking,
particularly for health visitors and GPs working in areas of deprivation. It
was felt that information should also be sought on how women in areas of
deprivation are targeted by the tobacco industry – this could then be used to
develop community action.

Participants were also keen to find out more about different initiatives at
area and regional levels. It was felt to be important to develop inter-agency
alliances, and to involve local traders and trading standards officers to improve
the enforcement of the law on sale of cigarettes to under-16s. Health promotion departments also needed to play a key role in providing training and
producing materials which were sensitive to the needs of local women,

especially those with low literacy. Training should involve not only smoking cessation but also how to approach health and well-being issues with women on low income, how to raise smoking in community settings, and how to evaluate initiatives.

Considerable concern was expressed about the fact that different stakeholders such as health promotion agencies, funding bodies and community workers often had conflicting agendas and placed value on different approaches. For example, some valued initiatives focusing directly on smoking cessation while others preferred rather more indirect approaches which addressed the underlying reasons for smoking. Stakeholders also utilized different measures of success, with some only interested in cessation whereas others were more concerned with empowerment and improving women's self-esteem. It was also felt to be important to focus on other settings, particularly schools, and to develop policies which make it easier for women to take action, for example increasing nursery provision. The training, resources and initiatives available in local areas needed to be more widely known and a network of local contacts established.

Several groups echoed the need expressed in the consultation phase for a comprehensive approach at national level encompassing action on reducing smoking through a tobacco control strategy along with a campaign against low income, poverty and deprivation (see Woodhouse, this volume). A strongly expressed view was that the government should ban all tobacco advertising and promotion and that the media should not promote positive images of women and smoking, for example in TV soaps or films. National agencies and organizations were seen to have a crucial role in facilitating developments at all levels by funding new initiatives, materials, evaluation, research and networking. Ideas for further work included more research on why women on low income do or do not smoke and how some manage to quit; the development of appropriate evaluation tools and measures of success; and a conference where women on low income could themselves discuss the issues around smoking. Greater communication and networking were highlighted as important. In particular the participants did not want the enthusiasm and commitment to action generated by the conference to be lost.

Moving foward: examples of innovative practice

'Under a Cloud' showed that there were more community initiatives trying to support smoking reduction among women living on low income than had been previously thought. There was also enthusiasm and motivation among those who work with women to develop initiatives and to become more involved. However, many were being hindered by the lack of funding, training, appropriate support and resources. People also valued the opportunity to discuss the issues of importance to them and to meet others with whom they could share information and experiences. It was concluded that the time was right for further developments in this area of work.

Drawing on the project recommendations, ASH Scotland sought and was awarded funding by the Health Education Board for Scotland (HEBS) for a 30-month project to facilitate community initiatives. This was to be done by developing a comprehensive database of community initiatives in Scotland which address smoking among women on low income, and using this to support a network in Scotland. In addition one-year grants of up to £3000 each were to be offered to community groups in Scotland to develop projects which support smoking reduction, directly or indirectly, among women living on low income. The aim was to encourage innovation and experimentation.

This project started in April 1996 with the first of two waves of community project funding available in Autumn 1996, and the second wave in Spring 1997. Applicants were encouraged to ensure that proposed project work was led by the needs and interests of the participants. Over 120 applications were received in the two waves and twenty projects were funded. These projects aim to use a diverse range of approaches including integrated programmes of educational and recreational activities, the development of a magazine for young women, and both peer- and tutor-led women's health programmes. Participants include young women, young mothers, homeless women, women from ethnic minorities and women with mental health problems.

Given the innovative nature of these projects, and previous concerns about evaluation, considerable emphasis has been placed on the importance of evaluating and monitoring funded projects. An advisory group of researchers and practitioners, with relevant evaluation experience, has focused on developing process and outcome evaluation methods and indicators which, while sensitive to different approaches and contexts, do not place an unnecessary burden on projects. The results will be fed back as part of a range of dissemination activities including a national conference and the production of a report which will review and assess the programme as a whole.

This Scottish project aims to support developments and identify principles of effective practice. However, as the original consultation exercise showed, community based initiatives are already emerging both in Scotland and elsewhere in the UK. Some have resulted from national funding initiatives, such as the Health Education Authority HELIOS funding for 13 local stop smoking projects (Bostock 1996), and local programmes such as the 1995/96 small grants scheme on smoking cessation and prevention funded by Hackney Environmental Services and East London and the City Health Promotion Department (Bimpe 1996). Some have been developed on a more individual basis by health promotion departments and community projects in response to the expressed needs of local women. These projects encompass a range of approaches and activities, including local conferences, women-centred support groups, peer education, providing breaks and offering support to health and community workers. Examples of each are given below.

Burning Issues Event – Lanarkshire

This event marked the 1996 'No Smoking Day' and 'International Women's Day'. Women from across Lanarkshire were invited to discuss and share their experiences of smoking and to participate in a number of fun workshops, e.g. pottery, photography, video work and dance. This event was attended by 20 women. It was part of a series of activities which form a joint initiative between Lanarkshire Health Board, Motherwell Health Project, social work, community education and local communities.

Further information: Lanarkshire Health Board, Strathclyde Hospital, Airbles Road, Motherwell, ML1 3BW Tel: 01698 258800.

Women and Smoking Project – Belfast

This project was inspired by the first International Conference on Women and Smoking held in Northern Ireland in 1992. The Health Promotion Agency, who funded the project, and the Women's Resource and Development Agency, a feminist community development organization who managed and housed the project, came together to work in partnership on the project. From March 1993 a series of three-week introductory courses for local women were planned in various locations. The participants came from areas of disadvantage. Focusing on the role of tobacco advertising, women's use of the health services and family and personal smoking history, these courses had a broad focus to stimulate further interest in stopping smoking.

A 12-week course involving around a dozen women was completed in December 1994. This course had a more personal focus, looking at assertiveness, stress, self-esteem, relaxation and support, though some environmental issues were also addressed. The women also had the opportunity to use aids such as acupuncture, nicotine patches or hypnotherapy to help them stop smoking. During the 12 weeks all of the women stopped. Although six months later all had re-started, their view of smoking and their own smoking behaviour had changed significantly, with most changing to lower tar brands or cutting down.

Further information: Health Promotion Agency for Northern Ireland (1996) *Stopping for Me: Women, Disadvantage and Smoking*. Belfast: Health Promotion Agency for Northern Ireland.

Women and Smoking Peer Education Programme – Wood End

This project was developed following publication of health statistics for the Wood End/Henely Green area of Coventry which highlighted high levels of smoking and smoking-related illnesses. Local women were recruited as peer educators to provide a range of cessation services. The seven-week training programme covers health issues relating to smoking; the history of women smoking; poverty and sources of help and support; stress/isolation and smoking; relaxation and alternative therapies; presentation skills; self-esteem;

smoking cessation techniques; and working in alliances/partnerships. After completing training peer educators are paid £5 per hour to undertake work with local stop smoking groups, women's groups and youth groups.

Further information: Health Promotion Services, Ground Floor Annexe, Christchurch House, Greyfriars Land, Coventry, CV1 2GA Tel: 01203 633066.

Benarty Local Services – Fife

Benarty Local Services has tried several initiatives to support smoking reduction among women living on low income. The most successful have been low-cost 'Women's Break-Away Weekends'. Fourteen women and two members of staff from corporate services, community education, social work, health visitors or nursery education participate in each. Both the transport and the accommodation have no-smoking policies. Although most of the women who participate smoke, at the 'away weekends' smokers smoke less – not because of the policy, but because enjoyable alternatives are offered to occupy their time. On returning from these weekends a significant number of women have found the motivation to stop smoking, and a few have succeeded.

Further information: Benarty Local Services, 6 Benarty Square, Ballingry, Fife, KY5 8NR Tel: 01592 414343.

Healthy Castlemilk – Glasgow

Healthy Castlemilk has been involved in various initiatives to support local people in smoking reduction. National 'No Smoking Day' is one of their main events. Several years ago the project acquired one of the units in the local shopping centre and has run a number of activities. Local schools are also encouraged to take part by designing posters, and the project supports local schools in running an event of their own by providing help, information and leaflets. As a result of activities on No Smoking Day a 'Quit and Get Fit' group has started which offers support to anyone trying to quit without putting them under pressure. Healthy Castlemilk has also produced a *Quitters' Guide* which includes stories of local people who have managed to stop. Feedback on the guide has been very positive. Healthy Castlemilk also offer smokers different ways to cope with stress, such as relaxation, aromatherapy and tai-chi.

Further information: Healthy Castlemilk, 33 Dougrie Drive, Castlemilk, Glasgow, G45 9AD Tel: 0141 634 2679.

Women and Tobacco Network – Fife

The network emerged out of a one-day seminar designed to raise the issue of women and smoking with those working in women's health and education in Fife. The network was launched in March 1994. A core group of

members was established which consisted mainly of health service professionals along with a broader group who did not attend meetings but were
forwarded information. Network members were updated every six months
with information about past activities and future plans to enable members
to follow up and exchange information with each other. In 1995 the network focused on smoking and pregnancy and developed a leaflet for pregnant women.

Further information: Fife Healthcare NHS Trust, Health Promotion Department, Glenrothes House, North St., Glenrothes, Fife, KY7 5PB Tel: 01592
754355.

Conclusions

Despite the importance of this issue to the health of disadvantaged women,
we are still at the early stages of developing a grounded understanding of
what makes for effective practice. Many initiatives are short-lived and under-
resourced, often lasting only a few months, and few have been properly
evaluated. However, a recent review which has drawn on the experiences
of HEA-funded projects and others (Bostock 1996) has identified several
principles which could help guide further initiatives. Many of these principles echo the 'Under a Cloud' findings and recommendations. They include
the need to build alliances between local health professionals, community
workers and local authorities; to ensure that all stakeholders share the same
agenda and objectives; to plan and consult in partnership with local people;
to ensure community ownership; to adopt an empowering approach; to have
a positive focus, e.g. using positive language, providing support and encouragement; and to redefine success more widely than just cessation.

Health professionals, the NHS and others concerned about improving the
health of women on low income by helping them to reduce their smoking
face a double challenge. First, they need to utilize current understanding of
the issues and principles of good practice to develop their own work and that
of others to tackle this problem. Second, they must ensure that the lessons
that they learn from their own work, whether through formal or informal
evaluation and assessment, are disseminated to other practitioners and policy
makers. Only through the critical assessment of such activities will effective
practice be developed and adopted. It is hoped that initiatives like 'Under a
Cloud' will contribute to this process.

Acknowledgements

'Under a Cloud' was funded by the Health Education Board for Scotland
and the Chief Scientist Office of the Scottish Home and Health Department.
The opinions expressed in this chapter are those of the authors and not

necessarily those of the funding bodies. We would like to thank Deborah Nash for help with typing, and the members of the advisory groups, in particular Alison Hillhouse and Maureen Moore.

References

Amos, A., Hillhouse, A., Alexander, H. and Sheehy, C. (1992) *Tobacco Use in Scotland.* Edinburgh: ASH Scotland.

Bennett, N., Jarvis, L., Rowlands, O., Singleton, N. and Haseldean, L. (1996) *Living in Britain: Results from the 1994 General Household Survey.* London: HMSO.

Bimpe, O.K. (1996) *Small Grants Scheme: Smoking Cessation/Prevention.* London: Hackney Environmental Services and East London and the City Health Promotion.

Bostock, Y. (1996) *Empowering Smokers to Quit: Success Principles for Community Stop Smoking Projects.* London: Health Education Authority.

Crossan, E. and Amos, A. (1994) *Under a Cloud: Women, Low Income and Smoking.* Edinburgh: HEBS.

Graham, H. (1993) *When Life's a Drag: Women, Smoking and Disadvantage.* London: HMSO.

Graham, H. (1994) When life's a drag: women, smoking and disadvantage. In E. Crossan and A. Amos (eds) *Under a Cloud.* Edinburgh: HEBS.

Greaves, L. (1996) *Smoke Screen: Women's Smoking and Social Control.* London: Scarlet Press.

Marsh, A. and MacKay, S. (1994) *Poor Smokers.* London: Policy Studies Institute.

Nicotinell (1993) *Smoking Mothers With Young Children: The Hidden Dilemma.* London: Nicotinell.

Scottish Office (1992) *Scotland's Health: A Challenge to Us All.* Edinburgh: HMSO.

13

•

Gender and health promotion in two different settings

•

Norma Daykin

Introduction

Traditional health education and health promotion campaigns have often been underpinned by damaging assumptions relating to gender. These have been challenged by feminist critiques of health promotion (Daykin and Naidoo 1995). This chapter draws on these critical perspectives in order to discuss the factors influencing gender sensitivity in health promotion in two contrasting settings: primary healthcare and the workplace. The discussion is illustrated by findings from two studies of health promotion undertaken in south west England during the 1990s.

Critics of traditional health promotion strategies have drawn attention to the way in which social, as opposed to biological, differences between men and women influence their health. These factors include structured inequalities at societal level which mean, for example, that women are still concentrated in a limited range of jobs while continuing to earn lower wages than men despite the introduction of legislation to encourage equal opportunities and equal pay (OECD 1993). This in turn contributes to the legitimization of gender differences in income and wealth, as well as occupational and domestic conditions which exert significant influence on women's health (Dennerstein 1995; Doyal 1995).

Economic inequalities have widened in recent years, partly because of the restructuring of employment opportunities and the growth of low-paid, insecure and 'flexible' employment (Brown and Scase 1991; Brewster *et al.* 1997). These changes have led to the increased marginalization of particular groups, including poor single mothers whose smoking behaviour has been highlighted as a cause for concern (Marsh and McKay 1994; see also Graham, Woodhouse and Amos *et al.*, this volume). All these factors need to be recognized in the development of strategies for promoting women's health.

Conventional styles of health education have also been criticized for their failure to question commonly held stereotypes of the 'natural' roles of men and women. Assumptions about 'female' duties have influenced health promotion at a number of levels. For example, women have often been targeted in research and health promotion because of their assumed responsibility for others. Similarly, many campaigns around smoking, nutrition and healthy lifestyles are based on the assumption that women will maintain and protect the health of families and households by providing practical and emotional services, planning and budgeting, and liaising with external agencies (Graham 1984, 1993; Doyal 1991).

The failure to recognize the social and structural constraints on women's behaviour, coupled with the apportionment of duty in relation to health promotion, can be seen to leave women unsupported to face the consequences of the paradox of responsibility without power. Differences in income as well as divisions of ethnicity, sexuality and disability mean that the responsibility for health promotion affects women in different ways. However, many share the same conflicts between their knowledge of socially approved principles of healthy living and their inability to provide the material resources necessary to support health, together with their lack of power to change the behaviour of others. These conflicts can result in women sacrificing their own health in order to maintain relationships and the health of others. Examples of this have been identified in several areas including smoking (Graham 1987, 1993; Oakley 1989); nutrition (Charles and Kerr 1987); and sexual health (Thomson and Holland, 1994; Wilton 1994, 1997).

Recent developments in health promotion have been marked by a focus on the (ungendered) individual. This was reflected in the *Health of the Nation* strategy which targeted coronary heart disease and stroke; cancers; mental health and suicide; HIV/AIDS and sexual health; and accidents for reductions in mortality and improvements in health status. Similar targets have also been adopted in its successor, *Our Healthier Nation*. It is often assumed that these improvements can be achieved solely through individual changes in lifestyle, including reducing smoking, improvements in diet and increased physical exercise. However, the strategy has been criticized for overlooking the 'landscapes of risk' faced by disadvantaged groups (particularly women) in their attempts to secure health and well-being (see Graham, this volume). The health priorities of these groups may reflect day-to-day preoccupations and the need for survival in often difficult environments rather than more abstract and distant risks.

The targets also prioritize the reduction of threats to life expectancy at the expense of quality of life issues. Whilst women currently enjoy greater life expectancy than men (79 years at birth compared to 73 years for men) they also experience greater ill health, impairment and disability (Miles 1991;

Arber 1996). Yet problems such as arthritis, back pain and osteoporosis which contribute to women's excess morbidity are not addressed as key targets within the strategy.

Poverty, gender and health promotion in primary healthcare settings

These problems were clearly reflected in the approach taken to implement the *Health of the Nation* strategy. The primary healthcare (PHC) setting has been seen as particularly important with significant resources being channelled towards encouraging primary healthcare teams, led by general practitioners, to introduce health promotion activity.

Primary healthcare does have a number of advantages in relation to delivering effective health promotion to women. It is more accessible than other settings, and is also particularly familiar to many women who make more visits to the doctor than men (HEA 1995). However, its current mode of organization creates barriers to achieving health promotion goals. First, the resources available for health promotion in this setting tend to be channelled through GPs themselves rather than through other professional groups or agencies. Yet GPs are trained to be primarily concerned with the cure of existing illness, rather than focusing on prevention. Second, the role of the GP exemplifies the individualist approach with the one-to-one consultation at the centre of most practice. Valuing the individuality of patients is an important core value within primary healthcare, but the ethos of individualism can be at odds with the need to address collective problems (Blackburn 1993).

Whilst individual women experience their gender identity in different ways, gender itself is a basic social division which is related in complex ways to other social inequalities. The links between gender and poverty for instance are well recognized, resulting from the unequal position of women in the formal structures of the labour market and the social security system as well as their assumed dependency on men within families and households (Payne 1991; Graham 1993; Millar 1996). Hence the issue of poverty in health promotion is one of particular significance to the development of gender-sensitive practice.

In a study carried out in the South West during 1993 and 1994, 50 primary healthcare staff were interviewed about their health promotion work (Daykin *et al.* 1995). Many demonstrated sophisticated levels of understanding of poverty issues in health promotion, particularly those working in inner-city, multi-ethnic localities. In their responses, this group drew attention to the way in which the *Health of the Nation* strategy focused on 'lifestyle choice' at the expense of broader issues. The emphasis on lifestyles was seen as inappropriate for all poor clients but particularly for women who had the responsibilities but lacked the resources to exercise the consumer rights assumed within the model.

I know you can still eat a healthy diet on a low income but it is a lot harder. People will buy white bread because you can get it cheap and it is more expensive to buy fruit and vegetables. If it is a family and they are living off benefits it is very hard to make changes even if they want to.

(Practice nurse cited in Daykin *et al.* 1995: 40)

Further, the strategy was seen as failing to respond to collective definitions of need, particularly those articulated by members of relatively deprived communities (Russell 1996).

We looked at 560 people in our community who were asked what they identified as the most important factors for their health and they said, decent housing, a job, enough money and a non-polluted environment. Now the Government has said it's smoking, alcohol, exercise and diet, so the Government and the deprived have two different agendas.

(GP cited in Daykin *et al.* 1995: 54)

The research also demonstrated that the current organization of primary healthcare creates structural obstacles to the delivery of health promotion to women. GP-led primary care services are often limited to those patients within the practice itself rather than being offered to more broadly defined communities. This narrowing of services to specified populations has been reinforced by the development of the role of the GP as purchaser of health services. Fundholding has also strengthened the position of the GP in relation to other members of the primary healthcare team. Our research showed that these developments have sometimes led to increased resentment among practices to what is perceived as 'freeloading' on community services by 'rival' colleagues. As a result primary healthcare staff, such as health visitors who have traditionally worked across practice boundaries, were facing increasing difficulties. Some of the health visitors in our study voiced concern that their increased accountability to financially independent GPs might threaten their health promotion work with women.

These accounts also raised questions about the way in which the effectiveness of health promotion is judged. Much of the health visitors' health promotion work was described in terms of processes such as support and encouragement designed to benefit women over a long term. Current attempts to identify immediate outcomes of practice were therefore greeted with mixed responses. Given that many women's health problems are chronic, evaluation methods need to reflect long-term and qualitative benefits. However, there is a danger that current techniques used to evaluate primary care services will increasingly emphasize only short-term, easily quantifiable gains which are visible to the GP.

Despite these limitations, primary healthcare workers have developed a range of strategies in response to the health promotion needs of their predominantly female clients. In our study these were reported as ranging from non-authoritarian advice-giving and personal counselling through to organizational changes to increase flexibility and extend consultation times. In addition, a number of healthy alliances with agencies such as Environ-mental Health Departments, local sports centres, community groups and interpreting services were described. Several innovative projects were under way including an 'exercise on prescription' scheme and a health and exercise group for Asian women. The need to move away from a victim-blaming model of health promotion was clearly acknowledged.

> On 'No Smoking Day' we put up posters and leaflets about the tobacco industry and how it affects things. I want to see it as wider. It's not just individual responsibility, it needs to be put in a wider context.
> (Practice nurse cited in Daykin *et al.* 1995: 42)

The tensions between the need to respond to individuals within the PHC setting and the relative ineffectiveness of strategies which do not recognize the collective nature of problems such as poverty appear to leave many health professionals feeling helpless and frustrated. This sense of frustration was certainly reflected in our interviews with PHC staff. For example practice nurses, who have achieved greater professional status through the development of health promotion within PHC, have at the same time felt disempowered by the narrow focus of the strategies they are expected to implement.

> We are finding it very hard to help the needy; what we think is import-ant they don't want. You usually get the worried well and not the needy.
> (Practice nurse cited in Daykin *et al.* 1995: 41)

The health professionals in our study constantly referred to women when giving examples of the difficulties of offering health promotion services to poor clients. Similarly, the examples of good practice almost always identi-fied female clients whether as individuals or within groups. Yet the issue of gender itself was rarely raised or problematized. Instead, the needs of women were usually defined with reference to their roles as mothers and carers. Similarly, the teaching of budgeting skills, the establishment of food and health discussion groups and the encouragement of cooperative food-buying activities were all examples of initiatives aimed almost exclusively at women and rarely at men. This illustrates the ever-present danger that pragmatic and well-meaning attempts to assist women in dealing with the constraints of poverty may serve to reinforce the patterns of gender inequality which shape their greater risk of deprivation in the first instance.

This discussion of primary care as a setting for health promotion points towards the need for a number of changes at policy level. First, the basis of current thinking on health promotion should be re-examined and its articulation with the diversity of women's health needs should be further explored. Second, the bias towards models of lifestyle choice needs to be addressed. At the same time, the current limitations of the primary healthcare setting in relation to the development of broader strategies need to be ac-knowledged and stronger mechanisms for enhancing the role of the primary healthcare team and facilitating multi-agency collaboration and community development approaches established.

When health promotion strategies in primary care are focused on issues related to poverty they are, of course, indirectly addressing gender inequalities since women represent the majority of the poor. However, there is also a need to address gender issues directly in order to avoid replicating assumptions and stereotypes which themselves contribute to women's difficulties in escaping deprivation. Hence models of good practice within primary healthcare, and the training of health professionals in these models, need to incorporate gender more explicitly alongside other forms of inequality.

Gender and health promotion in non-medical settings: occupational health and workplace health promotion

The workplace offers an alternative setting to that of primary care for the development of gender-sensitive health promotion strategies, and interest in it is growing in the UK. The workplace is attractive as a non-medical setting since working conditions are an important focus of strategies to address health inequality and improve social conditions. Workplace health promotion activities are popular amongst women workers who are more likely than their male counterparts to participate in programmes (Lovato and Green 1990; Wilson 1990; Alexy 1991; Glasgow *et al.* 1993). The perceived benefits of workplace health promotion to employers have also been highlighted, including reduced sickness absence, lower staff turnover and increased productivity as well as the reduced risk of litigation (Fingret and Smith 1995).

Workplace health promotion does have its critics. For example, it has been suggested that focusing on worker's health behaviour blames the victim, distracting attention away from hazards and poor working conditions which cause ill health (Watterson 1986). Indeed, in a review of the literature, Sanders (1993) noted that many programmes tend to concentrate on individual lifestyle change rather than addressing organizational and environmental problems. These wider influences are strongly affected by gender segregation in employment which helps to shape the occupational health risks faced by women (OECD 1993).

But despite these problems, workplace health promotion strategies can complement and extend traditional occupational health services in order to respond to the complex problem of work-related ill health. Whilst traditional occupational health services focus on the direct effects of work, such as industrial accidents and prescribed diseases, workplace health promotion addresses broader issues such as coronary heart disease and cancers which may be only indirectly related to employment. This is particularly important for women workers who are often perceived to be less at risk from traditionally recognized accidents and diseases and for whom occupational illness is often invisible to researchers and policy makers (Messing *et al.* 1993).

In fact, the distinction between directly and indirectly caused work-related illness cannot be clearly drawn. Many occupational health problems are multicausal, influenced by a combination of occupational and non-occupational factors. This too is especially significant for women workers, who are more likely to work part-time than their male counterparts, and who spend a greater proportion of time on domestic tasks (OECD 1993). These tasks involve hazards and risks which may compound those faced in paid employment (Doyal 1995).

Occupational hazards may also be compounded by 'lifestyle' activities such as smoking or alcohol consumption which can themselves be work-related. Occupational stress and boredom have been suggested as contributory causes of increased alcohol consumption and liver cirrhosis in a range of manual jobs (Leigh and Jiang 1993). These jobs include predominantly female occupations such as waitressing and bar work in which alcohol is readily available. Similarly, waitresses and bar staff may be exposed to a significantly higher risk of lung cancer than other workers (Seigel 1993). This may be due to a combination of both active and passive smoking (Kjaerheim and Anderson 1994). Hence lifestyle risk factors may be difficult to separate from other occupational health risks even though these behaviours may extend beyond the workplace.

Thus far, health-related services in the workplace remain extremely limited in the UK. There is no statutory requirement for employers to provide occupational healthcare and this type of provision is separate from other health services provided by the NHS. Traditional occupational health services and workplace health promotion activities are both more likely to be provided by large firms and by public sector organizations (Webb *et al.* 1988; HEA 1993; Johnson and Christie 1995). Hence workers in small firms and self-employed individuals are unlikely to benefit from current occupational health services of any kind. Changing patterns of employment, including increases in casual and temporary contracts and the growth of homeworking, further undermine the access of significant numbers of workers to employer-provided occupational health services (Pickvance 1996).

Recently, the NHS Executive has sought to improve occupational health provision for NHS employees. The 'Health at Work in the NHS' initiative, introduced in 1992, has raised the profile of health promotion in NHS workplaces. As the NHS is the largest employer in the UK, the complexity of implementing occupational health initiatives for its staff should not be underestimated (Johnson and Christie 1995). Nevertheless, both access and quality in occupational health services could be improved by further extending the role of the NHS to include occupational health promotion for the general population. Community-based occupational health services, such as those currently provided by non-medical personnel in a small number of primary healthcare settings funded by the NHS, offer a number of advantages, particularly for those who do not have access to employer-provided services (Pickvance 1996). As well as the unemployed and the retired, many of whom may need ongoing occupational health advice and support, this group includes the growing numbers of 'flexible' workers affected by changes in employment patterns in recent years.

Community-based services of this kind also have the advantage of being able to provide independent advice to employees and employers. Occupational health professionals often face ethical tensions between their respect for individuals' privacy and their obligations to employers (Lucas 1995). Workers themselves are likely to be suspicious of occupational health services if they are seen to be dominated by personnel functions or have responsibility for screening for health selection in recruitment and redundancy, particularly in a climate of growing job insecurity.

These issues were raised in a study of workplace health activity carried out during 1994 and 1995. The study involved a telephone survey of 101 organizations of different sizes and from different business groups. This was followed up by case study interviews with different workers in three organizations. Whilst the sample was relatively small (61 organizations responded to the survey) the findings mirrored that of a larger national study (HEA 1993) which found that workplace health activity was more likely to be provided in large public sector organizations.

Overall, the survey suggested that although women were more interested than men in occupational health promotion they faced significant obstacles in their attempts to use the services offered. More women than men were employed in small, private sector organizations and in retail organizations with the lowest levels of health promotion activity. In large organizations, women tended to be the lowest paid workers which meant that they tended not to benefit from services on offer. In one organization an extensive range of benefits was provided including sports facilities, a crèche and a counselling service. However, charges were made for the use of these facilities which, together with the transport costs involved, deterred low-paid women workers from using them.

Overall, the research demonstrated that health at work was not the greatest priority of employers. Whilst employers were keen to be seen as complying with statutory health and safety requirements, any provision beyond this was driven by considerations other than that of promoting health. For example, one of the most commonly provided facilities was private medical insurance (reported in 57 per cent of organizations). This was restricted to relatively highly paid staff, reflecting the commitment of employers to the preservation of status rather than the achievement of health benefits for all. A further illustration of priorities is the fact that organizations were five times more likely to provide company cars than they were to offer childcare facilities (provided by 59 per cent and 11 per cent of organizations respectively).

Nevertheless, the research also illustrated the positive potential of worksite health promotion in meeting some of women's concerns. In one organization (a large private sector manufacturing organization with a philanthropic reputation) a proactive occupational health nurse was employed. This nurse was concerned that women workers, who represented a minority of the workforce, were intimidated by the male-dominated culture of the factory. Consequently, she initiated a series of women's health forums on issues such as health screening, the menopause and toxic shock syndrome. These forums were extremely popular and whilst they did not address occupational health issues directly they were seen as successful in countering a shopfloor culture which made it difficult for women to express feelings and concerns in relation to their health.

The research identified a number of important issues relating to gender and the impact of health promotion. First, it demonstrated that, not surprisingly, health promotion affects different groups of women in different ways. For example, differences of status, power and control all influence the impact of working conditions on individuals. Consequently, health promotion strategies which address the concerns of one group of women may not be useful for others. In one organization (a small NHS hospital with a predominantly female workforce) staff identified job insecurity and the stress of uncertainty about the future as a major problem in their working environment. This uncertainty was the result of an announcement concerning the possible closure of the hospital, with relocation of staff to a distant site offered as the only alternative to redundancy.

Most of the staff were threatened to some extent by the changes, but important differences emerged between lower paid female staff and their female managers. More senior female staff faced anxiety caused by redeployment, changes in role and the potential loss of status as well as having to go through a new selection process. However, for the lower paid workers, who included catering staff and nursing assistants, it was the prospect of relocation that spelt disaster. Many faced practical difficulties such as the lack of private transport, the absence of convenient public transport and the increased childcare costs which would result from the need to spend more time travelling to work. These staff were also less likely than the higher paid employees to receive accurate and up-to-date information about the changes ahead. Hence, their problems were compounded by the circulation of what were sometimes inaccurate rumours.

Different groups of female staff also varied in their perceptions of good health promotion strategies. Whilst one female manager felt that an independent counselling service would address issues of stress and uncertainty, the lower paid workers distrusted this proposal, fearing that information about them might be misused by personnel. They were more in favour of practical remedies such as improving staffing levels (which had fallen since the announcement) and increasing the flow of information.

The success of workplace health initiatives depends upon a relationship of trust between health promotion providers and workers. Job insecurity, together with the perceived alignment of health promotion with management and personnel functions, can discourage workers from taking up services on offer. Hence, whilst workplace health promotion can extend and complement occupational health services, poor employment conditions and practices may undermine both of these, reinforcing surveillance and control. These are particular issues for women workers who are more likely than their male counterparts to experience the vulnerability of low-paid and flexible employment while also being more likely to be drawn to workplace health activity.

Conclusion

This chapter has examined the impact of health promotion on women in two different settings: primary healthcare and the workplace. In both of these settings, the focus on individual and biological as opposed to social definitions of health has been found to exert a significant influence.

In addition, problems with the way in which these settings are currently organized have been identified. The structure of the primary healthcare setting tends to limit the effectiveness of health promotion in responding to social inequalities including gender. Whilst individual health professionals may be committed to working with issues of poverty and inequality, their efforts are often constrained by the increasingly competitive environment of the NHS as well as by the channelling of health promotion resources through GPs towards disease-based targets.

The workplace offers an attractive setting for the development of social models of health promotion, but workplace initiatives can themselves reinforce the conventional individualistic bias by focusing on lifestyles and behaviours at the expense of environmental and structural problems. Yet a broad and dynamic response to work-related health needs is increasingly important given the changing nature of employment and the complex relationships between health and work. Community-based settings, including some primary care practices, are suitable for the development of independent multi-disciplinary occupational health services to complement those provided by employers. However, for such measures to be effective in addressing women's needs they need to be underpinned by a commitment to addressing social inequalities and making gender an explicit focus in the planning and delivery of health promotion.

Acknowledgements

The primary healthcare project was funded by the South West Regional Health Authority Research and Development Directorate. The workplace health promotion project was a joint initiative between the University of the West of England, Bristol and Bristol Area Specialist Health Promotion Service, funded by Avon Health Authority. The research could not have been completed without Zoe Cockshott, the researcher on the project. The project was advised by Linda Ewles, Jennie Naidoo, Judy Orme and Gill Velleman and by Lesley Doyal who also made extremely valuable comments on an earlier draft of this chapter. I am grateful to Jenny Dafforn and Emma Black for their help in preparing the manuscript

References

Alexy, B.B. (1991) Factors associated with participation and non-participation in a workplace wellness centre. *Research in Nursing and Health*, 14: 33–40.

Arber, S. (1996) Researching older women's health. In N. Daykin and L. Lloyd (eds) *Researching Women, Gender and Health: Report of a Conference*. Bristol: University of the West of England (UWE).

Blackburn, C. (1993) Making poverty a practice issue. *Health and Social Care in the Community*, 1: 297–304.

Brewster, C., Mayne, L. and Tregaskis, O. (1997) Flexible working in Europe: a review of the evidence. *Management International Review*, 37 (1) Special Issue: 85–103.

Brown, P. and Scase, R. (eds) (1991) *Poor Work: Disadvantage and the Division of Labour*. Milton Keynes: Open University Press.

Charles, N. and Kerr, M. (1987) 'Just the way it is': gender and age differences in family food consumption. In M. Brannen and G. Wilson (eds) *Give and Take in Families*. London: Allen and Unwin.

Daykin, N. and Naidoo, J. (1995) Feminist critiques of health promotion. In R. Bunton, S. Nettleton and R. Burrows (eds) *The Sociology of Health Promotion: Critical Analyses of Consumption, Lifestyle and Risk*. London: Routledge.

Daykin, N., Naidoo, J. and Wilson, N. (1995) *Effective Health Promotion in Primary Health Care. A Resource for Primary Health Care Workers*. Bristol: UWE.

Dennerstein, L. (1995) Mental health, work and gender. *International Journal of Health Services*, 25 (3): 503–9.

Doyal, L. (1991) Promoting women's health. In B. Badura and I. Kickbusch (eds) *Health Promotion Research*. Copenhagen: WHO.

Doyal, L. (1995) *What Makes Women Sick? Gender and the Political Economy of Health*. Basingstoke: Macmillan.

Fingret, A. and Smith, A. (1995) *Occupational Health: A Practical Guide for Managers*. London: Routledge.

Glasgow, R.E., McCaul, K.D. and Fisher, K.J. (1993) Participation in worksite health promotion: a critique of the literature and recommendations for future practice. *Health Education Quarterly*, 20 (3): 391–408.

Graham, H. (1984) *Women, Health and the Family*. Brighton: Harvester Wheatsheaf.

Graham, H. (1987) Women's smoking and family health. *Social Science and Medicine*, 25 (1): 47–56.

Graham, H. (1993) *Hardship and Health in Women's Lives*. London: Harvester Wheatsheaf.

Health Education Authority (1993) *Health Promotion in the Workplace: A Summary*. London: HEA.

Health Education Authority (1995) *Health and Lifestyle Survey of the UK Population, Part 1*. HEA: London.

Johnson, J. and Christie, D. (1995) Statutory right of access to occupational health services, Part 1. *Occupational Health*, 47 (1): 15–16.

Kjaerheim, K. and Anderson, A. (1994) Cancer incidence among waitresses in Norway. *Cancer Causes and Control*, 5: 31–6.

Leigh, J.P. and Jiang, W.Y. (1993) Liver cirrhosis deaths within occupations and industries in the California occupational mortality study. *Addiction*, 8 (6): 767–79.

Lovato, C.Y. and Green, L.W. (1990) Maintaining employee participation in workplace health promotion programmes. *Health Education Quarterly*, 19 (1): 73–88.

Lucas, J. (1995) Key ethical issues in occupational health practice. *Occupational Health*, June: 240–3.

Marsh, A. and McKay, S. (1994) *Poor Smokers*. London: Policy Studies Institute.

Messing, K., Dumais, L. and 'Romito, P. (1993) Prostitutes and chimney sweeps both have problems: towards a full integration of both sexes in the study of occupational health. *Social Science and Medicine*, 36 (1): 47–55.

Miles, A. (1991) *Women, Health and Medicine*. Milton Keynes: Open University Press.

Millar, J. (1996) Women, poverty and social security. In C. Hallett (ed.) *Women and Social Policy: An Introduction*. London: Prentice-Hall / Harvester Wheatsheaf.

Oakley, A. (1989) Smoking in pregnancy: smoke screen or risk factor? Towards a materialist analysis. *Sociology of Health and Illness*, 11: 311–55.

Organisation for Economic Co-operation and Development (1993) *Women, Work and Health: Synthesis Report of a Panel of Experts*. Paris: OECD.

Payne, S. (1991) *Women, Health and Poverty*. Hemel Hempstead: Harvester Wheatsheaf.

Pickvance, S. (1996) Towards multidisciplinary prevention services. *Occupational Health Review*, September/October: 27–32.

Russell, J. (1996) *A review of health promotion in primary care: from the GP health promotion contract to promoting health with local communities*. London: Greater London Association of Community Health Councils.

Sanders, D. (1993) *Workplace Health Promotion: A Review of the Literature*. Oxford: Oxford Regional Health Authority.

Seigel, M. (1993) Involuntary smoking in the restaurant workplace: a review of employee exposure and health effects. *Journal of the American Medical Association*, 270 (4): 490–3.

Thomson, R. and Holland, J. (1994) Young women and safer (hetero) sex: context, constraints and strategies. In S. Wilkinson and C. Kitzinger (eds) *Women and Health: Feminist Perspectives*. London: Taylor and Francis.

Watterson, A. (1986) Occupational health and illness: the politics of hazard education. In S. Rodmell and A. Watt (eds) *The Politics of Health Education*. London: Routledge and Kegan Paul.

Webb, T., Schilling, R., Jacobson, B. and Babb, P. (1988) *Health at Work? A Report on Health Promotion in the Workplace. Research Report No. 22*. London: Health Education Authority.

Wilson, M.G. (1990) Factors associated with issues related to and suggestions for increasing participation in workplace health promotion programmes. *Health Values*, 14 (4): 29–36.

Wilton, T. (1994) Feminism and the erotics of health promotion. In L. Doyal, J. Naidoo and T. Wilton (eds) *Women and AIDS: Setting a Feminist Agenda*. London: Taylor and Francis.

Wilton, T. (1997) *En Gendering AIDS: Deconstructing Sex, Text, Epidemic*. London: Sage.

14

•

Women and collective general practice: the Hoxton experience

•

Rosa Benato, Alison Clarke, Victoria Holt and Victoria Lack

Introduction

In the 1970s and 80s many women's health projects were established outside the mainstream of the NHS, some of them working as collectives. A significant number of these eventually secured statutory funding and became partially or wholly integrated into the mainstream (Foster 1989). Others remained outside the system, relying on the personal commitment of those involved to continue. Meanwhile, other women, and some men, tried to change the system from the inside, by setting up collective general practices, using the secure NHS funding of General Medical Services to provide democratic healthcare for a local population (Eisner and Wright 1984). Relatively few of these initiatives have survived into the 1990s but the Hoxton Health Collective in the East End of London is one of the exceptions.

The structure of general practice

A general practice is run as a small business, as part of the NHS, with the GP having independent contractor status. A doctor applies for a 'list' of patients and, once appointed by the health authority, employs the staff necessary to run the business and provide the services s/he feels able to offer. This is done within the constraints of both statutory regulations and health authority staff reimbursement limits. Sources of income include a fixed sum or 'capitation fee' per patient per year and individual payments for particular services such as the provision of contraception, as well as special deprivation payments to cope with the greater medical need in some areas. Rent and rates are fully reimbursed and GPs can also apply for a proportion of staff and computer costs.

In a larger practice, there may be a number of GPs, a practice manager, and one or more nurses as well as administrative and reception staff. Pay varies enormously. Though health authorities have introduced more stringent rules to promote fair employment practices, many administrative and reception workers are on low rates of pay and work part-time. Nurses have their own pay scale, varying according to experience and qualifications and, along with the rest of the staff, are usually managed by and answerable to the practice manager and/or the GPs directly. Pay for GPs varies hugely around the country, with the intended net remuneration being around £45,000 at present. Some GPs make more but many make less, particularly those in inner-city areas.

What is a collective general practice?

A collective general practice is exactly that: a practice which runs to collective principles, the primary principle being that of equality. Pay, power and responsibility, the three fundamental aspects of working life, are shared in Hoxton. This is achieved by paying an equal hourly rate to every person working in the practice, including the doctors and regardless of the number of hours worked. The practice is run by the collective as a whole, with routine decision making as well as strategic planning taking place in a weekly meeting at which all 'full' members of the collective are present. (Full collective members are those who work at least 18 hours per week.) All members of staff are responsible for their particular areas of work but are at all times accountable to the collective.

We aim to ensure a good quality of life for everyone by offering good terms and conditions. These are available to all members of staff and include childcare contributions, generous maternity and co-parenting leave as well as flexibility of working hours (as far as possible). A 36-hour week for everyone is intended and often achieved, depending on the workload.

How did HHC develop?

One doctor, inspired by other collectives in London and Sheffield, wanted to establish a similar general practice and therefore applied for a list in the traditional way. The practice in question was in a deprived, inner-city area on the borders of Hackney and Islington, in Shoreditch. Another collective in London, Leyton Green Neighbourhood Health Service, helped the doctor to interview and recruit two co-workers and assisted in setting up essential collective structures as well as providing much-needed support and advice. The new practice, Hoxton Health Collective, then started practising in 1987 from one small consulting room with a waiting area (Knight 1997).

The list had been inherited from a retiring GP who had had a long-standing relationship with many of the patients and an early priority was to sort the medical records so that they were clinically useful and could be handed to patients. Other early initiatives included setting up women's health clinics and counselling. The list rapidly increased in size and the practice soon found that it was necessary to move to larger premises, namely a converted three-bedroom council flat. This move enabled the practice to provide a wide range of services for a relatively small list. However, as the team expanded, more space was inevitably required and in 1997 Hoxton Health Collective moved into purpose-built premises, financed under the Private Finance Initiative, and developed in collaboration with the health authority and other small practices who work in separate surgeries in the same building. There are now 3000 patients who are a diverse mix including white working-class East Enders, Turkish and Kurdish refugees, West Africans, North African refugees, middle-class professionals and university and nursing students. Due to a visibly lesbian and gay friendly image we have large numbers of lesbian and gay patients.

The current team consists of two reception/admin. workers, one practice nurse, a women's health worker, a psychotherapist, two GPs and an administrator. Associate collective members include a finance worker, a cleaner and a sessional receptionist. The practice also works closely with the primary healthcare team members, such as the attached district nurse and health visitor.

How does a collective benefit women workers?

In the NHS where the vast majority of workers are women, most managerial and senior clinical positions are occupied by men (Doyal 1993). The hierarchy of the NHS therefore mimics the world outside the hospital: the traditional figure in authority is the male doctor who gives orders to and is assisted by the subservient female nurse. Indeed, men can be deterred from entering a profession such as nursing because it is defined as women's work and somehow inferior.

In a conventional general practice, this hierarchy is often echoed on a smaller scale. Cleaners, reception staff, nurses and other 'auxiliary' clinical staff are usually women who are employed by and receive orders from GPs, the majority of whom are men. Indeed, some GPs in traditional practices have been resistant to the employment of men in nursing and administrative posts, whilst others have required highly trained female nurses to perform such menial tasks as cleaning out their medical bags or providing tea and sandwiches.

The women at the lower end of the hierarchy are not the only losers in such a system. Women in positions of authority, such as female GPs and practice managers (as well as some men) may feel uncomfortable with the rigid hierarchical structure and with the power that accompanies their jobs. Relaxed social conversation is impeded by the imbalance of power and the awkward feelings this can provoke. Furthermore, GPs are not trained to be managers and are unlikely to have the skills necessary to provide good working conditions for their staff, however well-intentioned they may be.

A collective general practice strives to overcome these traditional barriers but it can be difficult to remove patterns of subservience which reflect wider social values and are reinforced during professional training. Doctors are encouraged to take the lead and make decisions while nurses learn to suggest things but never to make definitive statements (Melia 1987). By contrast, collective members are encouraged to communicate openly with each other, regardless of gender or job title.

In theory at least, the power in a collective general practice is equally distributed. This means that everyone has the authority and also the responsibility to contribute to the general running of the practice and to initiate new ideas while still being autonomous in their own area of expertise (Williams 1996). The female receptionist or nurse is not too intimidated to question the doctor and the female GP is enabled to ask advice from other members of the team in an atmosphere that fosters mutual respect. Thus equality facilitates communication for the benefit of both workers and patients.

Communication is formalized at a weekly collective meeting where practice business is discussed alongside clinical and social problems of patients as well as longer term projects. The meetings are chaired by a different collective member each week and everyone has an equal responsibility to take a full part. This open communication both in meetings and elsewhere in the practice ensures a mutual awareness of each other's skill and competence and workers can develop their abilities in the direction which is most beneficial to them and the practice. The atmosphere enables people to demonstrate what they can do well but also to state when they are unhappy with a work situation without fear of reprisal.

A nurse may be able to extend her role, for example, in a way that would help the practice without being concerned that she is intruding on traditionally medical spheres. A reception worker can ask for help with administrative work from other collective members without worrying that they will feel it is demeaning. This free communication and balance of power helps women workers in particular. On the one hand it gives greater freedom to those who have been socialized into silent acceptance. On the other, it helps women in positions of authority who may feel uneasy about abusing their power and are therefore deterred from taking a full part in the running of the practice.

The position of women's health workers provides an important illustration of some of these processes in operation. Over a period of years the various postholders have been helped by the collective to develop the role to its fullest potential. This development has been seen not as a threat to the power of doctors but as a major benefit for patients. In earlier collectives posts of this kind were held by women with a range of qualifications who learned the appropriate clinical skills from the nurses and doctors they were working with. New legislation in the 1990s (especially the 'new contract' for GPs) has meant that broadly based recruitment of this kind is no longer possible. All the women's health workers at Hoxton have been nurses and all have been committed to improving the health of women locally, to developing the relevant skills and to campaigning on women's issues in a broader context.

The current women's health worker is the main provider of services for 'well women' at Hoxton. Women patients have direct access to her for contraception, fertility advice, sexual health concerns, menstrual problems, body image issues, pre- and post-termination counselling and support around the menopause. The women's health worker is also responsible for the administration of the national cancer screening programmes and provides cervical cytology for all eligible women, as well as advising on breast awareness. These facilities are provided within the context of more general health promotion services. Combating coronary heart disease in women is an additional priority, still neglected in many practices (Freedman and Maine 1993; and see also Sharp, this volume) with the women's health worker focusing more on primary prevention, whereas it is the doctors and the practice nurse who are active in implementing secondary prevention measures. Each postholder has brought her individual expertise, skills and concerns and has developed the post in her own particular way, with the encouragement of the collective which has ultimately benefited from these endeavours.

On a very practical point, the collective enables women to work and to work effectively through generous terms and conditions. Because everyone is paid at a modest rate, the money saved from paying very high salaries at the top end of the traditional hierarchy can be used to improve life for all workers. Childcare costs are met by the collective and maternity and co-parenting leave are generous. Leave is also allowed for caring for a sick relative or partner; work traditionally done mostly by women without pay. Equal pension contributions are also paid by the collective. Job-sharing is always considered to be an option when a job is advertised and all workers have an adequate paid sick leave entitlement, all of which are benefits not consistently provided to employees in mainstream general practice.

Working in a collective general practice has great benefits for all workers, but they are more keenly felt by women, who tend to get a poorer deal in the NHS and in employment more generally. It can be extremely refreshing (but also challenging) to work in a place where all workers are committed to equality, where equality is built into the structure of the organization and where status and gender assume much less importance in the management of professional relationships.

How does the structure benefit women patients?

The higher levels of personal and professional satisfaction and enriched working lives experienced by collective members in turn enable us to provide a better service to all patients. However, we feel a special responsibility to women, and have therefore sensitized our service to meet their needs in particular. The framework we have used to achieve this is based on the principle of equality and the notion of shared responsibility between patients and ourselves. Crucially, it also reflects a clear understanding of the position women hold in society and the impact this has on their health (Doyal 1995). We are only too aware of the social, political, and economic barriers and restrictions that black and working-class women in particular experience in accessing healthcare and their greater need for services in the areas of both reproductive and mental health (Doyal 1995). Many of our patients exemplify the problems experienced by women with few resources and many burdens to carry. The reforms we have carried out in our practice are designed to remove some of these obstacles and help women promote their own health in ways of their own choosing.

Our priorities are the promotion of individual participation in health decisions, the facilitation of informed choices, and the development of relationships which reflect partnership and mutual respect. In order to achieve these we aim to provide services and support for all our patients that treat them in non-judgemental ways. We try to create a safe atmosphere and an environment where disclosures can be made which women may be reluctant to reveal in more conventional practices. A patient recently wrote thanking us for our 'attitude-free approach'. She went on to say, 'It can be unpleasant and difficult to get proper medical advice when you're in a relationship with another woman, and people can also make it difficult if you then fall for a man. I've appreciated the ease and naturalness with which I've always been treated at Hoxton Health Collective.'

Our equal opportunities policy works towards combating discrimination and recognizing social diversity, both in the recruitment of workers to the collective, and in the provision of services and subsequent access to them. We have been at the forefront of making lesbians' healthcare needs more visible and are very aware of the heterosexist assumptions inherent in many of their previous experiences of medical care (*Health Care for Women International* 1992; see also Wilton, this volume). We recognize the need to examine our own attitudes and prejudices, and collective meetings provide a forum to address these very difficult issues.

Partly due to the autonomous and independent practice of workers within the collective, a wide range of services is offered. Patients are able to choose between a male and female doctor. They may decide not see a doctor at all, but to refer themselves to the practice nurse, the women's health worker, or the counsellor. Appointments are varied in duration, timing and availability, and the women's health worker has appointments alongside the baby clinic to make things easier for mothers with small children.

Relationships between patients and workers reflect the same principles as those between the workers. All formal hierarchies are removed, although it is sometimes a struggle. Titles are discouraged and everyone uses first names as much as possible. Of course some patients find their lifelong deference to doctors difficult to change, but we believe that this dropping of titles is an important step in promoting and emphasizing equality and mutual respect. Communication is made more effective as a result of these open relationships, and aids appropriate and sensitive interactions with the patients. A woman who had survived incest and then incarceration in long-stay psychiatric hospitals registered at this practice with a deep mistrust of the medical system. When she moved on to better housing and had to leave the list she thanked us for 'the care and friendship that all of you showed me without judgement or question'.

In order to give our patients more power we encourage them to read their medical notes. Women seem to take advantage of this opportunity more often than men, initially with uncertainty but over time with confidence and an air of normality. Indeed, the option to do this is frequently quoted as a reason for not wanting to register elsewhere once they have moved away. We believe that encouraging patients to take responsibility is important in enabling them to increase the power they have over decisions concerning their health whether we as health workers agree with them or not. At first we were rather taken aback by one patient's letter in which she stated clearly that she actively chose not to have a cervical smear. However, she closed by commenting that 'this is not a criticism of your practice, rather a compliment that you have given me the guts to stand up and ask about something I have always been very unhappy about', which caused us, on reflection, to feel glad that she had been able to challenge both us and the screening system.

This access to personal medical records helps to demystify medicine, and reminds us to use language which is appropriate, easily understood, and legible. Having knowledge of what is written in their notes also encourages patients to ask questions for which we aim to provide full evidence-based information, and accurate explanations. This interest and involvement helps patients to participate more actively in decisions concerning their health and their treatments. Locum nurses working in the practice often comment on how well informed the patients are when they attend for appointments: 'they seem to know what they are coming for'.

Practice policies and protocols are accurately researched and referenced, used by all clinical workers and designed to promote choice and control for the patient and autonomy for the health worker. This is particularly true of the women's health protocols, one of which has been developed for dealing with menopause concerns. The general principles guiding this protocol are the need to support women to take control by sharing information and explanation; not to define menopause as a disease and to avoid negative language; to recognize that the hormonal system is very sensitive to other factors such as diet, exercise, and stress levels, which are often very high for women especially in the menopausal age group. Treatment for the relief of 'symptoms' is discussed on an individual basis, and includes self-help ideas and remedies. This protocol is supported by a separate hormone replacement therapy protocol.

Within the collective there is a wide and varied interest in issues pertaining to women's health, and workers are supported in their campaigning activities in local and national organizations such as London Lesbians in Health Care, the National Abortion Campaign and the local Maternity Services Liaison Committee. This has created a large network of contacts which can then be used to help women patients with particular problems or interests. The collective also provides a comprehensive selection of books and leaflets on women's health and gender issues for loan, or for reading in the waiting room. Collaboration between workers in the practice has resulted in successful menopause and women's assertiveness groups.

We are certainly not claiming that the particular way we choose to provide a general practice service is the only way of empowering women to have more control over their lives. Many feminist doctors and nurses are working in more traditional settings, and providing excellent standards of care to their patients. But what we hope to do is to provide one example of possible alternatives to a system that has rarely been designed with the needs of the majority of its patients – women – in mind.

Limitations of collective general practice

Working as a collective general practice has significant limitations, some obvious and some less immediately apparent. There are inevitable power imbalances which need to be acknowledged and discussed but which can never be entirely overcome, despite decades of radical health initiatives or, more recently, patients' charters. The collective is constantly relating with the 'outside world' where doctors' social and professional status is elevated. The majority of patients hold doctors in high regard and are somewhat awe-struck. Clearly, we cannot expect them instantly to understand our politics and feel 'equal'. They may therefore be impatient and even rude with desk workers, whilst continuing to treat the doctors with great respect and even reverence.

Outside agencies phoning into the practice often fail to entrust desk workers with information, treating them as incapable of taking a message or observing patient confidentiality and insisting on speaking to a doctor in person, even if clinically unnecessary. Other doctors can be the worst offenders and this serves repeatedly to undermine administrative workers. In addition, replies to referral letters written by the practice nurse or women's health worker are invariably addressed to the doctors. Furthermore, some outsiders assume that the male doctor of the team is in overall charge of the practice.

The financial value placed on a piece of work can be experienced as reflective of the true worth of that job. The health authority's reimbursement of 'ancillary staff' pay is inevitably done in accordance with national guidelines for different professions, typically rewarding the traditionally low status 'women's work' of reception very poorly. Thus the collective receives approximately twice as much money towards practice nurses' pay as they receive for reception workers. This money is then redistributed so that everyone earns the same hourly rate. However, this does not always deal with the associated feelings of those being 'subsidized' and the result may feel like benevolence rather than just rewards.

A further power imbalance is derived from the fact that some workers, especially doctors, have the potential for significantly increasing their income by moving on to a better paid job elsewhere. Administrative workers, on the other hand, may feel trapped by their relatively high pay which might be hard to match outside the collective, depending on their other qualifications. Doctors also have the potential to earn additional money outside the collective at a higher rate of pay. Previous collective practices, and ours initially, made it a rule that no one could work elsewhere, in order to overcome this inequality. However, once part-time contracts were introduced for those who chose them this measure of control of life outside the practice became untenable. The practice cannot exist in a vacuum and when we are employing locum doctors we have to comply with the norms of the medical world. Originally, the collective paid locum doctors at the collective rate until it became impossible to recruit holiday cover, since when we have had to pay the going British Medical Association rate.

Despite some radical measures to share workload, the doctors' working hours can frequently exceed those of other workers. This mitigates against full equality of pay, responsibility and stress. Obviously, a third doctor would solve this problem, but with a nationwide recruitment crisis this can seem a fantastical solution. The difficulty of recruiting a new doctor further heightens the collective's dependency on the doctors' personal commitment to the enterprise, yet the feeling that doctors are almost irreplaceable is good for no one's mental health. The burden of on-call compounds this problem but does have a solution in sight; our success in organizing local GPs to collaborate on an out-of-hours cooperative is due in part at least to our own experience of the benefits of working cooperatively.

Within any team of workers tensions are bound to arise, however similar the political philosophies and ideals of the team members. The causes can include unresolved differences of opinion, personal clashes or re-enactment of old hierarchical battles. For several years we spent one hour each fortnight with a group counsellor trying to overcome some of these difficulties and communication and understanding did improve. Other ways of resolving differences include less formal one-to-one or collective discussions, a formal collective grievance procedure or use of a mediator. However, it is important to recognize that in some extreme cases the only option remaining may be for an individual to leave so that the collective can survive.

Despite our ideals of power-sharing with patients many factors mitigate against the achievement of this. The often-quoted problem of time pressure in general practice inevitably limits the possibilities for information sharing. Moreover, some patients are reluctant to take responsibility for their health for a multitude of reasons. Most importantly, some of our patients are so vulnerable or so psychologically vulnerable due to past oppressions that they may only be able to relate to a fairly paternalistic style of care. Some will be so chronically disempowered by their experiences of deprivation, or even torture, that the process of sharing power will take decades to evolve. Thus a woman patient who has grown up in poverty in Hoxton, experiencing repeated male domestic and sexual violence, may not feel able to make active choices for herself about the use of contraception.

Collective working as an evolving process

Working in a collective general practice is a constantly evolving process. Although there are some traditions and 'rules' that have continued since its inception, much has also changed at Hoxton. Important pressures for change have included the arrival of new collective members questioning the status quo and the lessons learned from ongoing relationships with patients. The collective way of working, with its meetings where all can contribute and decisions are mostly reached by consensus, does allow for change. However, this has only been achievable by setting clear boundaries with patients. This process has been difficult but essential to our own mental health. At times it had seemed that in trying to be a caring practice we allowed patients an endless monopoly on our time, which prevented us from finding uninterrupted space and time to deal with the enormous administrative burden of general practice. Obviously, genuine emergency situations still have to intrude on our 'closed' periods but we have had to make positive choices to limit our availability. As well as decreasing our own stress levels this has been beneficial for patients. Our original idea that collective working necessitated fulfilling every patient request for time and attention was in reality patronizing and counter to fostering patients' independence and self-reliance.

The future

Like all general practices the collective is constantly forced to adapt to the seemingly endless changes to the 'system' of the NHS. Keeping up to date with advances in healthcare practice, although daunting, can seem minor compared to keeping abreast of NHS reorganization. The purchaser/provider split has been the source of much frustration; seeing the incredible wastage of money on managerial expenses, the pump-priming of fundholding practices and the decision of one of our local health authorities to refuse to allow referrals of patients to their most local hospital (St Bartholomew's) is all very disheartening and disempowering. In addition, increasing financial crisis is threatening the future of many local innovative health projects, several of which have provided support and services in a community setting, often prioritizing marginalized women.

We have yet to be involved in locality commissioning and are suspicious of the workload involved and uncertain whether doctors are really best placed to be deciding how to ration secondary care across a locality. It is unlikely that GPs will have the inclination or knowledge to prioritize women's services unless their needs are moved much higher up the national agenda. Moreover, the unformed but widely touted notion of a 'primary care-led NHS' seems to put GPs forward as leaders in community health, running the risk that more workers rather than fewer will be ineffectively managed by a professional group ill-equipped for the task.

Conversely, the increasing political support for the provision of salaried GP posts provides us with a dilemma. On the one hand, reorganizing primary care so that all staff are salaried professionals would be an improvement on the present arrangement of GPs as employers. On the other, it may be more difficult to organize a collective within such a system, compared with the freedom we are currently able to exercise as independent contractors.

The last two decades have been marked by the energy and commitment with which women have demanded information about and control over their own bodies. Informed in part by these politics the collective has tried to respond to their demands. This has produced benefits of increased autonomy and choices for women patients (as well as for women workers). In turn these benefits have inevitably been extended to our male patients, making the practice more sensitive to gender issues in particular and to the broader issues of equity and justice for all those involved in using and providing healthcare.

References

Doyal, L. (1985) Women and the National Health Service: the carers and the careless. In E. Lewin and V. Oleson (eds) *Women, Health and Healing: Toward a New Perspective*. London: Tavistock.

Doyal, L. (1993) Changing medicine? Gender and the politics of health care. In J. Gabe, D. Kellahar and G. Williams (eds) *Challenging Medicine*. London: Tavistock.

Doyal, L. (1995) *What Makes Women Sick: Gender and the Political Economy of Health*. London: Macmillan.

Eisner, M. and Wright, M. (1984) A feminist approach to general practice. In C. Webb (ed.) *Feminist Practices in Women's Health Care.* Chichester: John Wiley.

Foster, P. (1989) Improving the doctor/patient relationship: a feminist perspective. *Journal of Social Policy,* 18 (3): 337–61.

Freedman, E. and Maine, D. (1993) Women's mortality: a legacy of neglect. In M. Koblinsky, J. Timyan and J. Gay (eds) *The Health of Women: A Global Perspective.* Boulder, CO: Westview Press.

Health Care for Women International (1992) Special Issue on Lesbian Health: What Are The Issues? 13 (2), April–June.

Knight, J. (1997) Collective responsibility. *Guardian,* 22 January.

Melia, K. (1987) *Learning and Working: The Occupational Socialisation of Nurses.* London: Tavistock.

Williams, K. (1996) Equal partners, better care. *Nursing Standard,* 11 (4): 15.

15

•

Involving women as consumers: the Oxfordshire health strategy

•

Sian Griffiths and Jean Bradlow

Introduction

This chapter does not set out to be an exemplar on how to consult women within the NHS. Rather, it is a reflection on how one district health authority has grappled with its changing role and embraced the need to consult with the population for whose health it is responsible. As the consultation process has developed, it has been refined to take account of the views of the public, and in this chapter we will focus on women and their health.

First steps

In the summer of 1994 Oxfordshire Health Authority published its health strategy for the next five years. This was the first time the authority had attempted to involve the public in debate about the strategic direction of its services. The process was very much one of trial and error, and the learning process has provided insight into better ways of involving the population in decisions about their health services.

The health strategy was written by members of the public health and commissioning directorates, and prepared for publication by a journalist. The aim was to provide 'signposts' rather than a 'route map' for the direction of services over the next five years. The structure of the strategy was a series of chapters covering care groups (including women) and clinical conditions (which included breast cancer). The content of each chapter was based on the three questions:

- Where are we now?
- Where do we want to be?
- How should we get there?

Each chapter focused on the broad spectrum of healthcare from health promotion through prevention, treatment, rehabilitation and care. This framework was designed to ensure the use of a holistic approach to the health issues addressed. The chapters on clinical conditions were all based on available evidence of clinically effective practice. Where topics linked across the strategy between other chapters – women and mental health for example – these were cross-referenced in both chapters.

Where appropriate, clinicians, patients and carers were involved in drafting the chapters. However, this consultation process was patchy for a variety of reasons, reflecting the existing development of ideas and the degree of public and professional involvement with the health authority. The stroke strategy, for example, was the product of a working group across the county which had been working together for a considerable time, whereas the men's strategy was written by a registrar in public health as no group existed at the time. The chapter on women's health was drafted by the commissioning manager, with support from personnel in public health, but was commented on extensively both prior to and during the consultation process by clinicians, the community health council (CHC) and a number of women's groups.

The women's strategy

The women's strategy was written with the help of a strategy group with representation from clinicians, general practitioners, midwives, community nurses, local authorities and the CHC. It was underpinned by a set of principles including the need for all services to be responsive to the needs of women and the importance of using good research evidence on the effectiveness of procedures in both the planning process and in service delivery. The strategy recognized certain key issues: that women have specific health needs in addition to the general ones they share with men; that as a group they are high users of both primary and secondary care services; and that women from different cultures have particular needs which need to be taken into account when planning healthcare.

The 'Where are we now?' section of the strategy concentrated on the demography of women in the county, their health status, their use of health services and the services available to them. As with all exercises of this kind, information on gender differences was not always easily available. However, data from a variety of sources proved useful: population statistics, the public health common data set with its disease-specific death rates and a range of research findings on referral patterns. Health authority information systems also provided data on the current use of services by women. In addition, Oxfordshire was fortunate in having information from a health and lifestyles survey, which has been repeated every three years, which gave useful information on self-reported health status and gender-specific information on lifestyle (Wright *et al.* 1992).

The overall picture showed approximately 230,000 women over the age of 14 living in the county. This number was predicted to increase by 4 per cent over the next five years. The largest increases were predicted in the 40–54 year old age group (9.7 per cent increase) and the over 85s (16.3 per cent increase). The National Morbidity Survey (Royal College of General Practitioners 1990) gave us national information on rates of general practice consultations; women being seen on average 4 times a year in the 1980–1 survey in comparison to men who were seen on average 2.7 times. Local research on referrals from general practice to hospital outpatient departments showed that women were more likely than men to be referred to a specialist in ophthalmology, dermatology, rheumatology and plastic surgery (Bradlow *et al.* 1992).

Overall, females were more likely to be referred than males in all but the youngest and oldest age groups. Between the ages of 25 and 54 women were almost twice as likely to be referred to hospital as men. Women accounted for 56.7 per cent of all hospital admissions and for 65 per cent of joint replacements, 80 per cent of orthopaedic admissions and 71 per cent of rheumatology admissions. Conversely, women accounted for only 30 per cent of referrals for cardiac surgery.

The health and lifestyle survey carried out on a sample of 3500 Oxfordshire residents between the ages of 18 and 64 suggested that women were less likely than men to drink more than the recommended number of units of alcohol per week, but that smoking in young women had increased from 33 per cent to 38 per cent, making them more likely to be smokers than any other group (Wright *et al.* 1992). Surprisingly perhaps, 27 per cent of women reported long-standing illness or disability compared to 31 per cent of men. Overall, 87 per cent of women and 88 per cent of men reported their health to be good, very good or excellent. Whilst it was recognized that these statistics came from a relatively small sample they provided a useful guide, particularly in relation to young women smokers.

Having described the health status of the county and its current patterns of healthcare, questions about quality and future direction were addressed. National guidelines and policy documents including *Changing Childbirth* and the *Health of the Nation* strategy formed the foundation for 'Where do we want to get to?' Recommendations for clinically effective practice were also incorporated in the strategy. An intention was flagged for example to reduce the numbers of women under 40 receiving a dilatation and curettage (D and C) because there was no evidence that having this procedure achieved the reduction in heavy menstrual bleeding which was usually its desired outcome (Coulter *et al.* 1993). Another recommendation sought to transfer appropriate services to primary care by encouraging women to request straightforward contraceptive advice from their GP rather than from family planning clinics, thus allowing the family planning service to concentrate on developing targeted services for young people.

The section on 'How do we get there?' was a framework for implementation designed to show how developments could be achieved and by when. Resource constraints meant that they could only be undertaken either by reconfiguration of existing services or by setting priorities for the allocation of resources. Consultation with women using the services was an important part of determining these priorities.

Raising awareness and implementing the consultation process

The health strategy was distributed to a wide range of public bodies – local councils, the CHC and voluntary organizations including a number of women's groups. It was sent to all GPs and hospital staff and was also made available in public places, such as libraries. Brief summaries of all the chapters were produced to encourage general comment as it was recognized that many people would not wish to plough through detailed documents. The consultation process included:

- specific seminars on individual chapters;
- public meetings in different communities;
- consultation sessions with different interested groups;
- the receipt of written comments.

Though there was no gender-specific consultation process, two meetings on women's health were held by the health authority. The first was a small seminar on the implementation of the breast cancer strategy where consumers were represented by the CHC and by a patient who had received treatment. The main concerns expressed were not about the quality of clinical care but about communication and clinic organization. There was a feeling that providers focused too much on the medical issues with insufficient consideration given to the sensitivity of care. Long waiting times, failure to let women know what was going on and lack of emotional/psychological support were all mentioned as areas which needed to be addressed.

The second seminar examined the women's strategy more broadly, with representatives from the CHC, clinicians, GPs and hospital specialists, midwives and nurses based both in hospital and the community and representatives from the city council. This group suggested that more attention should be paid to smoking, particularly in young and pregnant women, mental health services including provision for those with eating disorders and counselling, and information for GPs relating to gynaecological services. The group also suggested wider consultation on the strategy through the circulation of the strategy leaflet, canvassing of healthcare professionals caring for women and the involvement of existing groups.

Table 15.1   Key issues from consultation

Service	Comment
Maternity	The strategy should be wider than *Changing Childbirth*
	Breast feeding should be given a higher profile
	Clear and consistent criteria are required for deciding on home or community hospital delivery
Gynaecology services	Need for specialist uro-gynaecology services
	GPs need better information on the availability and appropriate use of services, particularly the organization of specialist services
Mental health services	Better access needed to services for eating disorders
	Better information needed for women and health professionals on the availability of counselling
	Women with particular needs should have specially tailored service (e.g. women from ethnic minorities, women with disabilities and homeless women)
General issues	Outpatient departments need to be much more sensitive to the needs of women with dependants
	Better access to services is required, particularly for women in rural areas with poor public transport

One of the main conclusions of the group was that if we were to consult with the public we had to use appropriate routes and give clear comprehensible messages. Hence the strategy was further discussed at a variety of meetings which included the women's subcommittee of Oxford City Council, the providers of family planning services, the Maternity Strategy Implementation Group, Women in Medicine, the women's centre at the local hospital and some Women's Institute branches. In addition to these meetings the health authority received written comments.

Overall, consultation on the strategy highlighted significant areas of omission. Despite good intentions it was (rightly) criticized for not presenting a holistic approach and for not taking account of the needs of women as carers or of women in rural areas. In particular, the strategy was narrowly focused on the needs of women for individual services rather than more general issues, such as providing crèches in outpatient departments, sensitivity to school times for women outpatients and the availability of women doctors, particularly for patients from ethnic minorities.

Through the consultation process it became apparent that one of the greatest perceived deficiencies across all areas was lack of clear, consistent information. If the authority was to promote informed choice it had to improve the information on which both individual and collective decisions could be reached. Other key issues which were highlighted by the consultation process are included in Table 15.1.

The first year of the strategy represented the first attempt to obtain the views of women in the county about the health issues which concerned them. It was recognized that the process was not participative enough and had not been coordinated with the CHC. Although the consultation was welcomed by some, others were cynical, particularly since the resources involved were so limited. This did not deter the health authority from its commitment to making the strategy an iterative process, but this has not always been an easy task.

In the second round of the consultative process comments came mainly from health and social care professionals, who raised specific points about the quality of some services, such as cervical screening. The lack of direct input from the public was disappointing but probably reflected the nature of the consultation process itself. No leaflets were made available for the second year and much of the health authority's energy had been absorbed by internal reorganization. On the other hand, earlier failure to involve the CHC was redressed in the second year, and the CHC report on *Women's Perceptions of Maternity Care in Oxfordshire* (CHC Women's Group 1996) was helpful in raising issues about women's perceptions of the services they receive and the relationship of these to the objectives of *Changing Childbirth*.

The majority of women felt there were many good aspects of maternity care, but specific areas were highlighted for improvement, including the need for clearer and more consistent information as well as much more sensitivity to women's preferences and desires. Continuity of care and well worked up birth plans were also cited as aspirations that had not yet been achieved. These results highlighted the value of seeking comments directly from women and emphasized the gap between the rhetoric and reality of service provision. Professionals might well believe that information exists but if pregnant women say they are not getting it or that they are not being listened to then this disparity needs addressing.

The CHC Maternity Services Report also highlighted the need to develop networks which provide ongoing public involvement. This was reflected in the process devised for the third update of the health strategy which is formally 'owned' by the county and all five district councils. Exploration of the links between elected members and their constituents suggested avenues for soliciting views on the strategic plans of the authority alongside more formal links with women's groups. The Women's Institutes across the county are now actively involved in the consultation process and have expressed particular concern about the health of older women in rural areas.

Moving ahead

The Oxfordshire strategy has been updated annually since its inception, and through this process has become a more focused and useful document. Ideas from the continuing consultation process have been instrumental in developing some important new initiatives for women including the following:

- A liaison project was set up between the gynaecology department in the largest provider in the county and general practice, to explore ways of improving the interface between primary and secondary care. This resulted in improved communications between specialists and GPs, enabled joint education between the two groups, initiated general practitioner involvement in the patient information group and led to the production of a guide for GPs referring patients to the hospital for both routine and emergency services. The CHC was a key partner in this exercise.
- The health promotion unit in the county produced a directory of counselling services for women.
- Guidelines for management of female incontinence in primary care were produced by a joint working group of GPs, hospital specialists and physiotherapists and were distributed to all primary healthcare teams.
- A uro-gynaecologist was appointed in one of the county's hospitals with responsibility for developing the continence services.
- Training was given to health visitors to improve the detection of post-natal depression and there is increased support to women in the community.

In other areas progress has been slower than anticipated. This reflects a number of obstacles, the most important of which are difficulties in reaching agreement between the different interest groups and the continuing pressures generated by lack of resources and increasing demands. Included among the aspirations constrained in this way are the following:

- development of agreed policies for ante-natal screening tests;
- improved policies for the promotion of breast feeding;
- strategies for the reduction of smoking in young women and pregnant women;
- better ways of addressing the needs of women in rural areas;
- more provision of clear and consistent information for women.

These initial experiences of consultation have continued the authority's belief that it should be part of the everyday process of planning and purchasing. In order to achieve this goal six requirements have been identified as the basis for local consultation.

- a clear consultation plan with stated aims, defined methods and timetable;
- corporate support in developing the content of the consultation as well as a clear commitment to the process;
- identification of specific groups to be consulted;
- active search for and welcoming response to input from individuals and groups;
- involvement of other agencies such as local authorities and voluntary groups in the process;

- the provision of feedback which is structured and open and is linked to specific action;
- continuity in the consultation process.

The future direction of services is now being discussed in a variety of forums whether they are concerned with a specific health issue such as breast cancer or form part of the annual work programme of the health authority. However, the early experience of turning up to village halls on wet and windy nights to discuss the health strategy with a handful of people has suggested that such an approach to consultation has limitations. It has also highlighted the need to explain clearly to those participating, the structure of the NHS and the reality of who can do what for whom.

The role of the health authority as guardian of the health of the population is not an easy one to communicate to individual women. Resources for healthcare are limited and there may be conflict between concern for 'the greater good' of the population, and the desire to support the choice of individuals. The health authority also has to make difficult choices in allocating resources and whilst the views of the local population are an important factor in determining how the health authority spends its money, these views have to be balanced against issues such as the available resources, clinical effectiveness and competing priorities across the spectrum of healthcare. The important thing is to seek and take account of the views of local women and to make the process of priority setting explicit.

Experiences from consultation on the health strategy have played their part in reshaping the planning approach in Oxfordshire Health Authority. The health authority now has a specialist team working on public involvement with an ambitious programme of work around the health strategy. In future women in the county can expect to be consulted on an ongoing basis.

References

Bradlow, J., Coulter, A. and Brooks, P. (1992) *Patterns of Referral*. Oxford: Health Services Research Unit, University of Oxford Department of Public Health and Primary Care.

CHC Women's Group (1996) *Women's Perception of Maternity Care in Oxfordshire*. Oxford: Oxfordshire Community Health Council.

Coulter, A., Klassen, A., MacKenzie, I.Z. and McPherson, K. (1993) Diagnostic dilatation and curettage: is it used appropriately? *British Medical Journal*, 306: 236–9.

Royal College of General Practitioners (1990) *Morbidity statistics from general practice – 3rd National Study, 1981–2*. London: HMSO.

Wright, L., Harwood, D. and Coulter, A. (1992) *Health and Lifestyles in the Oxford Region*. Oxford: Health Services Research Unit, University of Oxford Department of Public Health and Primary Care.

16

•

From theory to practice: the Glasgow experience

•

Sue Laughlin

Introduction

In Glasgow, there has been a localized movement actively advocating for women and their health for the past 15 years. It has had both great highs and demoralizing lows but has served as a constant reminder of the importance of promoting women's health, not only for the benefit of women themselves but for the population as a whole. None of its gains have been easily achieved. Indeed, they are often derided because the work challenges fundamental assumptions about gender relations and about the ways in which policy decisions are made and services organized.

Arguably, there has been a consistency to the work in Glasgow which runs counter to recent trends in women's health politics in the UK. The active women's health movement of the 1970s and early 1980s has now waned and appears to have made little significant impact on organizational structures or health policy (see Doyal this volume). In Glasgow the pattern has been very different. Although developments there have some roots in the women's health movement they are allied more closely to a related but different campaign concerned with creating a new public health agenda. Here the major goal is to replace the medical model with a social one as the dominant framework for healthcare and health promotion. This difference has often made the experience in Glasgow isolated and isolating but it also provides an illustration of the fact that progress is possible even in unpromising times.

The focus and activity of the work has been evolving over the years but a number of inter-related characteristics have remained central throughout:

- it has sought to link women's health with women's social role although only recently has it developed a language of gender inequality. Reproductive rights and reproductive health have formed one aspect of this focus;
- it has had a strategic perspective on the need to change existing organizations. Initially, this was implicit but it has become more explicit over the years. Funding has been sought for women's health projects or activities but this has not been the only goal of the work;
- it has sought to engage with the full range of statutory and voluntary organizations in the city and not just with the health service;
- it has had a strong community perspective;
- the struggle for change has combined action from within organizations with pressure from outside;
- it has co-existed alongside and often linked with parallel activity within a more general women's movement.

In this account, the historical development of the work will be described and discussed in order to highlight some of the ingredients which have made developments possible both within the local health authority and also in a wider multi-agency context. It highlights some of the opportunities for change and the action taken to realize their potential, some reactive, some proactive. Opportunities obviously vary from city to city and area to area but the themes and the direction of the work are readily transferable to other parts of the country. Some of the key milestones for Glasgow are summarized in Figure 16.1.

Developing the strategy

Establishing the way forward

It is now recognized that one of the main catalysts for recent work on women's health in Glasgow was the 'Women's Health Fair', held in 1983. This, together with a similar event held in Edinburgh, was a local response to the WHO 'Year of Women's Health' and highlighted the importance of celebratory events.

Women's health fairs later became common occurrences but at that time such an event was an innovation. Over 6000 women of all backgrounds attended the fair in Glasgow, many travelling considerable distances from rural Scotland to participate because of the lack of local opportunities and services. Seven issues formed the core of the fair. They were the changing role of women; the family; employment and unemployment; social factors in health; social policy; food and exercise; and fertility. Their range was indicative of a desire to extend the debate on women's health beyond a medical perspective and beyond reproduction and it is this analysis that has dominated the work described here. Concerns about access to existing facilities were also addressed by providing a drop-in well woman centre in the heart of the city in a famous art gallery.

Development of women's health in Glasgow 1982-1995		
	Community/voluntary participation	Organisational development
1982		WHO Year of Women's Health
1983	Women's Health Fair, Glasgow	
1983 awards	Local women's health fairs and groups	
1984 awards	Clydeside women's health campaign	
1985/6		Review of well woman services
1986	Model well woman clinic	
1987	Proposal for centre for women's health	
1989		Women's Action Group Strathclyde Regional Council Women's Unit
1990	HCP Women's Health Working Group	
1991	Women's Health Policy Framework	
1992	Women's Health Policy	
1993	Women's Health Policy Community Launch Glasgow Women's Health Directory	Agreement for Centre for Women's Health
1994	'Glasgow's Health, Women Count' publication (aimed at agencies, policymakers, employers)	'Purchasing for Women's Health' GDC Women's Health Policy Group
1995	Centre for Women's Health open	

Figure 16.1   Key milestones for women's health in Glasgow

The organization of the fair was notable for the range of women who participated in the working group comprising health service, social work and community education staff together with representatives from a trade union, a voluntary organization campaigning for the rights of single parents and community groups. Although instigated by staff in the Health Education Department of the local health authority (Greater Glasgow Health Board) the engagement with other agencies and groups also set the tone for future activity. At this stage, however, much of this involvement was reluctant or covert. Managers of local authority departments found it difficult to recognize either the link between their work and the promotion of health or the importance of women's health, while many health service staff and managers were bound by the medical view of women's health. These perceptions still exist and continuing debate is therefore a necessity.

Campaigning for change

The interest generated by the 'Women's Health Fair' and the concerns voiced by many of the women who attended it metamorphosed into a vocal and focused set of demands. These were then promoted by the Clydeside Women's Health Campaign which was launched very visibly in Glasgow's Council Chambers in 1984. For the next few years this became a formidable alliance with many hundreds of women involved from the health service, local authorities, trades unions, women's groups, education and voluntary organizations as well as many individuals.

Although it established a *Women's Health Charter* for the area with explicit demands, the efforts of the campaign eventually crystallized around the struggle for a Centre for Women's Health. It was intended from the outset that the activities of such an initiative should be informed by the broad range of factors which affected women's health and that it should receive mainstream funding. Such a centre, it was hoped, would then create a model for other types of provision within the health service as well as in local authorities and large voluntary organizations around the city. Although there were ten years of unsuccessful struggle to establish a Centre, the existence of the campaign made a significant contribution to raising the profile of women's health with key organizations responsible for the services, policies and resources which had such an enormous impact on their lives.

Consultation and dialogue

It is axiomatic that the likelihood of achieving any difficult change will be enhanced by the active involvement of as many people as possible. The quality of that change will also be improved by ensuring that the involvement is democratic and inclusive. Attempts to involve a large cross-section of women and men in strategies to promote the health of women have continued to be explicit in all aspects of the Glasgow work. Constant review of the form and process of campaigning has highlighted the difficulties involved in genuine consultation and participation and has led to a number of different types of initiative.

The 'Women's Health Fair' in Glasgow triggered many similar, smaller events in local communities. These were supported and facilitated by a range of professional workers and their agencies as a result of the growing recognition of the interest in women's health especially at community level. Together with the feedback from women's health groups, discussion groups with women, small-scale research and the issues raised by women participating in the Clydeside campaign, a web of ideas and informal linkages was created between organizations and local women and this was consolidated by later actions.

Legitimization

The adoption of Glasgow as one of the founding cities in the World Health Organisation's 'Healthy Cities' Project in 1988 helped to provide a more formal space for the work on women's health since it already embodied the principles of *Health For All*. A pre-existing Women's Action Group, chaired by the then Lord Provost (mayor), who was a woman, proposed that it should be re-formed as a Women's Health Working Group of the Glasgow Healthy City Project (1992). This Working Group was, and remains, a multi-sectoral group comprising representatives of the partner organizations of the 'Healthy City' Project (two local authorities: Strathclyde Regional Council, Glasgow District Council; the health authority; the Glasgow universities) and a range of voluntary organizations and community groups (see Figure 16.2).

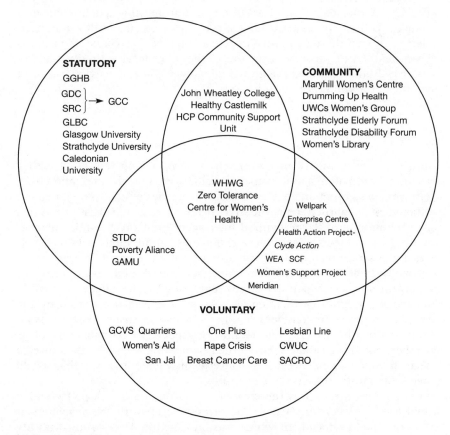

Figure 16.2 Organizations and groups in Glasgow involved in the Women's Health Working Group.

The aims of the group were to provide a forum for women to discuss health issues and to identify practical ways of establishing systems to promote the health of women. For the first time since women's health had begun to have a distinct voice in 1983, routes were opened up to take the concerns expressed into the heart of the city's organizations. The group was represented on the Steering Group of the Glasgow 'Healthy City' Project alongside senior officers and elected representatives of the partner organizations. Resources, although limited, could also be accessed via this steering group to facilitate the type of work that emerged from the Women's Health Working Group.

Also contributing to the growing acceptance of women's health concerns were parallel developments within some of the key organizations. Of particular significance was the Regional Council's *Social Strategy for the 1980s* (Strathclyde Regional Council 1980) which identified health and women's issues as two of its priority concerns. This enabled motivated politicians to lobby for the setting-up of a Women's Unit and the appointment of a Women's Officer, thereby providing a route for women's health to be considered both by the decision-making structures of that council and by its departments. An equivalent structure in the other local authority was not established until 1994 and the growth of women's health activism has been identified as a significant catalyst.

Policy development

Once established, the Women's Health Working Group was faced with a wealth of information about women's health needs and an expectation from both women's groups and professionals that change could be brought about. Although it comprised representatives from various organizations and a place within one of the recognized inter-agency initiatives within the city, its focus on women's issues and its willingness to question traditional policies and practices meant that it was also kept at arm's length by these same structures. In addition, many of the members found it difficult to convince the organizations or departments they represented of the value of the group and the implications of their representation. The challenges faced by the group were therefore considerable. Firstly, it had to ensure that it was an effective structure which could retain the support and commitment of its members but also facilitate them in their own work. Secondly, it required a means to take forward the health concerns of women in a way that would have a significant impact.

The strategy agreed was the creation of a women's health policy which could act as a lever for change. The process began with the development of a consultation document which was launched in 1991 to the 'Healthy City' Project partners, women's groups and individual women. This was an important step and the volume of responses was a testament to the interest

Aim
To improve the health and well being of women in Glasgow

Objectives
1 To raise awareness about women's health needs and an
   understanding of a woman's health perspective

2 To introduce this awareness into policy and planning processes of
   statutory and voluntary agencies

3 To ensure women's health needs and a woman's health perspective

Figure 16.3 The Women's Health Policy for Glasgow

aroused through previous activities. A policy document, the *Women's Health
Policy for Glasgow* (Women's Health Working Group 1992) was then launched
to the partner organizations the following year and adopted by them as well
as being taken back to a women's conference for endorsement.

The policy was designed to improve the health of women in Glasgow. Its
objectives and recommendations focused on structural change and were
concerned as much with the gender sensitivity of existing services as with
developing or consolidating services specifically for women (see Figure 16.3).
They were based on a more explicit understanding that gender inequality
and poor health are intimately linked and that there are sex differences in
the aetiology and outcome of health problems. The policy identified five
priority issues, generated through ongoing dialogue with women. These
were improving mental and emotional health; providing support for women
as carers; improving reproductive health; reducing the incidence of disease;
and improving women's safety in the home and workplace.

It is highly likely, and probably inevitable, that most women in Glasgow
have not heard of the policy that is attempting to make changes in their

Investing in women's health

This recognises the need to make women's health a priority in order to overcome the effects of disadvantage and discrimination

Social model of women's health

This recognises the importance of social, economic and environmental determinants of health as well as biological factors (which include women's reproductive function). It seeks to emphasise the significance of women's poverty in affecting health. A social model also facilitates an understanding of the heterogeneity of the female population and the inequalities which exist between different groups of women. The model emphasises the need to examine the specific needs of black and minority ethnic women, disabled women and lesbians, and develop appropriate responses.

Consultation and participation

This recognises the sovereignty of women's views whilst acknowledging that women have limited access to decision-making and limited opportunities to define their health needs. Mechanisms are necessary to enable the active involvement of women in decisions aimed at promoting health.

Interagency and organisational development

This recognises the importance of an integrated approach to women's health. Organisations which define policies and/or plan services that impact on health need to incorporate gender sensitivity into their processes and to co-operate in the implementation of policies and delivery of services which will improve women's health.

Strategic framework for action

The implementation of the following activity is the basis for taking the model forward:
- women-sensitive community development to help articulate women's health concerns
- the establishment of an intersectoral forum for women's health which brings together statutory, voluntary and community organisations to identify the agendas for change
- organisational structures and systems to raise awareness of gender inequality and its link to women's health, facilitate data collection by sex, gender monitoring and gender sensitive planning
- a model project to test and evaluate new methods for responding effectively to women's urgent health needs
- research and development into indicators of women's well-being

Figure 16.4   The Glasgow Model for Women's Health in a City

name. However, a recent unpublished survey indicates that many are familiar with some of the outcomes associated with the policy or with related activities. Thirty outcomes directly linked to the policy have been identified and recorded as part of a re-worked policy document which was relaunched in October 1996 (Women's Health Working Group 1996a). This was designed to maintain the profile of women's health in the context of changes in local government and associated reforms and also to address omissions in the original document.

It has also been possible to assemble the pieces of a complex set of arrangements into a framework (see Figure 16.4) which has been adopted through a WHO 'Healthy Cities' Project structure for joint work between cities, a Multi-City Action Plan for Women's Health. Engaging in such a process has not only been useful for the exchange of information and experiences across the United Kingdom and Europe, but helped to consolidate and legitimize further the local process. The production and launch of an action pack designed to show how women's health can be tackled by organizations should similarly aid the process of consolidation (Women's Health Working Group 1996b).

Impact on the health service

The historical development of women's health campaigning in Glasgow played an important role in laying down the foundations for recent developments within the health authority. Without these beginnings it is unlikely that current activity would have been as far reaching or as significant in its impact. Several important milestones were reached during the 1980s and four of these were especially notable – the appointment of a Consultant in Public Health for Women's Health (with support staff); the prioritizing of women-sensitive work within the health education department and its successor health promotion department; a review of well woman and family planning services; and the establishment and evaluation of a model well woman clinic in a deprived community.

Through their work together the individuals and groups involved in these processes have begun to demonstrate the potential of the health service for improving women's health as part of a social model of change. At the same time they have also been able to gather important data to inform the subsequent development of services and these will be considered below. Work aimed at improving reproductive services has also been ongoing. It will not be discussed in any detail here but two of its major aims have been to ensure that maternity services are women-centred and that screening services are run as efficiently as possible.

Structures

The adoption of the Women's Health Policy by the health board and the recent endorsement of the second phase document has allowed the establishment and maintenance of organizational structures for implementation. Both a working group, chaired by a non-executive board member, and the creation of a post to coordinate implementation were proposed by the board representatives on the Women's Health Working Group and agreed by the board. The former was set up in October 1992 and the latter appointment made in January 1993. This was done for an indefinite period in recognition of the fact that introducing changes of this kind into an organization can be a lengthy process. The coordinator is responsible to the Director of Public Health.

The original composition of the working group reflected an organization that had not yet been affected by the NHS reforms and was constructed to ensure representation from a cross-section of services and functions. With the introduction of the purchaser/provider split, there was agreement that implementing a women's health policy required a spirit of cooperation. As the reforms evolved, the group was therefore reconfigured to ensure managerial, commissioning, public health, health promotion and health economics representation from the purchasing organization, managerial representation from provider trusts and a general practitioner representative from the Local Medical Committee.

With no precedents to learn from, the role of the working group has been continuously evolving but for most of its existence it has functioned most effectively as an instigator of research and as an adviser to the coordinator and to the Consultant in Public Health for Women's Health who work together with a small public health/women's health team. This ensures integration between the medical and social aspects of women's health.

Priorities

In reviewing the implications of the policy for the work of the health board in 1992, the working group agreed five priorities for action which the board itself then endorsed. A further three were proposed and accepted in 1995. The eight priorities reflect a combination of immediate and practical requirements, a continuation of historical developments and an initiation of areas of work which go to the heart of the challenges facing a health authority seriously wishing to address health issues arising from gender inequality.

Awareness raising

Formal adoption of a women's health policy by a health authority, even after a decade of other activity, does not guarantee that women's health is accepted as a priority by the organization or its staff. It was agreed by those involved that implementation of the Glasgow policy should be action-led and not dependent on first raising awareness and understanding of women's health with all decision makers and practitioners. Nevertheless, a programme of seminars has been conducted with Trust boards, managers and practitioners to explain the origins of the women's health policy, its aims and its implications for service delivery. Although not formally evaluated, this programme has reached considerable numbers of the intended audience and anecdotal reports indicate that it has strengthened awareness. However, some people have remained resistant to the validity and utility of a women's health policy and the need to raise awareness continues.

Information about and for women

Gender blindness has meant that even where routine data is collected by
sex, the information is rarely made available and its use for planning and
policy purposes is even rarer. The women's health section of the Greater
Glasgow Public Health Department has worked in conjunction with the
Women's Health Working Group to begin to rectify this situation. This has
involved the publication of routine statistics together with local prevalence
data where they were available, as well as the preparation of research data
by sex and gender to serve as baseline data on the priority issues identified
in the Women's Health Policy. The combination of new evidence and continuing pressure has meant that in 1996, the annual report of the Director
for Public Health for Glasgow (Greater Glasgow Health Board 1996) con-
tained a discussion of gender as an important health determinant for the
first time. Gender guidelines have also been prepared and approved for use
by health board working groups examining ways of improving health gain.

The dominance of the medical model of women's health amongst the
mainstream producers of health-related literature has ensured that there has
been a preponderance of material supporting women in improving their
reproductive health or in their role as carers but little that examines general
health issues from a women's perspective (see for example, Amos 1993). In
order to improve the quality of information for women, the Health Promotion Department in Glasgow has used a participative model of practice to
produce a series of mini-magazines on health issues (the 'Women Talking
About . . .' series).[1] Using women's own accounts of their successes in making changes in their lives as the core, they cover risk factors such as smoking
and alcohol use, as well as mental health and becoming a mother. Preliminary evaluation has shown them to be extremely popular and negotiations are
under way within the local authority to develop a similar set covering social
issues such as housing and poverty and their effect on women's health.

Centre for Women's Health

The Centre for Women's Health represents the most tangible and practical
outcome of the Women's Health Policy. It was opened in 1995 and its objectives reflect the basic principles behind more than ten years of campaigning.
It aims, first, to identify and respond to women's unmet health promotion
needs; second, to provide training for professional staff and women's groups
on women's health issues and a women's health perspective and, third, to
develop ways of transferring good practice into mainstream service delivery.
Like the rest of the policy, it therefore has both a service role and a strategic
one.

Although funded by the health board and the local authority with personnel
and finance support from the community trust, it is led by a Management
Committee drawn from the funding bodies and voluntary groups representing
both the groups of women and the particular issues that have been identified
as priorities. This ensures representation from black and ethnic minorities,

disabled women and lesbians as well as advice on addressing the effects of poverty, on mental health, on women as carers and on domestic violence. To ensure continuity the health board is represented by the same non-executive member who chairs its Women's Health Policy Working Group. Issues of concern to the board are taken back through the same working group.

Comfortable and relatively well-resourced, the centre offers information, advice, counselling and support for self-help on three days and four evenings a week in a women-only environment with a full-time crèche. Training is offered for both sexes, on site and elsewhere, on women's health, gender issues and service development. By linking with the Women's Health Working Group and the Policy Coordinator, strategic issues that emerge through individual users are followed through with different service providers.

Model well woman services

Women consistently report their concerns about the way they are treated by medical care providers and this is often reflected in the way they subsequently use services. Women experiencing poverty and deprivation are often particularly alienated (see for example Blackburn 1991). Introduced as a model well woman service in the mid-1980s after a review of family planning and related services, the Ballantay clinic in a poor area of a Glasgow council estate improved uptake five-fold amongst some groups of women (Craddock *et al.* 1990). Based on guidelines prepared by the Association of Community Health Councils of England and Wales it provided a clinical service combined with counselling, self-help support and health education in a welcoming and women-sensitive atmosphere.

Evaluation highlighted those elements which were particularly successful and the model became the gold standard for other well woman and family planning services throughout the city. Prior to the introduction of the Women's Health Policy, the model was often greeted with scepticism or criticism from staff for its women-centred focus. However, it has now been introduced into the service agreement with the relevant Trust with resources provided for the minimum staff requirement. On this basis the Ballantay model is being implemented through an annual rolling programme supported by a model clinic coordinator and an advisory sub-group of the Policy Working Group. Overcoming resistance has often been difficult and the work highlights the problems of transferring the learning from pilot projects to the mainstream. However, nine out of twenty-two existing clinics are now at various stages of implementing the model.

Mental health strategy

All local surveys in Glasgow have consistently shown that women rate mental and emotional well-being as their first health priority (Hair 1994). Improving women's mental health cannot be achieved through the health service alone since it requires major social change. However, the health service does have an important role to play. The Policy Working Group, mindful of women's concerns, has examined the potential of the health service in this area very carefully and identified areas where change could be implemented to improve its effectiveness.

A sub-group comprising representatives from public health, health promotion and the Community and Mental Health Services Trust in Glasgow has been auditing current activity by practitioners in the community. It has also sought the perceptions of general practitioners on the incidence of mental health problems amongst their women patients and the role of counselling in supporting them. Informed by work from other areas (see for example Williams *et al.* 1993), the sub-group has a remit to advise on the commissioning process for mental health services and those community services such as health visiting with a bearing on the promotion of mental health. One practical outcome to date has been the systematic introduction and monitoring of screening for post-natal depression.

Domestic violence
The existence of domestic violence committed by men against women exemplifies the imbalance of power between the sexes and is probably the most sensitive indicator of gender inequality. Two decades of action have slowly moved the issue from the private to the public domain. Evidence to show the effect of domestic violence on women's health is mounting as is the recognition that it must be taken seriously by healthcare planners and providers. Hence no women's health policy with any credibility can ignore the issue. Following on from agreement by the health board to part fund a 'Zero Tolerance' Campaign, the policy working group therefore added domestic violence to its original set of priorities.

Given the sparcity of publications on good practice, the initial focus of the work has been to investigate ways in which practitioners in different settings currently respond to women who have experienced domestic violence. This evidence has then been used to develop better quality care through training of staff and the introduction of guidelines. The initial research process has been completed in two settings – an accident and emergency department and the family planning and well woman service – with mixed results. Training, using traditional and distance learning methods, has been shown to affect knowledge, attitudes and understanding but even when it is combined with the use of guidelines this has not been sufficient to produce significant changes in practice (McCartney 1996).

General awareness of the importance of this issue for the health service has been raised and currently workers in both pilot settings are examining other ways in which they can affect the climate and make organizational changes. New educational methods are also being developed and will be tested within two other settings, obstetrics and primary care. The attitudinal and organizational barriers encountered again highlight both the levels of creativity and the amount of time required to change aspects of mainstream service delivery even where there is encouragement to do so.

Women and heart disease

Nationally, the issue of women and heart disease has increasingly been highlighted (see Sharp, this volume) and it has been identified as one of the second wave of priorities for action to implement the Women's Health Policy. A gender audit of current data on diagnosis, referral, treatment, rehabilitation and outcome is under way. The results will determine what strategy, if any, is required to develop women-sensitive attitudes and practices. Preliminary findings in one rehabilitation unit has shown marked sex differences in uptake and the unit is working with women to examine ways of redressing this difference. An issue of the 'Women Talking About . . .' series has been devoted to heart disease in order to draw women's attention to their risk of heart disease and to the experiences of women who have suffered a heart attack.

The health of women staff

The final area of activity currently being taken forward concerns the health of the women who make up 80 per cent of the NHS workforce. Research coordinated by the Health Promotion Department has examined factors determining stress in a representative sample of staff in one acute hospital in Glasgow. Collaboration with the policy coordinator ensured that the study questions included a section targeting women and that the results of the entire survey were analysed by gender. The findings showed that women in particular are engaged in the types of jobs where they lack influence over their work, and have little opportunity to develop their knowledge and skills or future careers. They are also affected by having to balance employment with their domestic lives and the research identified a number of ways in which this could be ameliorated including the provision of counselling and on-site paramedical services (Houston *et al.* 1996).

These findings reflect the growing recognition that any strategy aimed at improving the health of female staff needs to move beyond the lifestyle approach which currently dominates thinking on health-promoting hospitals. A group comprising representatives from personnel, occupational health, nursing and public health is now reviewing the literature in order to produce a set of guidelines for both purchasing and provider organizations which will facilitate equality of opportunity for women as well as providing support for carers. It will also set out the requirements for a comprehensive occupational health service which is as capable of recognizing domestic violence as it is of providing immunization.

Support for purchasing

Determination of methodologies and guidelines for the implementation of the Women's Health Policy are regarded not only as ends in themselves but as tools for influencing the purchasing or commissioning process. Taking a policy as wide-ranging as this one into the heart of the purchasing process is not easy because of the current nature of purchasing (either by boards or GP fundholders), because it has implications for all service delivery and because a social model of women's health is either not fully understood or not accepted. The policy is now specifically cited in all quality arrangements with Trusts and evidence of implementation has been requested on monitoring visits. However, effective monitoring is still limited by the lack of well-constructed indicators and only the Centre for Women's Health, the model well woman services and post-natal screening for which there are monitoring tools are specifically included in contracts. At the next stage, it is planned that data recording systems for domestic violence will be introduced into all Accident and Emergency Departments including the Dental Hospital and that guidelines for the promotion of women's mental health by community and mental health services will be introduced. Gender guidelines have also been produced for working groups examining different aspects of health gain thereby facilitating a gender perspective on the recommendations that these groups make to purchasing commissioners.

Provider roles

Implementation of the Women's Health Policy cannot be dependent entirely on what is or is not included in contracts and creativity also needs to come from the providers. At present only the systematic introduction of the well woman service is being driven by providers themselves. However, a series of seminars hosted by each Trust in turn has enabled them to assess where current activities comply with the policy and to identify areas for development in the future. One example was the hosting of a women's health day for patients and staff to give voice to their concerns, while another initiated its own series of seminars for staff on domestic violence with a view to introducing a cascade model of training to improve recognition of signs and symptoms, support and referral.

But what about men's health? Conclusions and the future

It should now be clear that Glasgow has had considerable success in gaining acceptance of the importance of women's health. A number of major gains have been achieved as any review of the past 15 years will confirm. In no little measure this progress can be attributed to persistence, to a willingness to work across boundaries and to grasp opportunities as they occurred, combined with the support of some key politicians and officers in the organizations concerned. A strategic perspective together with some fine examples of good practice by women's projects have also been vital.

In terms of the health service, it has been possible to build on earlier initiatives and to use the available structures to begin to construct the methodologies needed to promote women-sensitive and women-specific ser-vices. However, a lack of historical precedents has meant that this process is often laborious and prone to short-term failures. Future progress is now dependent on being able to consolidate existing work; to define new areas of potentially valuable work; to maintain and strengthen the links with agencies in the other city organizations; and to gain new recruits desirous of change. It is gratifying that recent proposals for organizational change within the health board have acknowledged the volume of work that has been carried out together with the clarity of its aims and objectives even if the board has not yet committed itself wholeheartedly to placing the issue of gender at the heart of its planning.

More problematic, however, is the challenge that is posed for many men and some women by the move to widen women's health from reproductive rights to gender equality. This requires a fundamental change in the status quo which for many is unacceptable. The growing amount of rhetoric about men's health is no coincidence and requires to be constantly countered. It threatens to re-route the limited resources available for taking the policy itself forward as well as preventing the development of a wider strategy that can incorporate a men's health programme. The argument that creating equality for women enhances the lives of all therefore needs to be reiterated often and loudly.

Note

1 The Women Talking About series of mini-magazines is available from the Health Promotion Department, GGHB, Dalian House, 350 St Vincent Street, Glasgow, G3 8Y2.

References

Amos, A. (1993) In her own best interest? Women and health education: a review of the last fifty years. *Health Education Journal*, 52 (3): 141–50.

Blackburn, C. (1991) *Poverty and Health: Working with Families*. Buckingham: Open University Press.

Craddock, C., McIlwaine, G., McKoy, M., Read, M., Robertson, M. and Wilcon, E. (1990) *The Ballantay Project: A New Approach to Well Woman Services*. Glasgow: University of Glasgow.

Glasgow Healthy City Project (1992) *The Health of the City, A Shared Concern – The Glasgow Healthy City Project 4 Years on*. Available from Glasgow Healthy City Project, Corporate Policy & International Affairs, City Chambers, 40 Cochrane Street, Glasgow, G1.

Greater Glasgow Health Board (1996) *The Annual Report of the Director of Public Health 1994/95*. Glasgow: GGHB.

Hair, S. (ed.) (1994) *Glasgow's Health: Women Count*. Women's Health Working Group, Glasgow Healthy City Project.

Houston, K., Elder, A. and Laughlin, S. (1996) *An Investigation of Staff Health in the West Glasgow Hospitals University NHS Trust.* Glasgow: Health Promotion Department, GGHB.

McCartney, S. (in press) Case study: domestic violence. In D. Hunter and S. Griffiths (eds) *Perspectives on Public Health.* Edinburgh: Radcliffe Medical Press.

Strathclyde Regional Council (1980) *Social Strategy for the 1980's.*

Williams, J., Watson, G., Smith, H., Copperman, J. and Ward, D. (1993) *Purchasing Effective Mental Health Services for Women: A Framework for Action.* Canterbury: University of Kent.

Women's Health Working Group (1992) *Women's Health Policy for Glasgow.* Glasgow: Glasgow Healthy City Project.

Women's Health Working Group (1996a) *Women's Health Policy for Glasgow: Phase 2.* Glasgow: Glasgow Health City Project.

Women's Health Working Group (1996b) *Action for Women's Health: Making Changes Through Organisations. A Resource Pack for Workers and Organisations.* Available from Centre for Women's Health, 6 Sandyford Place, Glasgow G3 7NB.

Conclusions: the ways forward?

●

Lesley Doyal

The National Health Service has brought major benefits for women but more remains to be done if the care they receive is to be optimized. This final chapter will draw together some of the key issues identified in earlier sections and explore some of the strategies that can be used to tackle them. In particular it will highlight policies adopted in other countries to deal with similar concerns. The first section will look at gender issues in medical research and options for change in its organization and funding. This will be followed by sections on the planning of health services and on their delivery. The conclusion will indicate some of the broader policy initiatives that will be needed for the promotion of women's health across the lifespan and in diverse communities.

Reconfiguring health research

Research provides the foundation for practice in healthcare but we have already identified a number of ways in which it fails to recognize the specificity and the diversity of women's needs. The scientific questions that are asked in medical research and the answers that are sought sometimes depend more on who has the power to do the asking than on which biological or social questions need answering. As yet, these concerns have received little attention in Britain though evidence of their importance is beginning to accumulate (see Sharp, this volume). If they are to be taken seriously, lessons need to be learned from those countries where these issues are already on the agenda – Canada, the United States and Australia all offer important illustrations (Narrigan *et al.* 1997; Ruzek *et al.* 1997).

The most important aim of any reform will be to improve existing knowledge of health problems specific to women and also to gain a better understanding of sex and gender differences in those illnesses that affect both women and men. One strategy for achieving this is to divert significant resources into research designed specifically to address some of the key health problems affecting women. In Canada this has been achieved through the creation of five centres of excellence for women's health set up in 1996 and funded by the Federal Government. In the US and Australia on the other hand, large-scale, longitudinal research projects have been set up to explore both the biological and the social influences on women's lives.

'Women's Health Australia' began in June 1995 as part of the National Women's Health Policy (Brown *et al.* 1996). It involves six cohorts of women selected on the basis of age and ethnicity to represent a cross-section of Australian women and is interdisciplinary in approach. The main themes of the study are time use; health, weight and exercise; violence against women; life stages and key events; and use of and satisfaction with health services. It was initially funded for three and a half years but has been designed with the potential to be continued for twenty to thirty years.

In the US the 'Women's Health Initiative' (WHI) is more clinically focused and addresses some of the major health concerns of post-menopausal women (Rossouw *et al.* 1995). It is designed to test whether long-term preventive measures will decrease the incidence of cardiovascular disease, certain cancers and fractures and it has three major components: a cluster of randomized controlled trials; an observational study to identify predictors of disease; and a study of community approaches to encourage the development of healthy behaviours. Launched in 1991, the WHI is designed to enrol some 250,000 women in its various studies and the answers to its main questions will be available by the year 2007.

These are important initiatives that will greatly increase our knowledge of some of the major health problems affecting older women in particular, and the potential value of similar studies in the UK need to be explored. However, there is also an urgent need to 'mainstream' women's issues in medical research. In a report published as early as 1985, a task force of the US Public Health Service recognized that women were not well served by medical researchers and that the government as the major funder had a responsibility to address this situation (US Public Health Service 1985). Lengthy campaigning following this report resulted eventually in the setting-up of an Office of Research on Women's Health (ORWH) in 1991.

The Office was given three broad mandates: to strengthen research related to diseases that affect women; to see that women are adequately represented in studies funded by the National Institutes of Health (NIH); and to support more women in taking up biomedical research careers. It has developed a number of strategies in pursuit of these goals, all of which have relevance to the situation of medical research in the UK. As a starting point, ORWH worked with a number of different constituencies to develop a research agenda for women's health (US National Institutes of Health 1992). Four 'understudied' areas were then selected for priority funding – occupational health; autoimmune diseases; reproductive health; and women's urological health.

The Office also worked extensively with a number of interest groups to ensure the 'appropriate and sensitive recruitment and retention of women, particularly minority women, in clinical studies' (Mastroianni *et al.* 1994). This was facilitated by the passing of the NIH Reauthorization Act of 1993 which required that all studies funded through NIH should include women and people from minority groups in sufficient numbers such that 'valid analyses of differences in intervention effects can be accomplished'. Not surprisingly, the law has thrown up considerable ethical and methodological challenges for those involved in its implementation (Mastroianni *et al.* 1994). However, it offers an important illustration of one approach to the problem of gender inequity in medical research which could usefully be explored as an option for the UK.

In pursuit of its goal of increasing the numbers of women in medical research, ORWH convened a task force to examine both the content of the medical curriculum and also gender issues in education and career advancement. Its aim was to ensure that more women were involved both in the execution of medical research and in the evaluation of proposals and allocation of funds. The importance of this review process was highlighted by a recent study on medical research in Sweden which showed that female applicants needed to score much higher than men if their projects were to be funded (Breen 1997). While there is no formal proof of similar bias in the UK, anecdotal evidence indicates the need for further investigation and possibly for remedial action.

It is clear that a number of different strategies are required to ensure that topics of particular relevance to women receive more priority in the allocation of resources and also that women themselves are more appropriately represented in medical research as subjects, decision makers and as creative scientists. However, these approaches alone will not suffice. A full understanding of the influences on the health of women (or men) requires not only the insights to be gleaned from the biomedical approach but also the knowledge generated within a variety of disciplines using a range of different methods.

Both the 'Women's Health Initiative' in the US and 'Women's Health Australia' have recognized this need for methodological diversity, with the latter in particular placing much of their research emphasis on the social sciences. While biomedicine can play a major part in understanding biological or sex differences in health and illness, the social or gender dimension requires a different approach. This will necessitate clinicians working together with sociologists, anthropologists, psychologists and others to understand the broader social, economic and cultural context of women's lives as well as the particularity of their experiences of healthcare (Orosz 1994).

Sometimes quantitative methods of various kinds will be the most appropriate tools for such investigation. However, other research questions will require the use of qualitative techniques such as interviews, observation or focus groups to explore the more subjective dimensions of sickness and well-being (Brems and Griffiths 1993). If this broader perspective on health research is to flourish in the UK, a more flexible approach will be required by funding bodies to ensure that research proposals using a variety of different approaches receive equal treatment in the review process.

Planning women's health care

Developing services that are sensitive to women's needs will also necessitate significant changes in the frameworks used for policy and planning (see Griffiths and Bradlow; Laughlin, this volume). Some countries have chosen to facilitate these developments through a national women's health policy which provides an institutional mechanism for promoting greater gender awareness, for funding new initiatives and for monitoring subsequent progress. This approach has been adopted by a diverse group of countries including Brazil, Colombia and Australia and a number of others are in the early stages of developing such policies (Doyal 1995: ch. 7; Irish Department of Health 1995; Plata *et al.* 1995; Wainer and Peck 1995).

The Australian Women's Health Policy was the first of its kind and has also been the most extensively documented (Broom 1991; Wainer and Peck 1995). Based on a social model of health it was launched in 1989 and provides a framework and a strategy to meet the healthcare needs of all Australian women to the year 2000. The policy operates a dual strategy of funding a number of women's health services directly while also encouraging the mainstream health services to be more responsive to the needs of women. It represents the outcome of extensive campaigning by women and their advocates over a lengthy period of time and evaluations suggest that it has made a notable impact on the quality of care women receive (Davis *et al.* 1995).

Different countries have developed their policies in different ways. Some have been centrally organized but with a large element of decentralized implementation as in the Australian model. Others have been mainly regional or local in their approach. In the new South Africa for example, the emphasis has been on a 'grass-roots' model (Klugman *et al.* 1995). In some countries such as New Zealand, non-governmental organizations have been given a lead role in the change process. Here the Federation of Women's Health Councils is regularly consulted by professional and government bodies and its representatives are members of major working parties and committees.

As yet there has been little debate in the UK on possible frameworks for managing policy development and implementation in the area of women's health. The potential benefits of a centralized approach would include political legitimization and easier access to government resources, though these might be outweighed by the stifling of local innovation. Conversely, the apparent freedom of a 'bottom-up' policy might in reality be severely limited by lack of funds. Similarly, the choices offered to some groups by a concentration on 'women only' services might be outweighed by the advantage to the majority of a 'mainstreaming' approach that brings gender sensitivity into all areas of the healthcare system (see Wilton, this volume). These are complex issues but discussion of their relevance in the UK context is urgently needed. Without government backing and clear allocation of responsibility for policy development, little progress is likely to be made in moving women's issues up the NHS agenda.

The choice of an institutional form for the development of women's healthcare is important, but whatever strategy is devised there is now a growing consensus on the key issues that need to be addressed. A wide range of governmental and non-governmental organizations have drawn up frameworks of principles and priorities within which progressive approaches to the organization of women's healthcare can be developed. Despite the diversity of the constituencies involved, a remarkable similarity of themes has emerged, with most women's health advocates making broadly similar recommendations.

The first priority is the creation of better databases on the health and healthcare needs of women. In comparison with most other countries, the UK has always been relatively advanced in the collection of official statistics. However, significant gaps remain. The concentration on mortality rather than morbidity data, for instance, is a significant problem for both sexes but tends to be particularly serious for women who suffer more often than men from chronic, less easily classifiable health problems. In the context of service delivery, attempts to introduce the policies recommended in *Changing Childbirth* have highlighted many gaps in our existing knowledge of maternity care (Macfarlane 1997). Similarly, the 'Stress on Women' campaign highlighted the absence of national data on issues such as women-only wards or choice of male or female worker (Sayce 1996).

There is also an urgent need for the development of more effective indicators to monitor different aspects of women's well-being. Both older women and young women may have less access to routine healthcare and appropriate indicators are needed to monitor their health status and assess their needs. Better data is also required on a range of women's health problems that receive relatively little attention.

Violence against women, for instance, is a serious public health hazard that continues to be inadequately monitored both inside and outside the NHS (see Laughlin, this volume; Heise *et al.* 1995; WHO 1996). In the home we need more information on the nature and the gender distribution of domestic accidents (Doyal 1995: ch. 2) while in the workplace the development of more specific occupational health indicators could help identify the particular hazards facing women at work (Messing *et al.* 1995).

Alongside the development of better information on women's health status there is also a growing recognition that women themselves need to be more actively involved in the planning process. In the UK context this will certainly require further efforts to increase the numbers of women on the authorities that purchase services and also on the boards of Trusts that are responsible for providing them. But this alone will not ensure that their diverse interests are represented. There is also an urgent need for the development of new strategies for consulting women about their needs and their preferences. Different communities will require different approaches and planners need to be constantly reviewing who they consult and how to ensure that all women's voices are heard.

The last few years have been marked by a growing debate about the best methods for involving the public in the planning of services across the public sector (Allen 1988; McGrath and Grant 1992). In the UK this has included the development of new approaches to working with users' groups in the fields of mental health and disablity in particular. The MIND 'Stress on Women' campaign provided an important illustration of good practice in this area (Sayce 1996). Lessons can also be learned from projects in other countries which have focused on helping female participants to understand more about policy issues and to make their views known (Berer 1992; Klugman 1994).

Insights learned from these various sources need to be incorporated wherever appropriate, as a routine part of planning in the NHS. Key issues to be addressed will include the time and place of meetings, the way language is used, the way information is presented and the mechanisms of facilitation offered to those who have little experience of participating actively in the public arena. These developments cannot be left to chance but will require adequate funding and a coherent infrastructure to ensure that they are effectively carried out.

Finally, it is essential that purchasers and planners ensure that gender issues are built into the activities of monitoring and evaluation as part of the broader process of quality assurance. Unless this is done the differential impact of services on women and men are likely to be ignored. At the clinical level this will require the explicit inclusion of sex and gender as variables in the audit process and in the work of the new National Institute for Clinical Effectiveness (Department of Health 1997). In the broader context of health services research it will necessitate careful assessment of the way both men and women experience healthcare and a commitment to remedy any gender inequalities that are identified. This will require special attention in the annual patient surveys outlined in *The New NHS* (Department of Health 1997). Recent research findings from a number of different settings have highlighted some of the major issues that are likely to be important here.

First and most importantly, there is a need to ensure that women's access to services is not hindered by what are often gender-related obstacles (Timyan *et al.* 1993). The geographical location of facilities, their physical layout and their opening times can all pose problems especially for those who care for dependants. Lack of transport and of alternative carers can make the journey to a health facility more difficult. The large numbers of older women with chronic health problems and little social support may also find it difficult to access services unless they are tailored to meet their needs. If these problems are to be solved, services need to be decentralized wherever possible, the physical form of the buildings needs to reflect the varied needs of those who will be using them, and substitute care needs to be available, such as on-site crèches.

Access may also be limited by a range of other, less immediately obvious, factors. As we have seen, those whose first language is not English may not be able to use services effectively unless translation is offered (see Starkey, this volume). Women from some ethnic minorities are most at risk if they arrived in the UK as adults because they may have fewer social and linguistic capacities for interaction in the public arena. Groups of women arriving as refugees may have especially acute needs in this area. Cultural factors may also be important if female staff are not available since contact with a 'strange' man may be seen to put the woman's honour at risk. Hence physical, psychological and cultural barriers specific to women may still exist despite the elimination of many of the economic barriers of the past.

Once women have accessed care it is important to ensure that the quality of the treatment they receive is optimized. Within the biomedical tradition, it is the technical aspect of quality that has been emphasized, and as we have seen that continues to be a cause for concern. However, there is now a growing consensus that we also need to take into account a more diffuse constellation of factors centred around the interpersonal relationship between the health worker and the service user. These have received less attention from service planners but are of central importance to users themselves and will often impact directly on the effectiveness of clinical care (Bruce 1990).

We have seen that many women experience problems with these more qualitative aspects of their medical encounters. Areas of concern include lack of choice, inadequate levels of information and sometimes lack of respect shown by workers to their clients. While these manifestations of inequality come from a number of different sources, the doctor–female patient encounter clearly mirrors many other pieces of gendered social interaction. If these problems are to be properly addressed practical strategies need to be identified and put in place. One approach to this problem has been to change various aspects of the way care is organized.

General practice has proved to be the easiest area for such innovation since GPs have traditionally had more freedom than other health workers in organizing their services (Webb 1984). Women doctors in particular have attempted to exploit such opportunities, though many have experienced considerable difficulty in changing the traditional relations of hierarchy between doctor and patient and between doctors and other health workers (Eisner and Wright 1984; see also Benato *et al.*, this volume). As part of this process 'well woman' centres have been set up in some parts of the country; a survey in 1987 revealed the existence of around a hundred initiatives of this kind (Foster 1989).

These services have sometimes led to improvements in quality of care, particularly in terms of the amount of time available for women to discuss their problems and to explore alternative courses of action. However, most have been relatively limited in what they offer and in the degree to which they have challenged existing models of care (Craddock and Reid 1993). In the United States and Australia, on the other hand, 'women-centred' services have proliferated widely (for the Australian experience see Broom 1991; Davis *et al.* 1995). In the latter case this has reflected the greater availability of federal and state funding as part of the Women's Health Policy, while in the former most services are now provided on a commercial basis.

Not surprisingly, these initiatives vary markedly in the quality of what they offer to women and in the US in particular there has been growing concern that what began as feminist ideas have been coopted by mainstream providers in ways that water down their original potential (Worcester and Whatley 1988). However, there can be no doubt that some of these centres offer exciting versions of more holistic care in which women can be active participants as both users and workers. The models they offer therefore need to be carefully assessed to determine their relevance in an NHS that is to be increasingly 'primary care-led'.

However, organizational restructuring is not the only route for improving the quality of care women receive. An additional strategy is to strengthen women's own capacities to get the most out of their medical encounters. More information is an important element here, including better educational material tied directly to women's needs and interests (McIver 1993). This can give women the right kind of knowledge which they can then use to make better informed choices. Sometimes the decisions they have to make will be difficult and the information provided needs to reflect that, admitting medical uncertainty wherever appropriate.

Traditionally, voluntary organizations have been much better than the NHS at providing this kind of material, particularly the self-help groups in which women are often the major participants. This needs to change with mainstream health service providers learning from the good practice of the voluntary sector and developing new materials. The material being developed to empower women under the *Changing Childbirth* initiative provides a good example of how this can be done, and the initiative needs to be extended to other areas of care.

In some instances, however, information alone will not suffice and the structure of the medical encounter itself needs to be reformed to facilitate women's exercise of their own autonomy but also their sense of being cared for. This may involve the provision of counselling and advocacy services so that those women who need it can be helped in their decision making (see Harcourt and Rumsey, this volume). At present, services of this kind are provided in individual centres but an expansion of their availability would mean that more women could benefit. In some cases the provision of female staff or the organization of women-only support or therapy groups may also be an important element in enabling women to overcome both the structural and the psychological barriers imposed by gender inequalities.

If any of these initiatives are to succeed, those who work in the NHS will also need to change. However, relatively little effort has so far been made to achieve this despite the existence of a growing number of resources. *Health Workers for Change*, for instance, produced by WHO in collaboration with the Women's Health Project in Johannesburg, is now being used in a number of countries around the world (WHO/UNDP/World Bank 1996). This is designed to address gender issues in first-line care. A recent pack on gender and health from the Pan American Health Organization takes a wider perspective, offering important lessons for both policy makers and practitioners in that region (PAHO 1997). Despite their diverse cultural origins, all of these initiatives offer important lessons for the NHS.

In the UK, attempts have been made in some educational institutions to inculcate greater gender awareness among doctors, nurses and other health workers during their initial training. We need to make a much more careful evaluation of the impact these have had on subsequent practice and to ensure that they are incorporated into the educational experience of all student health workers. Just as importantly, however, programmes need to be put in place for those already working in the NHS who were trained before these new courses came on stream. These should include not only more general awareness of gender issues but also specific knowledge on women's health problems that have not been covered in initial training. In the US, for example, many health workers now undergo formal programmes on the recognition and appropriate treatment of women who have been abused, and similar programmes in the UK could greatly improve the care women receive in a number of settings (Council on Scientific Affairs, American Medical Association 1992).

Overall then, considerable gains could be made by the introduction of a range of education and information initiatives both for women who use the service and for the health workers who look after them. However, these are unlikely to be enough, and a number of other approaches may be helpful in enabling women to exercise their right to determine their own treatment and particularly to give their informed consent to a particular intervention (Faulder 1985).

Women in Australia, for instance, have been at the forefront of public debate about informed consent and national guidelines are now in place to ensure that both sexes are able to maximize their role in decision making. In the US these matters have been taken still further with specific legislation enacted in some states to deal with the particularly complex issues relating to informed consent in breast cancer surgery (Montini and Ruzek 1989). Recent *Guidelines to Informed Consent* issued by the Royal College of Surgeons have paved the way for improvements in what has always been a contentious area. However, these will need to be accompanied by a more sensitive response on the part of clinicians to the gendered inequalities inherent in the communications taking place in so many medical interactions (Tong 1997).

Finally, it is important that health service providers are also aware of the significance of equal opportunities issues for health workers themselves. While more women in positions of influence and power will not in themselves guarantee higher quality care for female patients, they certainly have an important part to play. Initiatives are under way to improve the situation of women in medicine and some progress has been made in recent years. As part of the national 'Opportunity 2000' programme, the NHSME has set targets for increasing the percentage of women consultants and schemes have been launched in conjunction with some of the professional bodies (NHSME 1992). Plans have also been put in place to increase the proportion of women in general management posts and the numbers on authorities and Trust boards. As part of the 50th anniversary celebrations of the health service, the NHS Executive has introduced a Quality Through Equality Awards Scheme.

Some progress has been made with these initiatives but like all policies of this kind they are heavily dependent for their success on the willingness of those involved to take them seriously. This is likely to be a particularly acute problem in medicine where the weight of tradition is substantial, affecting both women in the profession itself and also those other health workers over whom doctors still exert a considerable influence. Medicine as an institution is profoundly 'male' and has consistently employed strategies of exclusion on a gender basis (Witz 1992). It remains unclear, therefore, how effective a largely voluntaristic approach to equal employment opportunities will be in changing the division of labour between men and women in the NHS workforce.

Widening the agenda

We have now examined some of the most important dimensions of change that will be required in the NHS if women's healthcare needs are to be more effectively met. We have also identified the inextricable links between women's health and their economic, cultural and social circumstances. Of course, many of these factors lie beyond the remit of the NHS itself and it would be both unreasonable and counterproductive to expect health workers to take on responsibility for all aspects of the lives of the women and men they care for. However, that does not mean that either the planning or the delivery of services can ignore these broader determinants of health.

At the level of individual care, it is essential that the material, cultural and social reality of women's lives is taken seriously in both the diagnosis and treatment of whatever problems they are presenting. Of course, the relevance of these issues may not seem as obvious in the case of a broken leg as it might in trying to make sense of depression but the complexity of the relationship between gender, health and well-being can never be over-estimated. Even in the case of the broken leg, a woman's domestic circumstances and her own feelings about them may have a significant impact on the effectiveness of strategies for rehabilitation.

In the context of NHS planning, it is now evident that there will not be a significant reduction in health variations between different groups nor health gains for the wider population unless bridges continue to be built across the health and social care divide. The breaking down of these barriers and the development of integrated services are especially important for women who are the major users of these facilities both on their own behalf and in their role as the carers of others. There is also an urgent need for health policies to be linked to wider social policies such as housing and income support and for regular audit across all these policy areas to assess their differential impact on women and on men. Hopefully, this can be one of the main tasks on the agenda of the Health Action Zones. Techniques for gender audit of this kind are now becoming increasingly sophisticated in other parts of the world and their adoption in the UK context would provide an important tool in the campaign to identify and reduce inequalities between women and men.

We have noted throughout this book the importance of both biological and social differences between men and women and the ways in which these shape their health status and their need for healthcare. We have stressed the need for these differences to be properly understood and used as the basis for effective planning. If this is to be achieved, we all need to be active as citizens, as service users and as health workers to ensure that these principles are taken seriously by those responsible for managing the NHS of the future.

References

Allen, I. (ed.) (1988) *Hearing the Voice of the Consumer*. London: Policy Studies Institute.
Berer, M. (1992) *Women's Groups, NGO's and Safe Motherhood*. Geneva: WHO (WHO/FSE/MSM/92.3).
Breen, G. (1997) Nepotism and sexism in peer review (letter). *Nature*, 25 September.
Brems, S. and Griffiths, M. (1993) Health women's way: learning to listen. In M. Koblinsky, J. Timyan and J. Gay (eds), *The Health of Women: A Global Perspective*. Boulder, CO: Westview Press.
Broom, D. (1991) *Damned If We Do: Contradictions in Women's Health Care*. Sydney: Allen and Unwin.
Brown, W., Bryson, L., Byles, J., Dobson, A., Manderson, L., Schofield, M. *et al.* (1996) Women's Health Australia: establishment of the Australian Longitudinal Study on women's health. *Journal of Women's Health*, 5 (5): 467–72.
Bruce, J. (1990) Fundamental elements of quality of care: a simple framework. *Studies in Family Planning*, 21(2): 61–91.

Council on Scientific Affairs, American Medical Association (1992) Violence against women: relevance for medical practitioners. *Journal of American Medical Association,* 267 (23): 3184–90.

Craddock, C. and Reid, M. (1993) Structure and struggle: implementing a social model of a well woman clinic in Glasgow. *Social Science and Medicine,* 36: 67–76.

Davis, J., Andrews, S., Broom, D., Gray, G. and Renwick, M. (1995) *Changing Society for Women's Health: Proceedings of 3rd National Women's Health Conference.* Canberra: Australian Government Publicity Service.

Department of Health (1997) *The New NHS: Modern, Dependable.* London: HMSO.

Doyal, L. (1995) *What Makes Women Sick: Gender and the Political Economy of Health.* London: Macmillan.

Eisner, M. and Wright, M. (1984) A feminist approach to general practice. In C. Webb (ed.) *Feminist Practices in Women's Health Care.* Chichester: Wiley.

Faulder, C. (1985) *Whose Body Is It? The Troubling Issue of Informed Consent.* London: Virago.

Foster, P. (1989) Improving the doctor/patient relationship: a feminist perspective. *Journal of Social Policy,* 18 (3): 337–61.

Heise, L., Moore, K. and Toubia, N. (1995) *Sexual Coercion and Reproductive Health: A Focus for Research.* New York: Population Council.

Irish Department of Health (1995) *Towards a Health Policy for Women.* Dublin: Department of Health.

Klugman, B. (1994) Feminist methodology in relation to the Women's Health Project. In P. Wijeyaratne, L. Arsenault, J. Roberts and J. Kitts (eds) *Gender, Health and Sustainable Development.* Ottawa: International Development Research Centre.

Klugman, B., Stevens, M. and Arends, K. (1995) Developing women's health policy in South Africa from the grass roots. *Reproductive Health Matters,* 6: 122–31.

Macfarlane, A. (1997) Maternity statistics: what are the problems and how do we solve them? *Changing Childbirth Update,* Issue 10.

Mastroianni, A., Faden, R. and Federman, D. (eds) (1994) *Women and Health Research: Ethical and Legal Issues of Including Women in Clinical Studies, vols 1 and 2.* Washington, DC: National Academy Press.

McGrath, M. and Grant, G. (1992) Supporting 'needs-led' services: implications for planning and management systems. *Journal of Social Policy,* 21 (1): 71–97.

McIver, S. (1993) *Obtaining the Views of Health Service Users about Quality of Information.* London: Kings Fund.

Messing, K., Neis, B. and Dumais, L. (1995) *Invisible: issues in women's occupational health.* Charlottetown P.E.I. Canada: Gynergy Books.

Montini, T. and Ruzek, S. (1989) Overturning orthodoxy: the emergence of breast cancer treatment policy. *Research in the Sociology of Health Care,* vol. 8, Greenwich, CT: JAI Press.

Narrigan, D., Zones, J., Worcester, N. and Grad, M. (1997) Research to improve women's health: an agenda for equity. In S. Ruzek, V. Olesen and A. Clarke (eds) *Women's Health: Complexities and Difference.* Columbus: Ohio State University Press.

National Health Service Management Executive (NHSME) (1992) *Women in the NHS: An Implementation Guide To Opportunity 2000.* London: Department of Health.

Orosz (1994) The impact of social science research on health policy. *Social Science and Medicine,* 39 (9): 1287–93.

Pan American Health Organisation (1997) *Gender, Health and Development: Facilitators Guide.* Washington: PAHO.

Plata, M., Gonzales, A. and de la Espriella, A. (1995) A policy is not enough: women's health policy in Colombia. *Reproductive Health Matters*, 6: 107–13.

Rossouw, J., Finnegan, L., Harlan, W., Pinn, V., Clifford, C. and Macgowan, J. (1995) The evolution of the Women's Health Initiative: perspectives from the NIH. *Journal of the American Medical Women's Association*, 50 (2): 50–55.

Ruzek, S., Olesen, V. and Clarke, A. (1997) Conversing with diversity: implications for social research. In S. Ruzek, V. Olesen and A. Clarke, *Women's Health: Complexities and Difference*. Columbus: Ohio State University Press.

Sayce, L. (1996) Campaigning for change. In K. Abel, M. Buszewicz, S. Davison, S. Johnson and E. Staples (1996) *Planning Community Mental Health Services: A Multiprofessional Handbook*. London: Routledge.

Timyan, J., Brechin, S., Measham, D. and Ogunleye, B. (1993) Access to care: more than a problem of distance. In M. Koblinsky, J. Timyan and J. Gay (eds) *The Health of Women: A Global Perspective*. Boulder, CO: Westview Press.

Tong, R. (1997) *Feminist Approaches to Bioethics: Theoretical Reflections and Practical Applications*. Boulder, CO: Westview Press.

UNDP/World Bank/WHO (1996) *Health Workers for Change: A Manual to Improve Quality of Care*. Geneva: WHO.

United States National Institute of Health (1992) *Opportunities for Research on Women's Health*. NHI Publication 92–3457. Washington, DC: US Department of Health and Human Services.

United States Public Health Service (1985) *Women's Health: Report of the Public Health Service Task Force on Women's Health Issues*. Washington, DC: US Department of Health and Human Services.

Wainer, J. and Peck, N. (1995) By women for women: Australia's National Women's Health Policy. *Reproductive Health Matters*, 6: 114–21.

Webb, C. (1984) *Feminist Practices in Women's Health Care*. Chichester: Wiley.

Witz, A. (1992) *Professions and Patriarchy*. London: Routledge.

Worcester, N. and Whatley, M. (1988) The response of the health care system to the women's health movement: the selling of women's health centres. In S. Rosser (ed.) *Feminism Within Science and Health Care Professions: Overcoming Resistance*. Oxford: Oxford University Press.

World Health Organisation (1996) 'Violence against women'. WHO Consultation, 5–7 February 1996. Geneva: WHO.

Index

References in *italic* indicate figures or tables.